Nature and Extent of
Alcohol Problems
Among the Elderly

George L. Maddox is Professor of Sociology and Chairman, Duke University Council on Aging and Human Development.

Lee N. Robins is Professor of Sociology in Psychiatry, Washington University School of Medicine.

Nathan Rosenberg is Health Scientist Administrator, National Institute on Alcohol Abuse and Alcoholism.

Nature and Extent of Alcohol Problems Among the Elderly

Sponsored by the
National Institute on Alcohol Abuse
and Alcoholism

in collaboration with the
National Institute of Mental Health
National Institute on Aging

George Maddox, Ph.D.
Lee N. Robins, Ph.D.
Nathan Rosenberg, Ph.D.
Editors

SPRINGER PUBLISHING COMPANY

Springer Publishing Company, Inc.
536 Broadway
New York, NY 10012

86 87 88 89 90 / 5 4 3 2 1

Library of Congress Cataloging-in-Publication Data
Main entry under title:

Nature and extent of alcohol problems among the elderly.

  Reprint. Originally published: Rockville, Md.: U.S. Dept. of Health and Human Services, Public Health Service, Alcohol, Drug Abuse, and Mental Health Administration, National Institute on Alcohol Abuse and Alcoholism, [1984]. (Research monograph; no. 14)
  Bibliography: p.
  1. Geriatric psychiatry—United States—Congresses.
  2. Alcoholism—United States—Congresses. I. Maddox, George L. II. Robins, Lee N. III. Rosenberg, Nathan. IV. National Institute on Alcohol Abuse and Alcoholism (U.S.) V. National Institute of Mental Health (U.S.) VI. National Institute on Aging. [DNLM: 1. Alcoholism— in old age—congresses. WM 274 N285 1983]
RC451.4.A5N38   1986   618.97'6861   85-25018
ISBN 0-8261-5480-8

Printed in the United States of America

FOREWORD

This volume is another in a series of research monographs from the National Institute on Alcohol Abuse and Alcoholism (NIAAA). The series sets forth current information on a number of topics relevant to alcohol abuse and alcoholism as reported through workshops in the research, prevention, and treatment areas, as well as through state-of-the-art reviews on selected subjects.

NIAAA has had a long standing commitment to broad dissemination of information. This monograph series informs researchers, clinicians, program administrators, and other interested persons about significant findings that may be useful in strengthening alcoholism research and improving alcoholism programs.

> Robert G. Niven
> Director
> National Institute on Alcohol Abuse
> and Alcoholism

PREFACE

The elderly in America constitute a group that is growing in size and as a percentage of the total population. Furthermore, this percentage is expected to become larger as medical research leads to improved treatment for illnesses especially prevalent among the elderly. In view of the growing importance of this special population, the National Institute on Alcohol Abuse and Alcoholism (NIAAA) believes that it is important to view alcohol problems among the elderly in a realistic perspective. No one really knows the extent of alcoholism and alcohol-related problems among the elderly, nor is there yet a reliable basis for making sound estimates.

Perhaps in the past there was a tendency to believe that alcohol-related problems were not important among the elderly. Data from the American Drinking Practices Studies suggest that persons over the age of 50 do reduce their drinking. We also know that alcoholics and problem drinkers have a higher mortality rate, and consequently the surviving older population contains fewer heavy drinkers. Based on this line of evidence, it seems reasonable to expect alcohol-related problem prevalence to be relatively low in an elderly population. However, even if alcohol-related problems are relatively fewer in an older group, we do not know the degree of severity and range of such problems in an absolute sense. It would seem that we need to ascertain this so that allocation of scarce dollars to underdeveloped research areas is made on a rational basis. The workshop at Washington University was intended as a beginning point in a systematic NIAAA effort to stimulate research interest and activity in the alcohol-aging area. NIAAA recognizes that there are many research questions in alcohol and aging that need to be addressed, and that data on the prevalence of alcohol-related problems only scratch the surface. It is hoped that publication and dissemination of these workshop proceedings will serve as a catalyst for research on a wide variety of topics in the alcohol-aging area. We saw this workshop as a necessary first step in moving ahead.

The investigator-initiated research grant programs of NIAAA have resulted in only a few studies that directly address alcohol-aging questions. These proceedings report findings on only some of the important questions in this area, but we believe that the papers provide a sound basis for encouraging further growth and development of a knowledge base in an important area.

Ernestine Vanderveen
Chief, Clinical and Psychosocial Research Branch
Division of Extramural Research
National Institute on Alcohol Abuse and Alcoholism

PARTICIPANTS

James C. Anthony, Ph.D.
Assistant Professor
The Johns Hopkins Medical Institution
The Hampton House, Room 447
624 North Broadway
Baltimore, Maryland 21205

Dan G. Blazer, M.D., Ph.D
Professor of Psychiatry
Division of Social and Community
  Psychiatry
Duke University Medical Center
Durham, North Carolina 27710

Jacob Brody, M.D.
Associate Director for Epidemiology,
  Demography and Biometry Program
National Institute on Aging
Federal Building, Room 612
7550 Wisconsin Avenue
Bethesda, Maryland 20205

Lois Chatham, Ph.D.
Director, Division of Extramural
  Research
National Institute on Alcohol Abuse
  and Alcoholism
Parklawn Building
5600 Fishers Lane
Rockville, Maryland 20857

Robert J. Glynn, Ph.D.
Statistician
Normative Aging Study
Veterans Administration Outpatient
  Clinic
17 Court Street
Boston, Massachusetts 02108

Tavia Gordon
Research Professor of Statistics
Biostatistics Center
George Washington University
Bethesda, Maryland 20037

John E. Helzer, M.D.
Professor of Psychiatry
Washington University School of
  Medicine
Department of Psychiatry
4940 Audubon Avenue
St. Louis, Missouri 63110

John A. Hermos, M.D.
Medical Director, Substance Abuse
  Treatment Program
Veterans Administration Outpatient
  Clinic and Veterans Administra-
  tion Medical Center
17 Court Street
Boston, Massachusetts 02108

Charles E. Holzer III, Ph.D.
Assistant Professor of Psychiatry
  and Sociology
Depression Research Unit
Yale University
904 Howard Avenue, Suite 2A
New Haven, Connecticut 06519

Ben Z. Locke, M.S.P.H.
Chief, Center for Epidemiologic
  Studies
National Institute of Mental Health
Room 18-105
Rockville, Maryland 20857

George L. Maddox, Ph.D.
Professor of Sociology and
  Chairman, Duke University Council
  on Aging and Human Development
Duke University
P.O. Box 2970
Durham, North Carolina 27710

Rudolf Moos, Ph.D.
Research Career Scientist
Palo Alto Veterans Administration/
  Stanford University
Social Ecology Laboratory
Department of Psychiatry and
  Behavioral Sciences
Stanford, California 94305

Matilda White Riley, D.Sc.
Associate Director, Behavioral
  Sciences Research Program
National Institute on Aging
Building 31, Room 4C-32
9000 Rockville Pike
Bethesda, Maryland 20205

Lee N. Robins, Ph.D.
Professor of Sociology in Psychiatry
Washington University School of Medicine
4940 Audubon Avenue
St. Louis, Missouri 63110

Nathan Rosenberg, Ph.D.
Health Scientist Administrator
Department of Health and Human Services
National Institute on Alcohol and
  Alcohol Abuse
Parklawn Building, Room 14C-17
5600 Fishers Lane
Rockville, Maryland 20857

Robert Straus, Ph.D.
Professor and Chairman
Department of Behavioral Sciences
College of Medicine Office Building
University of Kentucky
Lexington, Kentucky 405-0086

George Warheit, Ph.D.
Professor of Psychiatry
Department of Psychiatry
Box J256, JHMHC
University of Florida
Gainesville, Florida 32610

CONTRIBUTORS

Joanne B. Auth, M.H.Ed.
Department of Psychiatry
Box J256, JHMHC
University of Florida
Gainesville, Florida 32610

Philip B. Bednarski, M.S.
Depression Research Unit
Department of Psychiatry
School of Medicine
Yale University
New Haven, Connecticut 06519-8068

Glen R. Bouchard, S.M.
Normative Aging Study
Veterans Administration Outpatient
  Clinic and Veterans Administration
  Medical Center
17 Court Street
Boston, Massachusetts 02108

Kristian Carey, B.A.
Washington University School of
  Medicine
Department of Psychiatry
4940 Audubon Avenue
St. Louis, Missouri 63110

John W. Finney, Ph.D.
Social Ecology Laboratory
Department of Psychiatry and
  Behavioral Sciences
Stanford University and Veterans
  Administration Medical Center
Palo Alto, California 94305

Linda K. George, Ph.D.
Department of Psychiatry
Box 3880
Duke University Medical Center
Durham, North Carolina 27710

B. Kathleen Jordon, M.A.
Department of Psychiatry
Box 3880
Duke University Medical Center
Durham, North Carolina 27710

Philip J. Leaf, Ph.D.
Depression Research Unit
Department of Psychology
Yale University School of Medicine
350 Congress Avenue
New Haven, Connecticut 06519-8068

Joseph S. LoCastro, Ph.D.
Substance Abuse Treatment Program
Veterans Administration Medical
  Center
17 Court Street
Boston, Massachusetts 02108

Ken G. Manton, Ph.D.
Center for Demographic Studies
Duke University
2117 Campus Drive
Durham, North Carolina 27710

Richard H. Miller, Ph.D.
Washington University School of
  Medicine
Department of Psychiatry
4940 Audubon Avenue
St. Louis, Missouri 63110

Jerome K. Myers, Ph.D.
Department of Sociology
Yale University
140 Prospect Street
New Haven, Connecticut 06519-8068

Gary L. Tischler, M.D.
Yale Psychiatric Institute
12A Yale Station
New Haven, Connecticut 06520

Myrna W. Weissman, Ph.D.
Depression Research Unit
Department of Psychiatry
Yale University School of Medicine
New Haven, Connecticut 06519-8068

Max A. Woodbury, Ph.D.
Department of Biostatistics
Box 3200
Duke University Medical Center
Durham, North Carolina 27710

CONTENTS

Page

Foreword--Robert Niven... iii
Preface--Ernestine Vanderveen.....................................   v
Participants... vii
Contributors... ix

Greetings

    Matilda White Riley, National Institute on Aging............   1

    Lois R. Chatham, National Institute on Alcohol Abuse
    and Alcoholism..   5

Introduction Session I: George L. Maddox, Chairman..............   7

Keynote Address

    Alcohol Problems Among the Elderly:
    The Need for a Biobehavioral Perspective--Robert Straus.....   9

Key Issues and Current Evidence

    The Mental Health and Social Correlates of Alcohol
    Use Among Differing Life Cycle Groups--George J. Warheit
    and Joanne B. Auth.. 29

Longitudinal Studies of Alcohol Problems Among the Aged

    Predictors and Correlates of Recovery in Older Versus
    Younger Alcoholics--John E. Helzer, Kristin E. Carey,
    and Richard H. Miller....................................... 83

    Changes in Alcohol Consumption Behaviors Among Men
    in the Normative Aging Study--Robert J. Glynn, Glen R.
    Bouchard, Joseph S. LoCastro, and John A. Hermos............ 101

    Influence of Cardiovascular Disease on Alcohol Consumption
    Among Men in the Normative Aging Study--John A. Hermos,
    Joseph S. LoCastro, Glen R. Bouchard, and Robert J. Glynn... 117

CONTENTS (Continued)

Page

Discussion: Session I

    George Maddox, Tavia Gordon, Rudolf Moos, Jacob Brody, Robert Glynn, John Helzer, and John Hermos................... 133

Reaction Paper

    A Systems Perspective on Problem Drinking Among Older Adults--Rudolf Moos and John W. Finney................ 151

Introduction Session II: Lee N. Robins, Chairman............... 173

Evidence from the Epidemiologic Catchment Area Studies

    The Epidemiologic Catchment Area Program of NIMH-- Ben Z. Locke... 175

    Introduction to the ECA Project as a Source of Epidemiological Data on Alcohol Problems--Lee N. Robins..... 201

    Antecedents and Correlates of Alcohol Abuse and Dependence in the Elderly--Charles E. Holzer III, Lee N. Robins, Jerome K. Myers, Myrna M. Weissman, Gary L. Tischler, Philip J. Leaf, James Anthony, and Philip B. Bednarski... 217

    Alcohol Abuse and Dependence as a Risk Factor Across the Adult Male Age Span--James C. Anthony................... 245

    The Elderly Alcoholic: A Profile--Dan Blazer, Linda George, Max Woodbury, Ken Manton, and Kathleen Jordan... 275

General Discussion Panel of Sessions I and II

    Jacob Brody.. 299

    Jacob Brody, Tavia Gordon, Rudolf Moos, Robert Straus, Lee Robins, J. Phillip Miller, Dan Blazer, Matilda Riley and Charles Holzer... 311

CONTENTS (Continued)

Page

Reaction Papers

    George L. Maddox... 323

    Lee N. Robins... 327

Closing Remarks and Postscript

    Nathan Rosenberg, National Institute on
    Alcohol Abuse and Alcoholism................................. 329

GREETINGS FROM NATIONAL INSTITUTE ON AGING

I am pleased to be here both personally and to represent the support and enthusiasm of the National Institute on Aging (NIA) for this workshop.

As a scholar myself, I am eager to become reinvolved with current research on a topic that I last reviewed over 15 years ago for our first volume in the series "Aging and Society." At that time, we had only begun to recognize the power of cohort comparisons in studies of aging. Among other analyses, we put together the 1963 survey by Mulford with the 1946 survey by my husband (published in the Quarterly Journal of Alcohol Studies). Thus we uncovered the increasing proportions of people who drink as members of a cohort move into middle adulthood, and the decreasing proportions of people who drink in the later years of life (especially women). This life-course pattern was supported by the finding that people 65 years old and older were more likely than young people to report they had stopped drinking (suggesting that the decline among older people was not due entirely to removal of drinkers from the cohort through death--a continuing challenge for research today).

While at that time we were able to tease from the data these changes with aging, we did not appreciate the striking differences in the life-course patterns of successive cohorts. However, those early data did clearly show that at every age the proportion of drinkers was higher in 1963 than it had been in 1946--a change obviously attributable to cohort differences and not to the process of aging. So these two tendencies (decrease in drinking with growing old and increase from one cohort to the next) were already apparent two decades ago. Also apparent were the higher rates of alcohol use for men than women. Of course, research was plagued then as now by the difficulty of identifying "problem drinkers," but here too the available clues pointed to some declines in the later years. Thus we were led at that early date to questions of antecedents and consequences of age changes in individual drinking behavior and of cohort tendencies for age-specific drinking to increase with changing norms and lifestyles in the society. We look forward to current formulations of these issues at this meeting.

As representatives of NIA's extramural program, Dr. Ronald Abeles and I can report at least three central foci in our program that are relevant to the issues before us here: demographic changes, broad cohort differences in patterns of aging, and the relation between health and behavior.

First, the demographic changes in regard to older people are startling, perhaps frightening, in the sense that we are not prepared for them. Repeatedly we are reminded of the projected increases in the number of older people. Those aged 65 and older will increase from 11 percent of the United States population today to 21 percent in the year 2030 when the baby boom cohorts reach old age (in absolute numbers from 25 million to 64 million). Even more striking and less widely recognized than these population changes are the unprecedented increases in <u>longevity</u>. As never before, we now live in a society in which most people live to be old. Today females surviving to age 65 can expect to live on the average at least another 18 years, males another 14 years. Over two-thirds of all the improvement in longevity in the entire world from pre-historic times until the present has taken place since 1900!

Thus as we look ahead to future problems and needs of older people (including those problems associated with alcohol), there will be many more old people, and many more of them will live to a very old age. Those aged 85-plus form the fastest growing segment of the population. And because women live longer than men, by the year 2000 there will be an estimated 150 women for every 100 men age 65 and over, and at age 85 and over, an estimated 250 women for every 100 men. So whatever the current alcohol-related problems associated with being old (and especially with being female and old), in the future these problems will bulk larger than they do now, both in the population and in the lifespan of individuals.

A second focus of concern is cohort differences. The people who will be old in the future will have grown old in very different ways from those who are old today; thus they will be very different kinds of old people. At NIA we are very concerned with research on the cohort differences in life-course patterns of aging, many of them with potential implications for problem drinking. It is clear that cohorts who are already old differ markedly from cohorts not yet old in education, income, diet, exercise, standard of living, medical care, and experience with chronic vs. acute diseases. Successive cohorts of young people are on the average taller than their parents, and successive cohorts of young women start to menstruate at younger ages. In respect to cigarette smoking (another behavior that tends to decline in later life), over the past decades each successive cohort of adult males in the United States--presumably responsive to the Surgeon General's warnings--has been less likely than its predecessors to smoke.

Even the most recent cohorts of women are beginning to follow this declining pattern.

There is also evidence that more recent cohorts are increasingly aware of their own future health and the importance of primary prevention of chronic disease. In the Framingham Heart Study, the lives of some 1,600 married couples have been traced for many years. Recently, a parallel study has been made of their offspring, comparing the offspring cohorts today with the cohorts of their parents 22 years ago when they were approximately the same ages. The differences between these two cohorts in three of the major risk factors in coronary heart disease are striking. The offspring, as compared with their parents, show lower blood pressure, lower serum cholesterol, and less cigarette smoking. Note that these differences are not due to age, since the ages of parents and offspring are the same at the time for which measures in these risk factors are compared. What the differences do suggest is that the cohorts who will be old in the future may be healthier, at least in certain respects, than cohorts already old today--a point worth considering in relation to public awareness (or unawareness) of the health problems of drinking alcohol.

Third, we at NIA are concerned with the interplay--the linkages--between the behaviors, attitudes, and characteristics of the successive cohorts of older people and their health. Highly relevant for questions of problem drinking at this meeting (as several background papers point out) is an understanding of the mechanisms linking genetic predispositions and biological aging processes with social, economic, cultural, and psychological components of growing older. (For example, how do life-course patterns of alcohol consumption relate to physiological and neurological changes in old age? Or to the drug therapies associated with the multiple chronic diseases of older people?) As many of you know, NIH (with NIA as the lead agency) collaborated with ADAMHA in supporting the Institute of Medicine program of conferences on health and behavior, which resulted in the volume by Hamburg, Elliott, and Parron (Health and Behavior: Frontiers of Research in the Biobehavioral Sciences). We have a continuing NIH Working Group on Health and Behavior, which I chair and which pursues common interests in collaboration with ADAMHA.

From these various activities, three important principles have been formulated with respect to aging. Let me state them as one potentially useful guide for our workshop discussions.

- Aging is a psychosocial as well as a biological process.

- Aging is not fixed for all time, but changes as society changes.

- Aging, because it is not immutable, is subject to a degree of human intervention and control.

I believe that each of these principles carries important implications for exploration of the nature and extent of alcohol-related problems among the elderly.

>
> Matilda White Riley, D.Sc.
> Associate Director
> Behavioral Science Research Program
> National Institute on Aging

GREETINGS FROM NATIONAL INSTITUTE ON ALCOHOL ABUSE AND ALCOHOLISM

For me to discuss the size and nature of the problems of alcohol in the aging is like bringing coals to Newcastle. Therefore, I will speak very briefly. This workshop is important because so little is known about alcohol use by the elderly.

Aging is of interest to all of us. Our skills, however, are varied. The science of aging itself is represented at this conference. The presence of Matilda Riley and Jacob Brody, from the National Institute on Aging, represents that agency's commitment to work with the National Institute on Alcohol Abuse and Alcoholism toward a more integrated analysis of this important problem. Together we should be able to assess the problem better than either institute could do alone. George Maddox's presence represents a non-Federal interface between alcohol and aging.

The science of mental health epidemiology is represented at this workshop not only by Lee Robins and a number of other NIMH grantees studying the epidemiology of alcohol, drug abuse, and mental health but also by Ben Locke of the National Institute of Mental Health--without whom the success of this conference would not be possible.

It is my hope that as a result of this meeting, NIAAA will be able to determine more intelligently how _many_ and what _type_ of resources should be channeled into studying alcohol problems among the aging.

For aging is of interest to most persons who survive youth, to scientists, and to politicians. This political interest resulted in a congressional mandate to establish an Alcohol Research Center for Aging. This mandate was carried out by the award of a grant to the University of Florida in Gainesville in 1982. George Warheit is here to represent that center.

Continued political interest is partly the result of an awareness of the size of the growing elderly population. According to the 1980 census, there are 25 million persons 65 years of age and older. In light of the size of the aging population, and the population's potential health care needs, we should try to identify preventable health problems—especially diseases as costly and deadly as alcoholism. If there really is a sizable alcohol problem among the elderly, NIAAA needs to channel some of its limited resources to study this problem. For if only 1 percent of persons over 65 suffer from alcoholism, 250,000 persons are seriously ill. However, if the conclusion of Schuckit and Pastor (Schuckit, M.A., and Pastor, P.A. The elderly as a unique population: Alcoholism. Alcohol Clin Exp Res 2:31-38, 1978) is correct—that from 2 percent to 10 percent of elderly individuals suffer from alcoholism—from 500,000 to 2,500,000 individuals would be afflicted. Determining the true nature and extent of the alcohol problem among the aging is very important. To do this, a number of issues will need to be addressed. One of the key issues is underreporting. Underreporting is probably due to a number of factors, some more subtle than others.

One of the reasons for underreporting is that there may be two peak periods for alcoholism: the first from 45 to 54 years of age, and the second from 65 to 74 years of age. (Bailey, M.D.; Haberman, P.W.; and Alkane, H. The epidemiology of alcoholism in an urban residential area. Quarterly Journal of Studies on Alcohol 26:20-40, 1965). If this is true, studies that show a decline in alcoholism after age 54 may have undersampled the over 65 group—thus missing the second peak.

Other reasons for underreporting may be

- The elderly tend to hide or deny their drinking.

- The elderly are unaware they have a drinking problem.

- The elderly may suffer from symptoms they do not associate with their drinking.

- Physicians and families are unable or unwilling to recognize elderly alcohol abuse.

It is hoped that the techniques used in collecting the data you present have overcome some of these problems of underreporting.

But, I promised not to bring too many coals to Newcastle so I'll turn the meeting over to you.

Lois R. Chatham, Ph.D.
Director
Division of Extramural Research
National Institute on Alcohol
Abuse and Alcoholism

INTRODUCTION: SESSION I

George L. Maddox, Chairman

Symbolism is important. Personally I attach significance to the statement of shared interest in aging and alcohol abuse illustrated in the opening statements by Lois Chatham and Matilda White Riley. The cooperation among Federal agencies that made this workshop possible is applauded.

There have been several references to history. Problems of aging and of alcohol abuse currently receive a great deal of attention. But, as you have read in the papers prepared for the workshop, these problems have a very long history. I became interested in alcohol abuse among young people over 30 years ago and, a decade later, became interested in aging. Nobody at that time was raising questions about the relationship between alcohol and aging. It has only been in the last 5 or 6 years that I have repeatedly received calls or letters suggesting that since I know something about alcohol and something about aging that I must know about alcohol and aging. I can honestly say that I know very little that I would take seriously or ask you to take seriously. This is why the Epidemiologic Catchment Area (ECA) project of the National Institute of Mental Health, which includes information on alcohol use among older adults, is so important. The workshop papers will illustrate that we have only a limited amount of scientific data that can be mobilized to answer reasonable questions the Congress or investigators in the scientific community might want to answer about aging and alcohol abuse. We will not promise that at the end of this workshop we will have all of the answers we want or need. But, perhaps some answers and some definitive directions about where we should go will emerge.

Matilda White Riley noted the history of how her interest in aging and alcohol merged. This reminded me of my own earlier interest in the political movement of Alcoholics Anonymous and in the principles of Alcoholics Anonymous that emerged. These principles declared that alcoholics are sick, can be helped, and should be helped. They are, in a general sense, related to Dr. Riley's principles, particularly her notion of the mutability of age-related problems. An important symbolic change is illustrated in this society by this kind of declaration. We are dealing with mutable, not immutable, processes. The implication is, therefore, that there is a public responsibility for responding. We have heard for 25 to 30 years similar principles being enunciated. It is important to have a sense of history. As we get older, we have a right to have a past about which we can speak with conviction. But we want, and need, official recognition of the past because, while history may teach us that history usually teaches nothing, this is not always the case.

Our keynote speaker, Robert Straus, has a sense of history about alcohol use and alcohol abuse in a society that is growing older. What are the origins of the issues we will discuss in this workshop? What have we learned about the important issues? What do we need to know?

It is a real pleasure for me to introduce to you Robert Straus, Professor and Chairman of the Department of Behavioral Sciences, University of Kentucky, Lexington, who will present the keynote address.

ALCOHOL PROBLEMS AMONG THE ELDERLY: THE NEED FOR A BIOBEHAVIORAL PERSPECTIVE

Robert Straus

ABSTRACT

The knowledge base for the study of alcohol problems among the elderly is reviewed from both a historical and a biobehavioral perspective. Changing perceptions about the variability of human responses to alcohol and the pharmacological versatility of alcohol are discussed along with relatively recent changes in the consumption of alcohol, the causes of intoxication, and the social and biological liabilities of alcohol misuse. It is suggested that alcohol problems be classified according to intoxications, alcohol-related diseases, and types of alcohol dependence and that dependency types be classified as physiological, psychological, and social as well as both generalized and situational. The changing nature and status of the aging population are described, and a number of questions are posed regarding both the relationship between alcohol use and misuse and selected biological, psychological, and social aspects of the aging process.

The planners of our conference suggested that this paper should include a historical perspective. Such a perspective is particularly appropriate because the alcohol studies field has experienced so many important changes during the last 40 years. There have been significant changes in patterns of alcohol consumption; in the social environments in which alcohol is used; in beliefs about the functions of alcohol; in its perceived liabilities; in the available medicinal, nonmedicinal, and industrial chemicals with which alcohol can interact; and in our knowledge about alcohol and the human body, our perceptions about the meaning of such knowledge, and our assumptions about what we can expect to learn.

The field of aging or gerontology has also changed rapidly, blossoming from a virtual nonentity 40 years ago to a major focus of social, scientific, and medical concern. This has, in part, been associated with the relatively recent recognition of the implications of expanding longevity of human life in industrial societies.

A changing degree of interest in alcohol and aging can perhaps be illustrated by the fact that the indexes of the first 10 volumes of the Quarterly Journal of Studies on Alcohol (1940-49) contained no references to aging, old age, elderly, or gerontology; in the next decade there was just one such reference, and in the 1960s there were 13. Comparisons beyond the 1960s are not truly valid because the journal expanded its content, becoming a monthly, and its indexing became much more detailed, but during the 1970s references to aging, gerontology, and the like became commonplace. By 1980, a substantial body of literature on alcohol and aging was also appearing in many other scientific journals, and there were at least two reviews of the field (Mishara and Kastenbaum 1980; Gomberg 1982).

One theme of this paper, therefore, is change. Primarily, we will consider change with respect to alcohol. More briefly, we will discuss the changing phenomenon of aging. Finally, we will consider what we know and do not know abut alcohol and aging and some of the questions we should be asking.

An implicit theme of this paper is the need for a biobehavioral perspective. The recent report from the Institute of Medicine on Health and Behavior (Hamburg et al. 1982) has identified numerous examples of the interface of biological and behavioral factors in relation to human health and disease. Both alcohol studies and gerontology appear to be entering a biobehavioral era of scientific thought and activity.

While both alcohol studies and gerontology have impressive records of multidisciplinary research, there have been few truly interdisciplinary studies and few efforts to explore fundamental interrelationships between biological and behavioral phenomena.

FACTORS OF CHANGE

Two factors of change to be discussed are conceptual in nature. They involve the variability in the way in which different individuals respond to alcohol and in the responses of particular individuals to alcohol under different circumstances, and the versatility of alcohol. Although neither of these concepts is new, each deserves examination and emphasis at this time.

INDIVIDUAL VARIABILITY

Interest in individual variability in response to alcohol has become a recurrent theme in some of the contemporary research of geneticists, biochemists, pharmacologists, and neuroscientists who have been studying alcohol-related phenomena. This was apparent at a conference on biological variability and alcohol held at Johns Hopkins University in 1979 (Lehninger et al. 1981), and it is apparent in the Institute of Medicine's report, <u>Alcoholism and Related Problems: Opportunities for Research</u> (1980). Simply stated, there is an emerging consensus that genetic factors, as yet not precisely identified, influence the relative sensitivity of the human body to alcohol and the vulnerability of individuals to alcohol-related problems. Not only is there variability between individuals in general, but within individuals there is variable sensitivity among different organ sites and even among different areas of an organ system like the brain. Furthermore, some aspects of sensitivity or vulnerability appear to vary with individuals according to changing circumstances, such as time in a circadian or menstrual cycle or age in the life cycle, and in relation to factors such as stress, fatigue, recent illness, and other conditions that can alter body chemistry. There are also changes and variability of special significance for aging that will be discussed later.

From a biobehavioral perspective, the significance of genetically influenced biological variations in degrees of hypersensitivity or hyposensitivity and vulnerability or resistibility to alcohol depends on an individual's actual exposure to alcohol and cumulative experiences with drinking. For individuals who never drink, vulnerability to alcohol will have little significance. On the other hand, for individuals who drink and who are hypersensitive or particularly vulnerable to alcohol, these traits may have bipolar effects. For some, the unpleasantness associated with exposure to even small amounts of alcohol may serve as a protection against drinking and exposure to further vulnerability. However, hypersensitive individuals who persist in drinking, in response to social or psychological forces, may experience problems earlier in their lives and in connection with amounts of drinking that would not be enough to cause problems for other people. At the opposite extreme, hyposensitive individuals may be able to consume relatively large amounts of alcohol without experiencing intoxication or other behavioral complications of drinking. Yet, if their hyposensitivity is restricted to brain function and does not include other organs, the fact that they are able to comfortably consume large amounts of alcohol may eventually expose them to other alcohol-related diseases that result from the cumulative impact of heavy drinking over long periods of time. It is not uncommon to have cirrhosis of the liver, peptic ulcer, or some other alcohol-related disease diagnosed in patients who deny that the disease can be due to alcohol. They will insist, and their friends and relatives will corroborate, that they have never been drunk in their lives. Usually, however, further discussion will reveal that they have regularly consumed reasonably large amounts of alcohol for long periods of time.

Although it has only recently received widespread scientific interest, the concept of variability in response to alcohol is certainly not new. Even the casual observer of drinking behavior will recognize that some people can "handle" very little alcohol while others can "hold their liquor" more than most people. Roger Williams, in his "working hypothesis" on the etiology of alcohol (Williams 1947), alluded to "a wide variability among individuals in the amount of alcohol required to bring about signs of intoxication or impairment of function" and to "the susceptibility of some individuals to the development of alcoholism in contrast to the apparent immunity of the majority." Williams also proposed a theory of causality that combined hereditary and environmental factors, suggesting that "alcoholics are not born and are not made, but . . . heredity and environmental influences are both important" and further "environmental factors are potent and indispensable for bringing about alcoholism, but they do not do so unless the person involved possesses the type of metabolic individuality which predisposes toward addiction." Unfortunately, Williams was arguing against the more accepted scientific thinking of the day. I well remember some disparaging remarks with which this paper was received at that time when prevailing beliefs held that evidence regarding hereditary predisposition toward alcoholism was unfounded; that problem drinking could be explained primarily by psychological, sociocultural, and environmental variables; and that the degree of alcohol-induced intoxication and incapacitation was consistently correlated with blood alcohol levels.

A decade later, Selden Bacon (1958) in his insightful paper "Alcoholics Do Not Drink" suggested that there must be some fundamental factors that differentiate people who can become alcoholics from those who do not. Variability among types of people who develop drinking problems was, of course, a major theme in Jellinek's (1960) classic volume on the disease concept of alcoholism. Yet, until the very recent biological interest in variability, alcohol studies have been more concerned with similarities than with differences in the ways in which people respond to alcohol.

If social and behavioral scientists are to capitalize on the important new leads that biological scientists are beginning to provide, they must become comfortable with such concepts as receptor sites and metabolic pathways; biologists must accept the significance of terms like reinforcement, reference group pressures, and norms. Both behavioral and biological scientists must be willing to go at least halfway toward the development of a common basis for further exploring the interface between heredity, those biological traits that are subject to change with human experience, and those behavioral factors that influence exposure to and cumulative experience with alcohol.

VERSATILITY OF ALCOHOL

Although the versatility of alcohol has long been recognized, there are some recent developments in the way in which the significance of versatility is being perceived. Historically, of course, alcohol has been important as a major source of human energy as well as for its numerous medicinal functions and mood modifying properties. In the 1940s, the high caloric value of alcohol was seen as a curse because prevailing beliefs blamed most of the alcohol-related diseases on malnutrition. It was assumed that alcoholics were obtaining so much of their caloric need from alcohol that they were neglecting foods that contained essential vitamins and minerals. It was also noted that the calories supplied by alcohol increased the need for certain other nutrients (Jolliffe 1945). Substantial support for this line of thinking followed the introduction of the practice of reinforcing such common food items as bread and cereals with what were believed to be daily minimal requirements of certain vitamins and minerals. The introduction of this practice resulted in a dramatic drop in the incidence of nutritional diseases such as pellagra and beriberi and nutritionally related brain syndromes among alcoholics being treated in public hospitals.

In more recent years, there has developed an increased recognition of the permeability of alcohol into virtually all body tissues, of the direct toxic effects of alcohol, and of its more direct role in disease causation. Still, the potential for heavy drinkers to incur nutritional disease remains, and this may be of greater significance for elderly people than for the population at large.

Studies of alcohol as a pharmacological agent have focused attention on the fact that, like all other drugs, alcohol can have both desirable and adverse effects. This, too, is not a new concept. In fact, the world literature is virtually dichotomized on the subject of alcohol, with most references either extolling its virtues or decrying its vices. A two-value orientation toward alcohol in the Old Testament is nicely illustrated in O'Brien and Seller's (1982) recent classification of positive and negative references to alcohol in the Bible.

Quite recently, however, the paradoxical effects of alcohol have been subject to more rigorous consideration. Like the effects of many other drugs, the effects of alcohol in small amounts can be vastly different from the effects of alcohol in larger amounts. Drinkers who experience a pleasant sense of well-being and euphoria from one or two drinks are usually sadly disappointed when they seek an intensification of these pleasant sensations from four or five drinks. Thus, in modest amounts, shortly after ingestion, alcohol can provide a stimulating sensation; yet, in larger amounts, its ultimate effect is sedation and depression. Alcohol is an effective analgesic; yet it is also an irritant to human tissues and a source of pain and discomfort when it causes such conditions as gastritis or pancreatitis. Alcohol, in small amounts, is a pleasant tranquilizing drug; yet in some drinkers and in excessive amounts, it can produce a sense of severe psyhic distress. Alcohol, in small amounts, relaxes inhibitions, facilitates comfortable participation in social functions, and enhances the enjoyment of personal interaction; yet too much alcohol can facilitate aggression, indiscretion, and other violations of social amenity or law. Moderate amounts of alcohol can provide sedation and induce sleep; yet alcohol-related sleep is often restless and unsatisfying. As Shakespeare and many others have noted, alcohol, in moderate amounts, can enhance sexual desire (by suppressing inhibition and anxiety); yet too much alcohol in the male can deflate sexual performance and in the female can obliterate pleasurable response. Small amounts of alcohol can help people engage in difficult or dangerous tasks, but too much alcohol can impair their capacity to complete such tasks successfully. These variations in the functions and dysfunctions that can be experienced by different amounts of alcohol involve a complex interaction of biological, psychological, cultural, and social factors. In part, they depend on individual variability in sensitivity to alcohol and in the reactions that different amounts of alcohol produce. In part, they are due to variable responses of different people to alcohol that have psychological and sociocultural roots. In part, they involve customs or norms that define varying degrees of acceptability or unacceptability for different kinds of drinking-related behavior and for individuals with varying roles and under varying circumstances. In part, they involve the degree of liability associated with alcohol-induced effects in persons engaged in particular kinds of human activity.

CHANGES IN ALCOHOL CONSUMPTION

It is difficult to grasp all of the changes that have been taking place with respect to alcohol use in our society over the past 40 years and the impact of various changes on each other. Clearly, during this period, there has been a significant rise in the annual per capita consumption of alcohol in most countries of the Western World. In the United States, per capita consumption has risen by about one-third since the 1960s. To a limited degree, this rise in consumption reflects an increase in the number of users, especially among youth under 18 and among women. However, it is primarily a reflection of increased consumption by drinkers. Since problem drinkers account for a significant amount of the alcohol consumed in a society, much of the rise in per capita consumption includes an increase in the number of people who are drinking too much alcohol. The rise in consumption has also been associated with an increase in the types and numbers of social situations that define drinking as appropriate or expected behavior. This is particularly evident with respect to the expansion of leisure time activities that has accompanied a shortening of working time for many segments of society and with respect to specific recreational activities. For example, 40 years ago, most bowling alleys were primarily designed for bowling. They usually included at most a soft drink machine for refreshment. My high school friends and I often enjoyed an evening's recreation for 50 cents while bowling three 15-cent strings and consuming a 5-cent coke. Today, there are few bowling establishments that do not have fully equipped bars, and alcohol consumption has become an accepted accompaniment of bowling events. Similarly, alcohol use has become increasingly integrated with attendance at the theater and at ballgames, and with a substantial amount of home entertainment via television.

Alcohol availability is also a major factor in the highly competitive convention industry. Competition between communities for the lucrative convention business has been directly associated with a relaxing of controls on the numbers and locations of outlets where alcohol can be served or purchased, with the legalization of alcohol sales in some areas that were formerly "dry," and with an expansion in the numbers of days and hours when alcohol has been legally available.

The extent to which alcohol consumption permeates certain types of social situations in our society is well illustrated by a quote from the late James Jones' novel <u>Whistle</u> (1978). Jones' leading character, Sgt. Winch, has been advised by his physician that because of his heart disease, he must get used to the idea that he can never drink again. Winch indicates that he is "used to it" but then Jones goes on to write:

> but he wasn't. When he thought about it, it was enough to have him almost biting the walls. It was astonishing when you got down in and noticed it, how much almost everything in America has to do with drinking. Every dinner. Every meal. Almost every social occasion. If you were chasing

some girl. And at night, when everybody was philosophizing about life and the war and death, or dancing and trying to make out with some broad, if you did not drink, you were outside everything. And bored to death by all of it.

When Winch went back into town for an evening after he had been out of bed for a week, he found "the whole place was totally impossible if you did not drink."

Studies of alcohol consumption in historical perspective suggest that the amount of alcohol consumed per se is not necessarily correlated with the perception of drinking problems in a society. As Lender and Martin (1982) have pointed out, the consumption of absolute alcohol in the United States 200 years ago is estimated to have been at least twice as great as it is today. Yet they note that there are few references in contemporary literature of the 1780s and 1790s to concern in the society over problems of drunkenness or of other adverse effects of drinking. Lender and Martin suggest that our ancestors were able to consume large amounts of alcohol without untoward effects in part because of the functions alcohol provided as a source of human energy, in part because drinking tended to be spaced over time in a pattern that limited its intoxicating effects, in part because there were strong family and community sanctions against intoxication, and in part because a higher level of alcohol-induced effect could be achieved without its being perceived or labeled as drunkenness.

CHANGING LIABILITIES OF ALCOHOL MISUSE

Such reasoning leads to the consideration of another major change that has occurred with respect to alcohol use in our society. This is the increase in the liabilities that occur for people who are intoxicated in an urbanized and industrialized society. The recently intensified social concern with drinking and driving highlights an example of an alcohol problem that did not exist in the last century and that has intensified with the expanded use of automobiles and airplanes. Safety in modern transportation depends on operators whose capacities for perception, judgment, motor control, and rapid response are free from impairment. Concern over the threat to the health and well-being of the innocent victims of drinking and driving is matched by an increasing concern about the extent to which alcohol impairment is compromising the quantity and quality of industrial production. Although these are not new problems, the degree of social concern has increased as both the real and perceived threat to human safety and economic well-being has expanded. This change is quite dramatically illustrated by our military organizations that are currently struggling to overturn a long tradition that supported the use of alcohol and rewarded individuals who were perceived to be able to hold their liquor at a time when the functions of alcohol as a source of human energy and as an antianxiety and an inhibitory drug were valued. Today, when most military personnel are expected to be able to handle complicated machinery requiring fine line brain function, the dysfunctions of alcohol impairment are seen as outweighing its traditional but now anachronistic functions. Changes in the nature of concern about the liabilities of problem drinking are also widespread in industrial circles. The pressures created by foreign competition have finally forced American industrial management to face squarely the extent to which alcohol misuse has contributed to the problems of quality control that have plagued their products.

The liabilities of alcohol use are not all associated with intoxication. Another significant change has involved the recognition of the extent to which the cumulative impact of drinking appears to be a contributing etiological factor in the major causes of death and disability in the United States. The documentation for this association was summarized in the volume Healthy People (Richmond 1979) in which the 10 leading killers and disablers of people in the United States are identified, and it is noted that alcohol in one way or another is a contributing factor to each of these. In the age group 15 to 24 years old, alcohol's impact is experienced primarily through motor vehicle and other accidents and through alcohol-related acts of violence. For the population as a whole, however, the relationship involves the cumulative effect of drinking as a contributing factor to major degenerative diseases. Since degenerative diseases are primarily experienced with advancing age, the role of excessive drinking appears to have a dual effect on the aging process. In part, it acts as a factor of selection since people who drink too much tend to have shorter lives. In part, it can contribute to the disabling conditions experienced by those who survive to become elderly.

CHANGES IN CAUSES OF INTOXICATION

Over the past 40 years, one of the most significant changes affecting alcohol's impact on human beings has been the introduction of a vast number of intoxicating substances that are now used by substantial numbers of people. In 1940, with the exception of barbiturates that were being prescribed on a limited basis primarily to induce sleep, most intoxication in the United States was associated with alcohol consumption. Since that time, the nature and status of intoxication have become immeasurably more complicated. There are now in common use a vast array of medicinal drugs, both prescribed and available for self-medication, that interact with alcohol in ways that are additive or synergistic. Some drugs may combine with alcohol to produce metabolites with unique toxic properties. Three classes of such drugs should be mentioned because they are being used very widely and because their use in combination with alcohol is very common.

Antihistamine drugs are today included in most over-the-counter remedies for colds and sleeping aids and are prescribed for the relief of a wide variety of allergic conditions. It has been estimated that, depending upon the season, between 25 and 40 million people in the United States may be using antihistamines at any particular time. Because these are sedative drugs that can cause drowsiness, it is not uncommon for individuals who are taking antihistamines to find that their reaction to one or two drinks is more like what they would expect from three or four. The combined use of alcohol and antihistamines is common because few people recognize the potential adverse effects of the combination and because many people believe that alcohol is also good for colds and as an aid to sleep.

Antianxiety drugs represent another class of pharmacological agents that were not available in the 1940s. Although prescriptions for antianxiety drugs appear to have decreased since 1978 in response to warnings to physicians about their abuse, it is estimated that at least 15 million people are still taking antianxiety drugs for some significant period of time within each year. These drugs, too, can interact in a synergistic way with alcohol. Also, it has been found that many people use alcohol and antianxiety drugs for the same purpose, and it is reported by many alcoholics that they commonly use antianxiety drugs in association with or in place of alcohol. Like alcohol, such drugs appear to create a high risk for dependency in susceptible individuals.

Since World War II and particularly during the last 20 years, we have been experiencing an epidemic of drug abuse involving numerous nonmedicinal and illegal substances. Of these, marijuana is of special significance because of its widespread use. Marijuana, though long known and widely used in many parts of the world, became a drug of common use in the United States only during the 1960s. Initially, marijuana use tended to be isolated around so-called pot parties but, quickly, its use became more widespread through different segments of the population. Use also became more casual and more commonly associated with drinking. Although marijuana use is today rare among the elderly population, its significance for the subject of alcohol and aging lies in the impact of alcohol-marijuana interaction in the cohorts of people who will become elderly in two or three decades.

As will be mentioned later, one distinct problem of drug interactions with alcohol and aging stems from the increased use of numerous medications by people as they get older. This is associated with an increased risk for a wide variety of potentially dangerous alcohol-medication interactions.

PERCEIVING THE PROBLEMS OF ALCOHOL

One of the problems faced by persons interested in alcohol-related matters, whether from the perspective of research, education, or public policy, has been the absence of broadly accepted terminology. For example, the terms alcoholic and alcoholism have been used by some temperance-oriented groups to include everyone who uses alcohol; sometimes they have been applied to everyone who ever has had an alcohol problem or who is perceived as drinking to a point of intoxication; and sometimes they have been restricted to persons who manifest a syndrome of alcohol dependency and its medical and behavioral concomitants. References to alcoholism as a disease are as old as the use of the term itself.

In 1942, Haggard and Jellinek published a book called <u>Alcohol Explored</u> in which they tried to introduce some precision of terminology by suggesting that all persons who expose themselves to the gross effects of alcohol be called intemperate drinkers to differentiate them from habitual social drinkers who drink regularly but not in amounts to cause disease, and moderate drinkers who only occasionally use small amounts of alcohol. Among intemperate drinkers, they suggested that those whose behavior is definitely affected by frequent intoxication be called inebriates. They suggested a subclassification of inebriates into normal excessive drinkers (motivated by recklessness, exuberance, or mistaken good fellowship), symptomatic drinkers (whose drinking is a symptom of their psychotic state), stupid drinkers (the feebleminded who cannot resist temptation), and addicts (those with an uncontrollable craving who cannot break the habit). Haggard and Jellinek reserved the term "alcoholic"--they actually used "chronic alcoholic"--for those drinkers only who, from the prolonged and excessive use of alcoholic beverages--usually over many years--finally develop definite physical or psychological changes. They noted that chronic alcoholism was not the habitual drinking of large amounts of alcohol but <u>definite disease</u> conditions resulting from such habits.

The publication of <u>Alcohol Explored</u> coincided closely with the "breaking out" of Alcoholics Anonymous from its small beginnings and just preceded the nationwide establishment of specialized alcoholism clinics modeled after the so-called Yale Plan and the development of a national voluntary health organization movement, which has evolved into the National Council on Alcoholism and its local affiliates. The concept of alcoholism as a disease has been an integral factor in all three of these movements.

The disease concept has been a topic of much controversy in recent years. Some critics believe that it was adopted primarily as a strategy for overcoming public stigma and to seduce or persuade health professionals into accepting responsibility for treating people with alcohol problems. Critics also stress that alcohol problems extend far beyond just alcoholism and that they have vast social, psychological, economic, and legal consequences that differentiate them from "real" diseases. They also point out that medical responses alone are generally inadequate.

A SUGGESTED CLASSIFICATION FOR ALCOHOL PROBLEMS

In response to the continuing controversy over alcohol problem terminology, I believe it is useful to think in terms of three major consequences of the use of amounts of alcohol that are "too much" or excessive for particular individuals. These are intoxication, alcohol-related diseases, and dependency.

<u>Intoxication</u> is generally manifested in the compromising of brain function. Since people vary with respect to the areas of the brain that are particularly sensitive to alcohol, intoxication is expressed in many different ways, including sleep, aggression, indiscretion, slurred speech, and deficiencies in motor control, judgment, perception, memory, or response time. Intoxication is an acute condition associated with the immediate impact of alcohol or its metabolites on organ systems. Intoxication is not restricted to the central nervous system; it can also be manifested through the incidental compromise of liver function and such conditions as gastritis, pancreatitis, or other forms of organ irritation.

When people repeatedly or continually subject themselves to alcohol intoxication, they run the risk of developing chronic and sometimes irreversible conditions that result from such cumulative insults. These conditions are <u>alcohol-related diseases</u> such as liver cirrhosis, peptic ulcer, or cardiomyopathy. To some extent, all of the major contemporary fatal and disabling diseases are alcohol related because they appear much more frequently in persons who have histories of heavy drinking than in those who do not.

<u>Dependency</u> on alcohol occurs in many levels and forms. A very mild form of dependency on the mood-modifying effects of moderate amounts of alcohol probably exists in the millions of people who

are accustomed to always having one or two drinks in connection with a regularly recurring event such as between work and the evening meal. This drinking practice may be quite functional for such individuals--the benefits of the relaxation they achieve far outweighing the adverse effects, if any. Yet, it is a form of dependency if, whenever a person does not have the alcohol, it is missed and the individual does not feel right or is "out of sorts." A comparable sensation is experienced by millions of caffeine-dependent persons whenever they miss their morning coffee. Alcohol dependency becomes a problem when individuals feel compelled to drink in amounts that are too much or in circumstances that are inappropriate in spite of potential adverse consequences.

Dependency problems can be classified as generalized or situational; (related to inner felt needs or to needs that emanate outside the individual); and as physical, psychological, and social.

Generalized dependency is found in persons whose lives have become so permeated by the need for alcohol that they are not able to function without it. Even when they are not actively drinking, they are preoccupied with protecting their supply of alcohol. The acts of drinking or assuring access to alcohol take precedence over all other aspects of their lives. Some people with generalized dependency develop a physical dependence manifested by withdrawal symptoms when tissues that have been accustomed to the presence of alcohol as a normal state are suddenly deprived. While all people with generalized dependency do not experience physical dependency, physical dependency is generalized, and those who have it are psychologically dependent as well. Psychological dependency is manifested by strong sensations of craving or painful compulsive senses of need. These feelings are so dominant that dependent persons are unable to function in other activities without alcohol.

I believe that most contemporary references to alcoholism and the alcoholic encompass people who manifest a generalized dependency.

Situational dependence is found in individuals whose needs for too much alcohol tend to appear only in association with certain kinds of situations. Much situational dependence has a psychological (inner felt) origin and is exemplified by persons who feel they have to drink to face certain kinds of anxiety-provoking situations such as meeting with a boss, taking an examination, performing in public, having a date, or engaging in sex. Some dependency seems generalized for certain periods of a person's life but is subject to change as the person moves out of or back into different situations such as a difficult job or a stressful marriage.

Many people who repeatedly drink excessive amounts of alcohol are not motivated either by physical dependency or by deep-seated psychological needs for alcohol. Instead, they are responding to what they perceive to be a very strong need to comply with prevailing social expectations and to conform to the behavior of persons with whom they identify and whose approval they strongly desire. I have called this social dependency (Straus 1983). It tends to be situationally specific and is in response to needs that emanate outside of the individual from the society and from cultural norms. Yet it can be both pervasive and powerful. It is a particularly significant form of dependence for young people and for others who are in the early stages of problem-drinking careers. I have described it here because it rounds out a classification scheme for types of alcohol dependency rather than because of its special significance to alcohol and aging.

AGING

Whether viewed from a biological, a psychological, or a sociocultural perspective, aging is a relative term. My magnificent mother-in-law, who died at age 97 in January 1983, had traveled alone from Hartford to Wyoming the previous October and to Kentucky and Washington, D.C., in November. Until her final illness, she was a future-oriented person who never "acted her age." On the other hand, we all know some people who begin thinking, feeling, and acting old in their 40s or 50s. Many demographic studies use age 65 as the dividing line between middle and old age, and until a recent act of Congress added 5 years to our working life, age 65 was a common point for compulsory retirement from many jobs.

In 1900, there were an estimated 3 million persons in the United States 65 years of age and older. These represented 4 percent of the total population. Life expectancy at birth was estimated at 47 years. By 1940, the 9 million older (65+) persons represented 7 percent of the population, and estimated life expectancy at birth was 63 years. In 1980, the 65+ population of 25 million was over 11 percent of the total population. Life expectancy at birth had edged up to 75 years. Clearly, the older segment of our population is growing in both absolute and relative terms, and this trend is projected to continue.

One concomitant of longer life is an increasing risk of developing the degenerative diseases that today represent our most common causes of death and disability. In recent years, it has become evident that persons who drink beyond very moderate amounts (remembering that what constitutes moderate varies according to individual sensitivity) are at substantially greater risk than others for developing heart disease, stroke, certain forms of cancer, diabetes, emphysema, pneumonia, and other diseases common to later life and that when they do become sick they are often sicker than others.

In keeping with the diseases they develop and the aches and anxieties that they often suffer, older people consume a disproportionately large share of the medications--both prescribed and purchased over the counter--that are used in the United States. For many, aging and declining health are associated with diminished economic resources, the loss of self-esteem, restricted activities, the illnesses or deaths of spouse and friends, enforced retirement, the need to uproot a home, or other stressful life events.

ALCOHOL AND AGING

We noted earlier in this paper that the topic of aging was, until quite recently, almost totally absent from the scientific literature on alcohol. To perhaps an even greater extent, the literature on aging is devoid of references to alcohol. Until very recently, alcohol use has not been perceived to be a problem of aging. Quite to the contrary, it has been assumed that alcohol problems tended to disappear beyond "middle" life.

At first glance, indeed, the good news about alcohol and aging appears to outweigh the bad. Epidemiological studies have told us that the percentages of men and women who use alcohol begin to decrease after age 50 and that there is a drop in the percentage of persons with drinking problems among women over age 50 and men beyond age 60 (Gomberg 1982). It is not clear whether the studies on which these observations are based reflect all types of alcohol-related problems and, particularly, whether they account for certain kinds of alcohol problems that are particular to aging.

The biological aging process includes a number of changes that can influence one's responses to alcohol. There are hormonal changes. The relative amount of body fat increases while the volume of body water tends to decrease. There are changes in rates of absorption, metabolism, and elimination. Storage time may be prolonged. There appear to be changes in tissue sensitivity. Associated with these changes, which vary in frequency and intensity from person to person, there is often an increase in the impact experienced from a given amount of alcohol and a decrease in the amount that can be comfortably consumed. Put another way, as many people get older, they experience a decrease in the amount of alcohol that they can drink if they want to maximize the desirable effects and minimize the adverse effects.

SOME QUESTIONS ABOUT ALCOHOL AND AGING

I will now change the focus of this paper from a historical and descriptive framework to a conjectural one. The nature and extent of alcohol problems among the elderly are just now beginning to be studied. It is hoped that the reports of research findings and the discussions of this conference will chart a course for further inquiry. To help launch this process, I will suggest several probable or possible types of alcohol problems that should be considered in relation to the aging process.

(1) What do we know about surviving alcoholics? Despite evidence that alcoholics tend to die earlier than their nonalcoholic counterparts, we really do not know to what extent some alcoholics manage to persist with their alcoholic drinking patterns and still survive the odds against longevity and become members of the elderly population. Furthermore, even though alcoholic drinking may persist, we should be asking what significant changes, if any, are occurring within these patterns. Do older alcoholics tend to drink less alcohol? Do they drink less frequently? Do they change, for example, from steady to periodic drinkers (or from periodic to steady drinkers)? Do they change from seeking a peak effect from alcohol to seeking a plateau (or from plateau to peak)? Do they change the types of alcohol they consume or the context of their alcoholic drinking? Do the problems that they encounter change with advancing age?

(2) What is the status of former alcoholics who have achieved sobriety? What do we know or would it be useful to know about alcoholics who are able to survive to old age, perhaps primarily because they have been able to achieve sobriety? To what extent are former or recovering or "dry" alcoholics afflicted with the degenerative diseases of aging? How does their alcoholic history appear to have an impact on their lives as senior citizens and on their deaths? To what extent does the task of maintaining sobriety change with advancing age? Does the point in their lives when they achieved sobriety appear to be associated with their longevity?

(3) To what extent are elderly persons who have never previously been identified as having alcohol problems or experiencing frequent intoxication afflicted with alcohol-related diseases that appear to be associated with the cumulative effects of regular consumption of significant amounts of alcohol?

(4) To what extent do drinking problems appear among older people who have simply carried over into their later years drinking practices that did not cause problems earlier in their lives? How many people experience with aging a decrease in the amount of alcohol that they can consume without experiencing intoxication or other adverse effects? How many of these people have been able to adjust their drinking downward in order to accommodate their decreased capacity? How many experience problems because they do not accommodate their drinking to their reduced capacity?

(5) What do we know about alcohol and nutrition among the aged? Does alcohol preempt the use of more nutritional foods by some older people? There is evidence that some aging people experience reduced appetites, less capacity to handle food comfortably, less sensitivity of taste, and less interest in food. Some of the degenerative diseases of aging limit the ability to ingest, absorb, and metabolize certain foods. It has also been suggested that the need for certain vitamins and minerals may increase with aging. Since alcohol meets caloric but no other nutritional needs, to what extent do older people who consume significant amounts of alcohol risk incurring nutritional diseases because the alcohol they use is satisfying their appetites, thus adding to their loss of interest in foods that supply major nutritional requirements?

(6) To what extent does alcohol contribute to the various accidents experienced by older people and to the injuries that they incur?

(7) To what extent do older people begin to use alcohol or use too much alcohol in order to ease the task of coping with changes that are particularly common to the later years of life? How is alcohol use related to retirement, unfulfilled leisure time, widowhood, reduced income and other financial problems, the pains and anxieties of illness, the gradual loss of friends and family members, and the loss of self-esteem, meaningful activities, and a purpose for living? To what extent does the capacity to cope with stress decrease as people get older, and is the use of alcohol a significant response to such a change?

(8) What are the benefits of alcohol use for older persons? Alcohol has a long and honorable history as a very versatile form of medication. Many of its medicinal uses have been supplanted by drugs with more specific and sometimes more controllable actions. Yet its use as a folk medicine persists, and there have been recent suggestions

that moderate alcohol users may experience less cardiovascular disease than either heavy drinkers or abstainers. Although this paper has focused on the potential problems of alcohol misuse among the elderly, the potential benefits that older people experience from moderate alcohol use should also be examined.

(9) What are the implications of alcohol and medication interactions for the elderly? As noted earlier, along with the aging process and the onset of a wide variety of degenerative diseases, there is a dramatic rise in the use of medications by older people. Many elderly persons are able to function effectively in their jobs, families, and communities only because they are using medications that compensate for conditions that would otherwise be disabling. There is a growing literature on medication misuse among the elderly and particularly on problems of drug interaction among persons who are using multiple medications. To what extent does alcohol use contribute to problems of drug interaction? How many older people use alcohol in ways that offset or interfere with the desirable functions of certain medications? To what extent does alcohol provide an undesirable or potentially dangerous additive effect? How many people are using alcohol in ways that cause a synergistic reaction with their medications? To what extent are older people more vulnerable to the adverse effects of drug interactions because changes in absorption, metabolism, storage, and elimination processes intensify the risks of adverse effects?

CONCLUSION

The examination of problems of alcohol and drug interactions among the elderly is a fitting note on which to conclude this paper, for it illustrates explicitly both the concept of change and the need for a biomedical orientation. There have been significant changes in recent years in the medications that older people are taking and in the potential liabilities that exist when they are used with alcohol. There are even more significant changes occurring in the perceptions of the biological sciences regarding the processes of alcohol and drug absorption, metabolism, distribution, and clearance and how these processes can change with aging. Yet the acts of prescribing and obtaining drugs and of drug and alcohol utilization are behavioral. Alcohol, medication, and other drug use patterns are all substantially influenced by the beliefs, values, customs, and other norms that have a cultural basis and that are activated and reinforced through a social process.

REFERENCES

Bacon, S.D. Alcoholics do not drink. In: *Understanding Alcoholism. Annals of American Academy of Political and Social Science* 315:55-64, 1958.

Gomberg, E.S.L. Alcohol use and alcohol problems among the elderly. In: National Institute on Alcohol Abuse and Alcoholism, *Alcohol and Health Monograph 4: Special Population Issues.* DHHS Pub. No. (ADM)82-1193. Washington, D.C.: Supt. of Docs., U.S. Govt. Print. Off., 1982.

Haggard, H.W., and Jellinek, E.M. *Alcohol Explored.* Garden City, N.Y.: Doubleday, Doran and Company, 1942.

Hamburg, D.A.; Elliott, G.R.; and Parron, D.L., eds. *Health and Behavior: Frontiers of Research in the Biobehavioral Sciences.* Washington, D.C.: National Academy Press, 1982.

Institute of Medicine. *Alcoholism and Related Problems: Opportunities for Research.* Washington, D.C.: National Academy Press, 1980.

Jellinek, E.M. *The Disease Concept of Alcoholism.* New Haven, Conn.: Hill House Press, 1960.

Jolliffe, N. Alcohol and nutrition: The diseases of chronic alcoholism. In: *Alcohol, Science and Society.* New Haven, Conn.: Quarterly Journal of Studies on Alcohol, Inc., 1945.

Jones, J. *Whistle.* New York: Delacorte Press, 1978.

Lehninger, A.L.; McKusick, V.A.; and Santora, P.B. Proceedings of the Conference on Genetic and Biochemical Variability in Response to Alcohol. *Alcoholism: Clinical and Experimental Research* 5(3):435-468, 1981.

Lender, M.E., and Martin, J.K. *Drinking in America: A History.* New York: Free Press, 1982.

Mishara, B.L., and Kastenbaum, R. *Alcohol and Old Age.* New York: Grune and Stratton, 1980.

O'Brien, J.M., and Seller, S.C. Attributes of alcohol in the Old Testament. *The Drinking and Drug Practices Surveyor* 18:18-24, 1982.

Straus, R. Types of alcohol dependence. In: Kissin, B., and Begleiter, H., eds. <u>The Biology of Alcoholism</u>. Vol. 6: <u>The Pathogenesis of Alcoholism: Psychosocial Factors</u>. New York: Plenum Press, 1983. pp. 1-16.

Williams, R.J. The etiology of alcoholism: A working hypothesis involving the interplay of hereditary and environmental factors. <u>Quarterly Journal of Alcohol Studies</u> 7:565-587, 1947.

THE MENTAL HEALTH AND SOCIAL CORRELATES OF ALCOHOL USE AMONG DIFFERING LIFE CYCLE GROUPS

George J. Warheit
Joanne B. Auth

ABSTRACT

This paper presents data on the prevalence of alcohol use and its relationships to mental health and social well-being. It also describes how these relationships vary among differing social, demographic, and life cycle groups. The data are drawn from a review of tne literature and from the epidemiologic field research of the authors and their colleagues. Information on a probability sample of 4,202 adults is presented.

Although there is little epidemiologic field survey data on concurrent alcohol and mental health problems, what are reported are remarkably consistent. About 5 percent of the general population have an alcohol problem that approximates the dependence/abuse criteria of the American Psychiatric Association. Males are about four times as likely as females to have an alcohol problem, and those under 30 years of age have problem rates four times greater than those over age 30.

Statistical analysis of the relationships between the prevalence of alcohol problems and the scores on three psychiatric symptom/dysfunction scales are consistently significant. The statistical relationships between alcohol problems and depressive symptomatology are especially significant.

The data on alcohol problems and general well-being as determined by a variety of indicators, show that the age group 18 to 29 years old has the highest alcohol consumption rates and, further, that these higher rates are associated with increased levels of social, medical, and/or mental health problems. The lowest alcohol consumption rates and their concurrent dysfunctions are found most often among those 50 years of age and older. Overall, single males under age 30 are at highest risk for alcohol abuse and its related problems.

INTRODUCTION

Purpose

This paper discusses the relationships between alcohol use, mental health, and social well-being and describes how these vary among differing social, demographic, and life cycle groups. The data utilized to address these issues come from a review of the literature and from the epidemiologic research of the authors and their colleagues.

Background

The relationships between alcohol abuse and mental health problems have interested researchers, clinicians, and other human service providers for a long time. This interest is logical given the frequent observations that tie the two phenomena together. However, to date there has been very little epidemiologic research with general population samples regarding these relationships.

A recent review of the relevant literature conducted by the authors (Auth and Warheit 1982, 1983) revealed that there have been a large number of epidemiological field surveys conducted in both alcohol abuse and mental health, but only a few of these have investigated the two issues simultaneously. Moreover, the review indicated that the interrelationships have been addressed from two different perspectives. One of these has defined alcohol abuse under the rubric of a mental health problem, while the other has conceptualized the relationships between alcohol use and mental health from a more phenomenological, concurrence point of view. Each of these approaches will be outlined briefly to provide a background for the presentation of our findings on life cycle variations of alcohol use and their relationships to health and social well-being.

RESEARCH ON ALCOHOL AND MENTAL HEALTH

Alcohol Abuse As A Mental Health Problem

Examples of the psychiatric epidemiologic field survey approach to alcohol problems are found in the early Midtown Manhattan and Stirling County Studies and in the Epidemiologic Catchment Area (ECA) projects currently under way.

The Midtown Manhattan Study, a pioneering post World War II project, attempted a prevalence enumeration of alcoholics in the general population (Langner and Michael 1963). The criteria for determining the existence of an alcohol disorder included the interviewer's judgments of the respondent's appearance and the appropriateness of the times of inebriation. Another criterion was the admission of an alcohol problem on the part of the respondent. The Midtown researchers estimated that 4.6 percent of their sample could be classified as alcoholic. When controlled for socioeconomic status (SES), the data indicated that the highest rate, 6.6 percent, occurred among the lowest SES group. For respondents in the middle group, the rate was 4.5 percent, and for those in the highest category, the rate was 2.7 percent. Controls for other social and demographic variables were not reported.

A second early psychiatric epidemiologic survey, which included an alcohol use component, was the Stirling County Study conducted by the Leightons and their colleagues (1963). The standards they used to estimate the prevalence of alcohol problems were roughly equivalent to those outlined in the Diagnostic and Statistical Manual of Mental Disorders (First edition) (APA 1952). They reported that 4.3 percent of the sample met the criteria for alcoholism and, further, that the rate for males was about 10 times greater than the one for females. Other social and demographic controls were not used in their analysis, but the Stirling County group did analyze their alcohol data in terms of the respondents' scores on the Health Opinion Survey (HOS), a brief screening scale designed to measure psychoneuroticism (Macmillan 1957). The results of this analysis indicated that both males and females identified as being alcoholic had HOS scores significantly higher than those of the overall sample. For the most part, however, alcoholism was conceptualized primarily as a mental disorder, and no additional concurrence analyses were reported.

As noted above, the authors have recently conducted an extensive review of the epidemiologic literature on alcohol problems (Auth and Warheit 1982, 1983; Warheit and Auth 1984). A revised summary of this review is presented in table 1. When the alcohol findings reported by the Midtown and Stirling County researchers are compared to those presented by other investigators, one is impressed by their similarities. This is quite surprising given the differences in the methodologies utilized.

More systematic efforts to explore alcohol abuse/dependence from a psychiatric perspective are currently under way as part of the ECA projects. Since these projects and the data from them are to be discussed later by those directly involved in this research, we will not pursue them further in this paper except to indicate

Table 1.--Surveys of Adult Drinking Practices, USA

Year(s) of study	Reference(s)	Sample size	Percent abstainers			Percent heavy drinkers*			Percent problem drinkers			Problems
			Total	M	F	Total	M	F	Total	M	F	
1946	Riley and Marden (1947)	2,677	35	25	44							
1963	Mulford, (1964)	1,515	29	21	37	8	13	3	7	13	1	
1964-65 (ADP)	Cahalan et al. (1969)	2,746	32	23	40	12 (18	21 34	5 5)+	6	10	3	
1966	Gallup (1966)	1,500 (approx.)	35	30	39							
1967 (ADP follow-up)	Cahalan (1970)	1,359	29	30	36	7	13	2	5 5 8 37 2	6 5 11 49 3	5 3 5 29 2	Health Belligerence Symptomatic drinking Psychological dependence Job
1967 and 1969	Cahalan and Room (1974)	583 (1,561) 978							20			
1971-76 (Seven NIAAA funded national surveys)	Johnson et al. (1977)	1,071- 2,510	(6-year average) 35 27 43			11	(6-year average) 18 4		6-11 25			Problem Drinkers (Based on 4 Studies) (Potential problem drinkers)

32

Table 1.—Surveys of Adult Drinking Practices, USA (cont'd.)

Year(s) of study	Reference(s)	Sample size	Percent abstainers			Percent heavy drinkers*			Percent problem drinkers			Problems
			Total	M	F	Total	M	F	Total	M	F	
1974	Gallup (1974)	1,500 (approx.)	32	23	39							
1977	Gallup (1977)	1,500 (approx.)	29	23	35							
1979	Clark and Midanik (1982)	1,772	33	25	40	7	12	3	3	4	2	Health
									6	8	4	Belligerence
									14	20	9	Symptomatic drinking
									21	26	17	Psychological dependence
									4	7	2	Job
1981	Gallup (1981)	1,500 (approx.)	30	25	34							
1980–82 (ECA Program)	Myers et al. (1983)	3,058 (New Haven)							4.8	8.2	1.9	Alcohol Abuse/ Dependence
		3,481 (Baltimore)							6.1	10.4	1.7	
		3,004 (St. Louis)							4.5	8.5	1.0	

*Heavy drinking was determined by most surveys on the basis of some combination of quantity-frequency of alcohol consumption.
+Cities of more than one million population only.
‡Problem drinking criteria varied considerably among surveys; see references for descriptions of indexes.

that some ECA-generated data are now being analyzed so as to explore the interrelationships between alcohol abuse/dependence and other diagnoses made by means of the Diagnostic Interview Schedule (Boyd et al. 1983). When completed, these and related analyses will provide a new generation of mental health information on alcohol abuse/dependence in the general population.

Concurrent Alcohol Use And Mental Health Problems

To date, apart from the Stirling County Study and the ECA projects, our literature search found only two other large-scale epidemiologic field surveys that examined the interrelationships between alcohol abuse and mental health. These had a different focus in that they did not conceptualize alcohol problems within the framework of a psychiatric diagnosis but rather reviewed them as interrelated but different phenomena. One of these surveys had the prevalence and distribution of alcohol use as its central research issue but secured data on depressive symptomatology as well (Clark and Midanik 1982; Midanik 1981). The other field survey was part of the Florida Health Study (FHS), the primary purpose of which was to enumerate mental health problems but which also obtained data on alcohol use.

The National Drinking Practices Survey conducted by the Berkeley Survey Research Group in 1979 secured information from a probability sample of 1,772 person 18 years of age and over. Respondents were interviewed by means of a structured schedule, which included a large battery of alcohol items plus the Center for Epidemiologic Studies Depression Scale (CES-D). The CES-D has been used extensively by psychiatric researchers, and its validity and reliability have been reported in the literature (Radloff 1977; Weissman et al. 1977).

The relationships between depression scores and three alcohol problem scale scores were reported by Midanik (1981). The alcohol problem scales used were social consequences, loss of control, and alcohol dependence. Her most relevant findings, from the vantage point of this paper, have been summarized by us and are presented in table 2. The findings show that 11.5 percent of the drinkers and 18.5 percent of the nondrinkers had scores above the depression cutoff point. This finding is somewhat unexpected given the overwhelming evidence from the clinical literature that shows, perhaps without exception, very high correlations between alcohol consumption and depressive symptomatology. Explanations for this result are not offered by the author, but since our research has produced similar findings, we have completed analyses that included controls not used by Midanik. The outcomes of these analyses are not definitive, but they do suggest that the abstainer group (about one-third of the population) contains disproportionately large

Table 2.--Concurrence between Depression and Alcohol Problems*

	Percent with depressive symptoms	Percent with any alcohol problem	Percent with any alcohol problem who are also depressed+	Percent with either loss of control or alcohol dependence who are also depressed‡	Percent with loss of control and alcohol dependence who are also depressed@
Drinkers (N = 1,169)	11.5	16.7	22.4	22.5	27.7
Male (N = 562)	7.2	21.4	16.9	17.4	19.0
Female (N = 607)	16.2	11.5	33.8	33.1	56.7
Nondrinkers (N = 603)	18.5				
Male (N = 200)	10.8				
Female (N = 403)	22.7				
Total Sample (N = 1,772)	13.8				
Male (N = 762)	8.1				
Female (N = 1,010)	18.8				

* Adapted from Midanik, L. (1981).
+ Based on drinkers with any alcohol problem.
‡ Based on drinkers with either loss of control or alcohol dependence.
@ Based on drinkers with both loss of control and alcohol dependence.

numbers of persons of low SES, a subpopulation that has inordinately high levels of depressive symptomatology. Other factors, such as the existence of physical health problems and age and sex variations between users and nonusers of alcohol, may also be possible explanatory factors.

Midanik (1981) found that 16.7 percent of the drinkers had at least one alcohol-related problem, with males being almost twice as likely to have a problem as females: 21.4 percent contrasted with 11.5 percent. The data on the concurrence of alcohol problems and depressive symptomatology show that 22.4 percent of the drinkers with any of the three alcohol problems had depression scores above the cutting point. By contrast 13.8 percent of the entire sample had high depression scores. The concurrence of alcohol problems and depressive symptomatology increased as the criteria became more stringent. About a fourth (22.5 percent) of those reporting either loss of control or alcohol abuse also had high depression scores. For males, the percentage was 17.5 percent and for females, it was 33.1 percent. Among drinkers identified as having both loss of control and alcohol dependence, the depression scores were even more dramatically elevated. Strikingly, more than half of the females (56.7 percent) with both of these problems had high levels of depressive symptomatology. This compares to 19 percent for males with both problems.

Midanik's data are generally consistent with those reported by other alcohol and psychiatric researchers. And, importantly, they corroborate with general population data findings from the clinical literature that demonstrate high concurrence between alcohol abuse and depression.

The second epidemiologic field survey reporting concurrent alcohol and mental health data was conducted by the authors and a large number of colleagues in different regions of the United States. Between 1969 and 1982, the senior author has been directly involved with field surveys that have secured a broad range of mental health and other related data on approximately 12,000 persons 18 years of age and over. A listing of the projects, all of which employed probability sampling procedures, the sample sizes, and the investigators is provided in table 3. These projects used a common core of items drawn from the Florida Health Study. A lack of resources has kept us from completing an integrated analysis of all the data, and for this reason, the data used in this paper are confined to the work conducted in the Southeastern United States (N = 4,202).

Table 3.—Research Sites, Sample Sizes, and Principal Investigators of Projects Using Field Survey Assessment Model* Total $\underline{N}$ = 12,001

Location	Year conducted	Sample size	Principal investigator
Florida	1969-73	4,506	John Schwab George Warheit Roger Bell
Kentucky	1974-75	1,078	Roger Bell Martin Sundell John Schwab
California			
Mexican-American/ Anglo	1980	1,345	William Vega Kenneth Meinhardt
Guamanian	1980	312	David Shimizu
Mexican immigrants	1981	150	Luz Fernandez Pieda Garcia Sylvia Tello
Nebraska	1981	1,810	Peter Beeson
Ohio			
Northwest	1980	1,728	Richard Hunter Richard Naida
South Central	1980	1,072	Mary Stefl

*The senior author of this paper was a principal investigator, co-principal investigator, or active consultant on all of the projects.

The design and methods used in the FHS have been outlined extensively in the literature and will not be detailed here (Schwab et al. 1979; Warheit et al. 1983). It is important for purposes of this paper to point out that 5 mental health scales were developed from the 110 psychiatric signs, symptoms, and dysfunction items included in the schedule. The scales, which relied on factor and principal components analysis (Holzer and Selfridge 1978), have been tested extensively for reliability as well as content and construct validity (Warheit et al. 1983). Although all of the tests cannot be detailed here, the results of those that checked for the internal consistency of the scales with differing regional, social, and demographic subpopulations are presented in table 4.

Space limitations compel us to limit our analysis of the concurrence of alcohol and mental health problems to only three of the scales. These are: depression, anxiety, and psychosocial dysfunction. We are cognizant that depression and anxiety are frequently seen together in clinical situations; nonetheless, all three scales have more than one-half of their variance unexplained by the others. Moreover, these scales were selected because depression and anxiety are commonly observed among both the general population as well as among those being treated for alcohol problems. Also, the dysfunction scale identifies those with more serious mental health-related problems than do the depression or anxiety measures.

The alcohol items in the instrument included questions about drinking in general; the frequency of intoxication; the personal, social, and/or familial problems related to drinking; self-perceptions regarding the appropriateness of alcohol use; and the use of alcohol to face daily problems. Detailed analyses of the alcohol data led to the construction of an index that was used to dichotomize the population into low risk and high risk groups. These designations suggest the probability of having an alcohol-related problem as a consequence of drinking behaviors. The low risk group included abstainers as well as drinkers whose intake of alcohol was limited and/or had no reported deleterious effects.

As observed earlier, abstainers in our sample had higher levels of psychiatric symptoms/dysfunctions than those with low levels of alcohol use. At the same time, it should be stressed that abstainers had significantly lower psychiatric scale scores than persons in the high risk alcohol group.

The presentation of the FHS concurrence data consists of comparing the mean scores on the mental health scales with the problem drinking risk scores as determined by scores on the alcohol index. Analysis of variance (ANOVA) and t-tests were used to determine the within and between group differences. Multiple stepwise regression

Table 4.—Coefficients of Reliability for the Florida Health Study Scales in Seven Different Field Surveys

Variable	Florida	Kentucky	California (Anglos + Mexican Americans)	California (Guamanians)	California (All Mexican Americans)	Ohio	Nebraska
HOS*	.82	.81	.81	.78	.84	.81	n.a.
Depression	.84	.80	.83	.78	.83	.83	.81
Anxiety	.82	.89	.80	.77	.80	.81	.80
Psychosocial dysfunction	.88	.88	.90	.89	.93	.90	.91
Cognitive impairment	.71	.74	.73	.73	.81	.73	.70
General psychopathology	.72	.74	n.a.**	.72	n.a.	.73	.72

*Health opinion survey
**n.a. = not available

analysis was used to determine the amount of variance in mental health scores that could be attributed to drinking behaviors. The data were controlled for race, sex, age, marital status, and SES. The SES measure is an index that encompasses education, occupation, and income and is drawn from the work of Nam et al. (1975).

The concurrence of depression scale scores and alcohol risk are reported in table 5. The mean score on the depression scale for the entire sample was 14.3. For those in the low risk alcohol group it was 13.9; it was 20.8 for the high risk group.

The analysis of variance indicated that the within group scores for depressive symptomatology were statistically significant for the race, sex, age, marital status, and SES groups. The $\underline{t}$-tests revealed that the depression scores were significantly greater for the high risk alcohol groups than for the low risk and total sample ones in all of the social and demographic subpopulations. The data presented in table 5 confirm clinical observations that link depressive symptomatology and heavy alcohol use and are very similar to those of Midanik (1981). Alcohol use per se, however, was not significantly related to increased depression scores.

The information on the relationships between anxiety scale scores and alcohol risks is reported in table 6. The pattern observed for depressive symptomatology is found for anxiety symptoms as well. Those in the low risk alcohol group had the lowest anxiety scores in most instances although they were not markedly different from those of the general subpopulation. Once again however, those in the high risk alcohol group had higher anxiety scores than those in the low risk and overall population groups. And, in the overwhelming majority of instances, these differences were statistically significant.

The psychosocial dysfunction scale is a measure of the effects that worry, nervousness, and fears have on the ability to perform work and to fulfill family-related and other social role expectations. The data on the relationships between the scores on this scale and alcohol behaviors are outlined in table 7. The results are patterned much like those of the depression and anxiety scales. The psychosocial dysfunction scale scores of those in the high risk alcohol group were, in all but one instance, significantly higher than those of the overall sample and of the low risk alcohol group. And, for the most part, the data show this pattern holds for all of the social and demographic subgroups.

The concurrence of alcohol problems and increased levels of psychiatric symptoms and dysfunctions is well established for the populations from which our samples were drawn. Moreover, these same observations were found when the other symptom/dysfunction

Table 5.--Depression Scale Scores and
Problem Drinking Risks, By Sociodemographic Groups

	N	Overall mean depression scores	Problem drinking risk groups		t-test significance
			Low	High	
Race-sex					
White males	1,517	11.9	11.3	18.1	****
White females	1,952	15.0	14.7	24.4	****
Black males	274	15.9	15.1	24.6	****
Black females	433	18.6	18.3	32.6	****
ANOVA		****	****	****	
Age					
18-22	496	15.7	15.4	17.4	****
23-29	608	13.5	13.0	20.2	****
30-44	960	14.0	13.6	20.9	****
45-59	931	15.0	14.6	23.9	****
60+	1,199	13.7	13.5	28.8	****
ANOVA		****	****	***	
Marital status					
Single	527	15.5	15.0	18.6	***
Married	2,765	13.1	12.8	19.9	****
Widowed	535	16.3	16.1	23.5	*
Separated	130	22.1	21.2	30.3	***
Divorced	226	16.4	15.6	25.9	****
ANOVA		****	****	***	
SES					
Low 1	432	19.5	19.2	29.6	***
2	798	16.6	16.2	24.5	****
3	933	14.5	14.0	24.2	****
4	1,246	12.3	12.0	17.4	****
High 5	790	12.0	11.6	17.4	****
ANOVA		****	****	****	
TOTAL	4,199	14.3	13.9	20.8	****

**** p less than .001
*** p less than .005
** p less than .01
* p less than .05

Table 6.—Anxiety Scale Scores and Problem Drinking Risks, by Sociodemographic Groups

	N	Overall mean anxiety scores	Problem drinking risk groups		t-test significance
			Low	High	
Race-sex					
White Males	1,517	4.8	4.5	7.3	****
White Females	1,952	6.5	6.4	10.0	****
Black Males	274	7.7	7.2	12.4	**
Black Females	433	8.0	7.9	12.7	n.s.
ANOVA		****	****	*	
Age					
18-22	496	5.2	5.1	5.7	n.s.
23-29	608	4.5	4.3	6.9	***
30-44	960	5.2	5.0	8.9	****
45-59	931	6.7	6.4	12.0	****
60+	1,199	7.5	7.4	16.4	****
ANOVA		****	****	****	
Marital status					
Single	527	5.0	4.8	6.0	n.s.
Married	2,765	5.6	5.5	9.0	****
Widowed	535	8.3	8.2	13.1	*
Separated	130	9.8	9.5	12.9	n.s.
Divorced	226	6.6	6.3	10.9	*
ANOVA		****	****	**	
SES					
Low 1	432	12.1	11.9	18.5	*
2	798	7.7	7.5	11.5	***
3	933	6.0	5.7	9.8	****
4	1,246	4.5	4.3	6.7	****
High 5	790	4.0	3.8	6.1	****
ANOVA		****	****	****	
TOTAL	4,199	6.1	6.0	8.7	****

**** p less than .001
*** p less than .005
** p less than .01
* p less than .05
n.s. = not significant

Table 7.—Psychosocial Dysfunction Scale Scores
and Problem Drinking Risks, by Sociodemographic Groups

	N	Overall mean psychosocial dysfunction scores	Problem drinking risk groups		t-test significance
			Low	High	
Race-sex					
White males	1,517	1.3	1.1	3.7	****
White females	1,952	2.2	2.1	6.3	****
Black males	274	1.9	1.5	5.2	****
Black females	433	2.9	2.8	7.6	**
ANOVA		****	****	*	
Age					
18-22	496	2.6	2.6	2.5	n.s.
23-29	608	2.0	1.8	4.6	****
30-44	960	2.2	2.0	5.9	****
45-59	931	1.9	1.7	5.3	****
60+	1,199	1.3	1.3	7.3	****
ANOVA		****	****	*	
Marital status					
Single	527	2.3	2.2	3.3	*
Married	2,765	1.7	1.5	4.7	****
Widowed	535	1.8	1.8	5.0	**
Separated	130	4.8	4.2	9.6	***
Divorced	226	2.6	2.4	5.5	*
ANOVA		****	****	*	
SES					
Low 1	432	2.6	2.5	6.1	*
2	798	2.3	2.2	4.9	***
3	933	2.0	1.7	6.3	****
4	1,246	1.6	1.4	3.6	****
High 5	790	1.6	1.5	3.7	****
ANOVA		****	****	n.s.	
Total	4,199	1.9	1.8	4.6	****

**** p less than .001
*** p less than .005
** p less than .01
* p less than .05
n.s. = not significant

scales used in our research were analyzed. We do not, of course, make any claims for etiologic directionality, but from a phenomenological point of view, the two sets of constructs are correlated consistently within and between differing social and demographic subpopulations.

To examine more fully the relationships outlined in tables 5, 6, and 7, a series of multiple stepwise regression analyses were completed. The results of these analyses are presented in table 8. SES, sex, age, marital status, and race along with alcohol problem risk were included as variables in the equations.

The results for the depression scale show that all of the variables were significant in the equation and that together they explained 13.7 percent of the variance. More detailed analysis revealed that 6.6 percent of the explained variance was accounted for by SES and that 3.0 percent was attributable to high risk on the alcohol index. The over variables explained the remaining 4.1 percent.

The same variables explained 13.1 percent of the variance on the anxiety scale. Here, however, most of it was explained by SES, 10.7 percent. Alcohol risk accounted for only 1.0 percent of the explained variance, and the remaining 1.4 percent was assigned to other variables. Race was the only variable not significant in the equation.

Only 6.3 percent of the variance of the psychosocial dysfunction scale was explained by the variables in the equation. Of this amount, SES accounted for 2.2 percent and alcohol risk, 1.7 percent. Also, although all of the other variables except race were significant in the equation, they were not powerful predictors of high psychosocial dysfunction scale scores.

The interpretation of table 8 must be approached somewhat cautiously in that we did not test for interaction effects, and moreover, it seems logical to conclude that through colinearity SES is consuming some of the variance that might be explained by race and the other variables. The data presented suggest that alcohol problems and increased psychiatric symptomatology are highly interrelated. And, although alcohol risk was not a very powerful predictor of high psychiatric and symptom scores, it was a significant factor in the regression analyses when depression, anxiety, and psychosocial dysfunction were the dependent variables.

Table 8.—Stepwise Multiple Regression Analysis:
Psychiatric Symptom/Dysfunction Scale Scores,
by Alcohol Problem Risk and Sociodemographic Variables

Variables	Symptom/dysfunction scales						Psychosocial dysfunction		
	Depression			Anxiety					
	Std. Beta	Sig.	R^2 Change	Std. Beta	Sig.	R^2 Change	Std. Beta	Sig.	R^2 Change
Socioeconomic status	-0.248	**	0.066	-0.294	**	0.107	-0.102	**	0.022
Alcohol problem risk	0.178	**	0.030	0.120	**	0.010	0.149	**	0.017
Sex (male)	-0.149	**	0.022	-0.082	**	0.007	-0.117	**	0.011
Age	-0.092	**	0.010	0.077	**	0.005	-0.106	**	0.005
Marital status (separated)	0.082	**	0.008	0.048	**	0.002	0.088	**	0.008
Race (white)	-0.037	**	0.001	0.018	n.s.	0.000	0.006	n.s.	0.000
Constant	23.249								
R^2			0.137			0.131			0.063

** p less than .01
* p less than .05
n.s. = not significant

ALCOHOL RISK, HEALTH, AND SOCIAL WELL-BEING AMONG LIFE CYCLE GROUPS

The conceptual model that guided the FHS relied heavily on the assumption that health and social well-being are complex theoretical constructs that can be delineated most effectively when viewed within the context of a general systems perspective. This approach led us to gather information that would permit us to analyze the interrelationships between individual physical and mental health variables, alcohol and drug use, coping behaviors including interpersonal networks, life satisfactions, social role performance, social and demographic factors, social structural patterns, and cultural beliefs and practices. The acquisition of these data has permitted us to analyze both mental health and alcohol problems from a number of differing perspectives. In appendix A, we have included an abbreviated summary of the relationships between alcohol risk groups, defined in this instance as the probability of needing formal alcohol-related services, and a representative number of variable clusters that were presumed to be related to health and social well-being. It is not possible to discuss all of these relationships in this paper. Instead, attention is given to a selected number of them, with controls for life cycle and, to a lesser degree, sex groups. The life cycle groups consist of those ages 18 to 29; those 30 to 49; and those 50 and older. We recognize that other life cycle categorizations are frequently found in the literature. The rationale for these groupings grows out of our review of the alcohol epidemiologic literature, which indicates that the populations represented have significantly different patterns of alcohol use.

Alcohol Risk And Life Cycle Stages

The findings on alcohol risk for the entire sample and the three age groups are reported in table 9. The data show that 5.3 percent of the total sample were in the high risk category and, further, that there were statistically significant differences between the age groups. Those ages 18 to 29 had percentages (9.8) about four times as high as those ages 50 and older (2.3). The 30 to 40 year old group had scores between these two extremes; 5.7 percent of their number were in the high risk alcohol group.

Alcohol Risk And Life Cycle Stages By Sex Groups

These same data are controlled for sex and presented in table 10. They indicate that 9.0 percent of the males as compared with 2.5 percent of the females were in the high risk category. And, once again, those in the youngest age group of both sexes had the largest percentages of their number at high alcohol risk. Among

Table 9.—Alcohol Risk and Life Cycle Groups

Age	N	Alcohol risk Low (percent)	High (percent)
18-29	1,104	90.2	9.8
30-49	1,270	94.3	5.7
50 +	1,820	97.7	2.3
TOTAL	4,194	94.7	5.3

(x^2 = 78.6; p less than .001)

Table 10.—Alcohol Risk and Life Cycle Groups (controlled for gender)

Sex	N	Alcohol risk Low (percent)	High (percent)
Males	1,805	91.0	9.0
18-29	514	84.4	15.6
30-49	547	90.9	9.1
50 +	744	95.7	4.3

(x^2 = 47.2; p less than .001)

Females	2,389	97.5	2.5
18-29	590	95.3	4.7
30-49	723	97.0	3.0
50 +	1,076	99.2	0.8
TOTAL	4,194	94.7	5.3

(x^2 = 25.6; p less than .001)

males ages 18 to 29, 15.6 percent were in the high risk category; for females the percentage was 4.7 percent. Repeatedly, the lowest rates of alcohol risk were found among those ages 50 and older. Only 0.8 percent of the females in this age category were in the high risk group.

The findings reported in tables 9 and 10 are very similar to those presented most often by other alcohol researchers. (For comparative analyses see table 1.) This was true for the prevalence of problems and for their distribution among age and sex groups as well.

Alcohol Risk, Health, And Social Well-Being By Life Cycle Stages

In an effort to extend the import of the findings on alcohol use beyond its concurrence with mental health problems, a number of items from our data have been selected that report on the relationships between alcohol risk and a variety of other factors related to health and social well-being. The analyses are controlled for the life cycle age groups. We have analyzed these and a great many other health and social well-being variables controlling for sex. And, although there are many fluctuations in the score distributions for individual items, the overall patterns that are found in table 11 are repeated for both male and female alcohol risk and age groups. Those in the high risk group, regardless of sex, manifested more health, mental health, and social dysfunctionality than those in the low risk groups.

Selected information on health, social well-being, and alcohol risk for the life cycle groups is outlined in table 11. Data on nine items are summarized for purposes of illustration. The items presented are representative of the broader pool of items that are contained in appendix A.

Item 1. Times Moved in the Past Year. This item was included in the analysis because the literature on alcohol abuse suggests that problem drinkers are more transient residentially than nonproblem drinkers. The findings support this assumption by showing that those in the high risk alcohol group changed residences more frequently than those in the low risk one. This was true for all three life cycle categories and the differences were statistically significant for the 18 to 29 and 50 plus age cohorts. Overall, those in the 50 plus age group were the most stable residentially while those under 30 in both risk groups moved most frequently. It appears that, although alcohol risk is associated with increased mobility, age is a better predictor of changes in residence.

Table 11.--Alcohol Risk, Health, and Social Well-being

	Alcohol risk			
		Low		High
Item/age group	N	(percent)	N	(percent)

1. Times moved in past year

   18-29
No times	499	50.8	39	36.4
1 time	282	28.7	35	32.7
2+ times	201	20.5	33	30.8
	982		107	

   (x^2 = 9.39; p less than .001)

   30-49
No times	998	83.9	55	76.4
1 time	147	12.4	12	16.7
2+ times	44	3.7	5	6.9
	1,189		72	

   (n.s.)

   50+
No times	1,562	89.5	34	85.0
1 times	152	8.7	3	7.5
2+ times	32	1.8	3	7.5
	1,746		40	

   (x^2 = 6.56; p less than .05)

Table 11.—Alcohol Risk, Health, and Social Well-being (cont'd.)

		Alcohol risk	
Item/age group	$\underline{N}$	Low (percent)	High (percent)
2. Marital status			
18-29			
Single	428	83.9	16.1
Married	598	95.2	4.8
Widowed	4	100.0	0.0
Separated/divorced	70	85.7	14.3
	1,100		

($\underline{x}^2$ = 37.89; $\underline{p}$ less than .001)

30-49			
Single	49	91.8	8.2
Married	1,014	95.2	4.8
Widowed	46	91.3	8.7
Separated/divorced	158	91.1	8.9
	1,267		

(n.s.)

50+			
Single	50	98.0	2.0
Married	1,148	97.9	2.1
Widowed	484	98.6	1.4
Separated/divorced	127	93.7	6.3
	1,809		

($\underline{x}^2$ = 11.21; $\underline{p}$ less than .01)

Table 11.—Alcohol Risk, Health, and Social Well-being (cont'd.)

	Alcohol risk			
	Low		High	
Item/age group	N	(percent)	N	(percent)

3. Married, feel helpless to deal with family problems

18-29
Seldom, never	446	79.1	20	69.0
Sometimes	94	16.7	4	13.8
Often, all the time	24	4.3	5	17.2
	564		29	

(X^2 = 10.01; p less than .01)

30-49
Seldom, never	717	75.4	31	62.0
Sometimes	174	18.3	15	30.0
Often, all the time	60	6.3	4	8.0
	951		50	

(n.s.)

50+
Seldom, never	885	81.0	11	45.8
Sometimes	145	13.3	7	29.2
Often, all the time	62	5.7	6	25.0
	1,092		24	

(X^2 = 22.37; p less than .001)

Table 11.--Alcohol Risk, Health, and Social Well-being (cont'd.)

	\underline{Alcohol risk}			
		Low		High
Item/age group	$\underline{N}$	(percent)	$\underline{N}$	(percent)

4. Unmarried, life satisfaction at present

<u>18-29</u>
Very, fairly satisfied	343	81.7	57	73.1
Mixed	55	13.1	14	17.9
Not very, at all	22	5.2	7	9.0
	420		78	

(n.s)

<u>30-49</u>
Very, fairly satisfied	149	65.6	8	36.4
Mixed	57	25.1	7	31.8
Not very, at all	21	9.3	7	31.8
	227		22	

($\underline{X}^2$ = 12.16; $\underline{p}$ less than .005)

<u>50+</u>
Very, fairly satisfied	486	77.5	9	56.3
Mixed	88	14.0	6	37.5
Not very, at all	53	8.5	1	6.3
	627		16	

($\underline{X}^2$ = 6.88; $\underline{p}$ less than .05)

Table 11.--Alcohol Risk, Health, and Social Well-being (cont'd.)

	Alcohol risk			
		Low		High
Item/age group	N	(percent)	N	(percent)

5. Physical health at present

   18-29
Excellent, good	878	88.2	86	79.6
Fair	101	10.1	19	17.6
Poor, very bad	17	1.7	3	2.8
	996		108	

   (x^2 = 6.41; p less than .05)

   30-49
Excellent, good	966	80.8	52	72.2
Fair	188	15.7	15	20.8
Poor, very bad	42	3.5	5	6.9
	1,196		72	

   (n.s.)

   50+
Excellent, good	1,285	72.3	24	58.5
Fair	353	19.9	11	26.8
Poor, very bad	139	7.8	6	14.6
	1,777		41	

   (n.s.)

Table 11.--Alcohol Risk, Health, and Social Well-being (cont'd.)

	Alcohol risk			
	Low		High	
Item/age group	N	(percent)	N	(percent)

6. Times in hospital in past 3 years

18-29
No times	626	62.9	68	63.0
1-2 times	327	32.9	34	31.5
3+ times	42	4.2	6	5.6
	995		108	

(n.s.)

30-49
No times	831	69.4	51	70.8
1-2 times	326	27.2	17	23.6
3+ times	40	3.3	4	5.6
	1,197		72	

(n.s.)

50+
No times	1,184	66.7	22	53.7
1-2 times	509	28.7	13	31.7
3+ times	83	4.7	6	14.6
	1,776		41	

(x^2 = 9.27; p less than .01)

Table 11.—Alcohol Risk, Health, and Social Well-being (cont'd.)

		Alcohol risk		
		Low		High
Item/age group	N	(percent)	N	(percent)

7. Mental health at present

18-29
Excellent, good	873	87.8	88	81.5
Fair	106	10.7	16	14.8
Poor, very bad	15	1.5	4	3.7
	994		108	

(n.s.)

30-49
Excellent, good	966	81.0	38	53.5
Fair	191	16.0	28	39.4
Poor, very bad	35	2.9	5	7.0
	1,192		71	

(x^2 = 31.13; p less than .001)

50+
Excellent, good	1,366	77.8	25	61.0
Fair	327	18.6	8	19.5
Poor, very bad	62	3.5	8	19.5
	1,755		41	

(x^2 = 27.73; p less than .001)

Table 11.—Alcohol Risk, Health, and Social Well-being (cont'd.)

	Alcohol risk			
	Low		High	
Item/age group	N	(percent)	N	(percent)

8. Cantril ladder position at present

   18-29
0-2, Low	39	4.0	6	5.7
3-4	106	10.7	21	20.0
5-8	729	73.9	72	68.6
9-10, High	113	11.4	6	5.7
	987		105	

   (x^2 = 10.94; p less than .05)

   30-49
0-2, Low	39	3.3	9	12.5
3-4	85	7.2	10	13.9
5-8	786	66.7	49	68.1
9-10, High	268	22.8	4	5.6
	1,178		72	

   (x^2 = 28.13; p less than .001)

   50+
0-2, Low	66	4.0	2	5.1
3-4	73	4.4	3	7.7
5-8	890	53.5	27	69.2
9-10, High	634	38.1	7	17.9
	1,663		39	

   (n.s.)

Table 11.—Alcohol Risk, Health, and Social Well-being (cont'd.)

	Alcohol risk			
	Low		High	
Item/age group	N	(percent)	N	(percent)

9. Suicide attempts

    18-29

Yes	33	3.3	9	8.3
No	963	96.7	99	91.7
	996		108	

(X^2 = 5.41, p less than .05)

    30-49

Yes	24	2.0	7	9.7
No	1,171	98.0	65	90.3
	1,195		72	

(X^2 = 13.85; p less than .001)

    50+

Yes	27	1.5	3	7.3
No	1,747	98.5	38	92.7
	1,774		41	

(X^2 = 5.10; p less than .05)

Item 2. Marital Status. Research findings have generally shown that the single and those in disrupted marital statuses are more likely than the married to have an alcohol problem. The interpretations of these findings have included the propositions that the single drink more as part of their social life and/or that those with drinking problems are less likely to marry. It also has been suggested that alcohol abuse is a contributory factor to separation and divorce and, further, that widowhood leads to increased drinking because of unresolved object loss, social isolation, and loneliness, particularly among males.

The data presented for item 2 show that the differences between the low and high alcohol risk groups were statistically significant for those under 30 (p less than .001) and those 50 and older (p less than .01). Being single was highly associated with alcohol risk for those 18 to 29; 16.1 percent of those in this age group were in the problem drinking category. By contrast, just 8.2 percent of the single in the 30 to 49 age group were in the high risk category. The percentage for those 50 and over was even lower; it was only 2.0 percent. The separated and divorced had the highest alcohol risk rates among all age groups, but the rates for widowhood were not inordinately high except in the 30 to 49 age group. Perhaps the data for widowhood would be altered if controlled for sex, but as presented, this marital status was not highly associated with drinking problems. As would be expected from the literature, the problem drinking rates for the married were very low for all three age cohorts.

The findings for item 2 strongly indicate that age is a better overall predictor of alcohol problems than marital status per se. The high rates of alcohol risk for the single were confined to those younger than 30. In the 50 and older age group, the single and married had equally low rates, 2.0 percent and 2.1 percent respectively. Although those divorced or separated rated had higher than average rates of alcohol risk in all three age groups, there was a marked decline in those rates with increasing age. The risk rate for the separated or divorced aged 18 to 29 was 14.3 percent; for those 50 and older, it was only 6.3 percent.

There are, then, distinct alcohol risk differences among marital status groups when controlled for life cycle stages although the impact of age is overridingly important.

Item 3. Married: Feel Helpless to Deal with Family Problems. The item on feelings of helplessness to deal with family problems was asked as part of a larger set of questions dealing with locus of control, self-mastery, and powerlessness. The findings indicate that high alcohol risk in all three life cycle groups was associated with feelings of helplessness. For those 18 to 29 and 50 and older, the differences between the low risk and high risk alcohol groups were statistically significant. Only 24 married persons in the 50 plus age cohort were in the high risk alcohol group, so the numbers dictate caution in interpreting the findings. Nonetheless, it is worth observing that one-fourth of this number reported feeling helpless to deal with family problems often or all of the time. And, an additional 29.2 percent replied that they sometimes felt helpless. The findings also show a distinct pattern between the age cohorts: advancing age was highly associated with increased feelings of helplessness among the high risk groups. The feelings of helplessness to deal with family problems were most dramatic for those 50 and older. Among the low risk alcohol group, 81 percent indicated they experienced these feelings only seldom or never. This is in sharp contrast to the 45.8 percent of the high risk group that expressed similar feelings.

It can be concluded, then, that those at high risk for alcohol problems are likely to have feelings of helplessness in their family life.

Item 4. Unmarried: Life Satisfaction at Present. This item was included in the survey instrument as part of a subset intended to determine respondents' perceptions of life satisfactions. The belief was that these perceptions reflected and/or produced certain dysfunctional behaviors including alcohol abuse. Item 4 was designed to deal with an overall assessment of how satisfying life was at the time of the interview.

The results reveal that those in the high risk alcohol group were less satisfied with their lives generally than were those in the low risk groups. And, the differences within groups were statistically significant for respondents 30 to 49 and 50 plus. Among high risk groups, those 18 to 29 were much more likely to be satisfied with how their lives were going than were those in the 30 to 49 and 50 and over age groups. Among those 18 to 29 at high risk, 73.1 percent reported being very or fairly satisfied with their lives while only 36.4 percent of the 30 to 49 reported such satisfactions. The percentage reporting being very or fairly satisfied among the 50 plus high risk group was midway between the other two groups, 56.3 percent.

Those 30 to 49 in the low risk group also reported lower life satisfaction levels than either of the other low risk age groups. This may also be related to unfulfilled life expectations and other factors frequently associated with midlife crises. Overall, the findings for both the low and high risk alcohol groups aged 30 to 49 indicate comparatively low levels of satisfaction with their lives.

Item 5. Physical Health at Present. This question called for a self-assessment of the respondent's physical health and was asked largely because pretests with both general samples and patient subgroups indicated strong relationships between the responses to this item and a variety of other health and well-being variables. Also, the literature is replete with findings that show strong correlations between health problems and alcohol abuse. We recognize, of course, that self-reports of health are often unreliable and that denial of negative consequences is strong among alcohol abusers. Nonetheless, the item has produced some useful findings.

The data show that the high risk alcohol group in all life cycle cohorts reported having poor or very bad health more often than the low risk group. While the differences were statistically significant only for those 18 to 29, the overall pattern was consistent and in the anticipated direction.

Other analysis of this health perception variable has shown that the fair response was more frequently associated with pathology than well-being. With this the case, the findings for the 50 and older high alcohol risk group are even more noteworthy; 41.4 percent reported their physical health as fair, poor, or very bad.

Thus, the data on self-perceptions of physical health are consistent with the clinical literature on alcoholism that shows relationships between increasing age, alcohol abuse, and physical health problems.

Item 6. Times in Hospital in Past 3 Years. This item, as in the case of the preceding one, was presumed to be a good predictor of a variety of health, mental health, and social well-being variables.

The responses to the question concerning hospital stays were very similar for alcohol risk groups in the 18 to 29 and 30 to 49 age cohorts. Although the high risk alcohol subgroups had slightly higher rates of hospitalization than the low risk ones, the differences were very small. The variations between the alcohol risk groups in the 50 and older age cohort were, on the other hand, significantly different (p less than .01). Almost half (46.3 percent) of the high risk alcohol group 50 and older reported at least one hospitalization in the 3 years prior to being interviewed, and 14.6 percent had three or more inpatient stays.

These data strongly suggest that alcohol problems are associated with increased hospitalizations generally; further, they are especially related to increased hospitalizations for those 50 and older. These findings are reinforced by those that indicate that the rates of hospitalization for the low risk alcohol groups were very similar in all three life cycle cohorts. Alcohol use, rather than age alone, seems to be a better predictor of the kinds of health problems necessitating hospitalization.

Item 7. Mental Health at Present. The responses to this question have been found to be excellent indicators of high psychiatric scale scores on all of the mental health measures and to be significantly associated with physical health problems and services utilization as well.

Given the data on concurrence described above, the findings on this item are not surprising. The differences between the alcohol risk groups were not very great for those 18 to 29 (n.s.). The differences for the 30 to 49 and 50 plus groups were, however, highly significant (p less than .001). Nearly one-half (46.4 percent) of the 30 to 49 alcohol problem group viewed their mental health as less than good, and 39.0 percent of those 50 and older perceived their mental health in the same manner. Those in the high risk alcohol group over 49 had the largest percentage of respondents with mental health self-ratings of poor or very bad (19.5 percent).

Item 8. Cantril Ladder Position at Present. This item was drawn from Cantril's Self-Anchoring Striving Scale (Cantril 1965). The question is in three parts and asks respondents to place themselves on the rung of a ladder 5 years ago, at present, and 5 years in the future. This technique has been used extensively and has been found to be a valid and reliable indicator of overall wellbeing. Its inclusion in this analysis is predicated on the assumption that those in the high alcohol risk group will define their lives less positively than those in the low risk group.

The findings for item 8 indicate that those in all three life cycle groups at high risk for alcohol problems regarded their lives less favorably than those at low risk. The differences were statistically significant for both the 18 to 29 and 30 to 49 cohorts. The variations between the three low risk age groups are very modest especially when the scores 5 to 8 and 9 to 10 were collapsed. Importantly, from a life cycle perspective, those 50 and older in both risk groups placed themselves higher on the ladder than the two younger cohorts. The between group score comparisons for the 50 plus age cohort, while not statistically different, revealed that those at high risk judged their ladder positions less favorably than the low risk group.

Item 9. Suicide Attempts. The rates of suicide for older males living alone or in nonfamily settings is well-documented in the literature and, furthermore, it is commonly believed that this group is more prone to suicide when individuals are alcohol abusers. The data for this item, while uncontrolled for living arrangements and sex, do permit some preliminary observations about age, problem drinking, and suicidal behaviors. The number of respondents in the sample admitting suicide attempts was very small, and this imposes restraints on interpreting or generalizing from the data. Nonetheless, the information is of value and is worth reporting.

The findings indicate significant differences between alcohol risk groups for all three life cycle cohorts. Among the low alcohol risk group, those 18 to 29 reported the greatest percentage of attempts, 3.3 percent. The lowest rate for this risk group was among those 50 and over, 1.5 percent.

The percentages of those attempting suicide among the high risk alcohol groups followed the same pattern but were of greater magnitude. The highest rate was found for those in the 30 to 49 age cohort, 9.7 percent. The lowest rate was among those 50 and over, 7.3 percent.

As observed above, the overall rates of suicide in the general population are low and are greater for females than for males. Males are more likely to use and/or abuse alcohol than females. These two factors may be accounting for the small cells found in the table for this item. Notwithstanding the limited numbers, a trend can be seen; those with alcohol problems are consistently more likely to report suicide attempts than those without them.

SUMMARY AND CONCLUSIONS

Primarily, this paper has addressed two questions: (1) What is the prevalence of alcohol abuse in the United States and what is its relationship to mental health? (2) What are the associations between alcohol problems and health and social well-being among differing life cycle groups?

To date, relatively little epidemiologic research has been conducted that has examined the concurrence of alcohol problems and mental disorders in the general population. What has been completed has relied on differing theoretical models. In spite of these limitations, the findings from the available research are remarkably similar. They indicate that about 5.0 percent of the general population has a drinking problem that approximates the abuse/dependence criteria as outlined by the American Psychiatric

Association. The research also consistently shows males to have much higher rates of alcohol problems than females.

The data on the concurrence of alcohol abuse and mental health problems conclusively show that the two phenomena are highly correlated. At the same time, the data suggest that they have many individual and unshared dimensions.

The alcohol findings from the FHS are very much like those reported by other investigators. It was found that about 5.0 percent of the general population could be considered problem drinkers and that males were about four times more likely than females to have a drinking problem. Powerful correlations were also found between the prevalence of drinking problems and age. The highest alcohol risk rates were discovered among those under age 30, and the lowest rates were found among those 50 years of age and older. The ratio was approximately 4:1.

The findings on the relationships between alcohol problems and mental health and social well-being among different life cycle groups were patterned. Those at risk for alcohol abuse were also at increased risk for a variety of other problems. However, the distribution and magnitude of these associations frequently varied among life cycle groups.

At present, alcohol and psychiatric epidemiologists share a large number of common theoretical and methodological problems that impede their scientific inquiries. Probably the most complex of these are associated with the definition and measurement of their dependent variables. In our opinion, alcohol abuse, by whatever name it is identified, and the functional mental disorders, regardless of the rigidity of the classificatory system used to label them, remain in large part constructs whose dimensions have not been completely delineated and whose interrelationships have not been fully explored. The rationale for this opinion comes from the observation that there are remarkable similarities in the findings reported by both psychiatric and alcohol epidemiologists even though they have employed models that have varied extensively in their theoretical and methodological complexity. The similarity of findings, we believe, can be attributed in large part to the diffuse and systemic web of relationships that link our physiological, psychological, social structural, and cultural environments. Researchers focusing on any one aspect of these environments end up tapping other elements as well. Given this perspective, we believe that definitional closure in either field is presently premature and that such closure, if it were to occur, would be detrimental to our common scientific interests.

It appears to us that the development of a scientifically defensible body of data on alcohol abuse (and on mental disorders as well) will be facilitated by a continuing recognition that the boundaries of the independent and dependent variables are frequently blurred and sometimes indistinguishable. And, further, we believe that we need to expand rather than to limit the scope of the constructs that guide our efforts.

REFERENCES

American Psychiatric Association. Diagnostic and Statistical Manual of Mental Disorders. 1st ed. Washington, D.C.: The Association, 1952.

Auth, J.B., and Warheit, G.J. Estimating the prevalence of problem drinking and alcoholism in the general population: An overview of epidemiological studies. Alcohol Health & Research World 7(2):10-21, 1982-83.

Boyd, J.H.; Burke, J.D.; Gruenberg, E.; Holzer, C.E.; Rae, D.S.; George, L.K.; Karno, M.; Stoltzman, R.; McEvoy, L.; and Nestadt, G. The exclusion criteria of DSM III: A study of co-morbidity. Draft 1983.

Cantril, H. The Pattern of Human Concerns. New Brunswick, N.J.: Rutgers University Press, 1965.

Clark, W.B., and Midanik, L. Alcohol use and alcohol problems among U.S. adults. In: NIAAA. Alcohol and Health Monograph No. 1: Alcohol Consumption and Related Problems. DHHS Pub. No. (ADM)82-1190. Washington, D.C.: Supt. of Docs., U.S. Govt. Print. Off., 1982. pp. 3-52.

Holzer, C.E., and Selfridge, R.G. Using regression to look at variance components: Research on life events and mental health. Working paper. University of Florida, Gainesville, 1978.

Langner, T., and Michael, S. Life Stress and Mental Illness. New York: Free Press of Glencoe, 1963.

Leighton, D.C.; Harding, J.S.; Macklin, D.B.; MacMillan, A.M.; and Leighton, A.H. The Character of Danger. New York: Basic Books, 1963.

MacMillan, A.M. The Health Opinion Survey: Technique for estimating prevalence of psychoneurotic and related types of disorder in communities. Psychological Reports, Monograph Suppl. 3. Birmingham, AL: Southern Universities Press, 1957. pp. 325-339.

Midanik, L. Alcohol use and depressive symptoms. In: Draft Report on the 1979 National Survey (report prepared under NIAAA contract ADM 281-77-0021). Berkeley: University of California, Social Research Group, School of Public Health, April 1981. pp. 225-258.

Radloff, L. The CES-D scale: A self-report depression scale for research in the general population. Applied Psychological Measurement 1(3):385-401, 1977.

Schwab, J.J.; Bell, R.A.; Warheit, G.J.; and Schwab, R.B. Social Order and Mental Health. New York: Brunner/Mazel, 1979.

Warheit, G.J., and Auth, J.B. The epidemiology of alcohol abuse in adulthood. In: Michels, R.; Klerman, G.; Guze, R.; Solnit, A.; Cooper, A.; Judd, L.; and Brody, K., eds., Psychiatry. Philadelphia: Lippincott, in press.

Warheit, G.J.; Bell, R.A.; Schwab, J.J.; and Buhl, J.M. An epidemiologic assessment of mental health problems in the southeastern United States. In: Weissman, M.M.; Myers, J.K.; and Ross, R.S., eds. Community Surveys. NIMH Monographs in Psychosocial Epidemiology. New Brunswick, N.J.: Rutgers University Press, in press.

Weissman, M.M.; Sholomskas, D.; Pottenger, M.; Prusoff, B.; and Locke, B. Assessing depressive symptoms in five psychiatric populations: A validation study. American Journal of Epidemiology 106(3):203-214, 1977.

APPENDIX A

Alcohol Service Needs and
Their Relationships to Health and
Social Well-Being

A. Life Satisfaction Indicators and Alcohol Service Need

	\underline{Alcohol service need}					
	None		Possible		Probable	
	N	Percent	N	Percent	N	Percent

Table 1.

How satisfied with residence?

	N	Percent	N	Percent	N	Percent
Very satisfied	2,190	60.0	155	50.2	100	45.9
Fairly satisfied	976	26.7	96	31.1	63	28.9
Mixed feelings	240	6.6	27	8.7	26	11.9
Not very satisfied	149	4.1	14	4.5	22	10.1
Not at all satisfied	96	2.6	17	5.5	7	3.2
	3,651		309		218	

(N = 4,178)
$p < .001$; $X^2 = 48.10$

Table 2.

How often enjoy your work?

	N	Percent	N	Percent	N	Percent
All the time	348	50.4	36	40.4	25	44.6
Often	262	37.9	38	42.7	22	39.3
Sometimes	68	9.8	10	11.2	8	14.3
Seldom	11	1.6	4	4.5	1	1.8
Never	2	0.3	1	1.1	0	0.0
	691		89		56	

(N = 836)
n.s.

Table 3.

How often upset, not doing preferred work?

	N	Percent	N	Percent	N	Percent
Never	357	49.2	31	39.7	26	41.3
Seldom	139	19.2	22	28.2	11	17.5
Sometimes	132	18.2	12	15.4	13	20.6
Often	64	8.8	7	9.0	11	17.5
All the time	33	4.6	6	7.7	2	3.2
	725		78		63	

(N = 866)
n.s.

	Alcohol service need					
	None		Possible		Probable	
	N	Percent	N	Percent	N	Percent

Table 4.

Working women: upset not doing preferred work

	N	Percent	N	Percent	N	Percent
Never	165	40.2	6	27.3	4	28.6
Seldom	92	22.4	7	31.8	3	21.4
Sometimes	100	24.4	6	27.3	4	28.6
Often	30	7.3	1	4.5	3	21.4
All the time	23	5.6	2	9.1	0	0.0
	410		22		14	

(N = 446)
n.s.

Table 5.

How satisfied being housewife?

	N	Percent	N	Percent	N	Percent
Very satisfied	752	67.6	27	58.7	12	57.1
Fairly satisfied	253	22.7	14	30.4	5	23.8
Mixed feelings	67	6.0	5	10.9	3	14.3
Not very satisfied	30	2.7	0	0.0	1	4.8
Not at all satisfied	11	1.0	0	0.0	0	0.0
	1,113		46		21	

(N = 1,180)
n.s.

Table 6.

Housewife: role preference

	N	Percent	N	Percent	N	Percent
Part-time work	269	27.1	18	40.9	9	45.0
Full-time work	117	11.8	5	11.4	2	10.0
Housewife	607	61.1	21	47.7	9	45.0
	993		44		20	

(N = 1,057)
n.s.

Table 7.

Housewife upset, not doing preference

	N	Percent	N	Percent	N	Percent
Never	126	35.4	7	36.8	5	45.5
Seldom	68	19.1	5	26.3	1	9.1
Sometimes	92	25.8	5	26.3	2	18.2
Often	44	12.4	1	5.3	2	18.2
All the time	26	7.3	1	5.3	1	9.1
	356		19		11	

(N = 386)
n.s.

	Alcohol service need					
	None		Possible		Probable	
	N	Percent	N	Percent	N	Percent

Table 8.

Retirement satisfaction

	N	Percent	N	Percent	N	Percent
Very satisfied	251	55.9	8	61.5	5	62.5
Fairly satisfied	118	26.3	3	23.1	1	12.5
Mixed feelings	44	9.8	1	7.7	0	0.0
Not very satisfied	21	4.7	1	7.7	2	25.0
Not at all satisfied	15	3.3	0	0.0	0	0.0
	449		13		8	

(N = 470)
n.s.

Table 9.

	N	Percent	N	Percent	N	Percent

Married: life in present family

	N	Percent	N	Percent	N	Percent
Excellent	1,118	45.0	87	46.8	29	27.9
Good	998	40.2	77	41.4	46	44.2
Fair	326	13.1	21	11.3	26	25.0
Poor	35	1.4	1	0.5	3	2.9
Bad	6	0.2	0	0.0	0	0.0
	2,483		186		104	

(N = 2,773)
$p < .01$; $X^2 = 21.74$

Table 10.

	N	Percent	N	Percent	N	Percent

Unmarried: life satisfaction in general

	N	Percent	N	Percent	N	Percent
Very satisfied	443	38.4	41	33.3	24	20.7
Fairly satisfied	441	38.2	54	43.9	50	43.1
Mixed feelings	181	15.7	20	16.3	27	23.3
Not very satisfied	61	5.3	8	6.5	9	7.8
Not at all satisfied	27	2.3	0	0.0	6	5.2
	1,153		123		116	

(N = 1,392)
$p < .005$; $X^2 = 22.66$

	Alcohol service need					
	None		Possible		Probable	
	N	Percent	N	Percent	N	Percent

Table 11.

Unmarried: how satisfying relationship with opposite sex?

	N	Percent	N	Percent	N	Percent
Very satisfying	199	55.1	42	57.5	30	46.2
Fairly satisfying	112	31.0	12	16.4	25	38.5
Mixed feelings	41	11.4	16	21.9	6	9.2
Not very satisfying	7	1.9	3	4.1	2	3.1
Not at all satisfying	2	0.6	0	0.0	2	3.1
	361		73		65	

(N = 499)
$p < .05$; $x^2 = 19.59$

Cantril ladder scores striving self-anchoring

Table 12.

Ladder at present

	N	Percent	N	Percent	N	Percent
0-2 (low)	123	3.5	21	7.0	17	7.9
3-4	229	6.5	35	11.6	34	15.7
5-8	2,215	62.7	195	64.8	148	68.5
9-10 (high)	967	27.4	50	16.6	17	7.9
	3,534		301		216	

(N = 4,051)
$p < .001$; $x^2 = 90.70$

Table 13.

Ladder 5 years ago

	N	Percent	N	Percent	N	Percent
0-2 (low)	386	11.0	59	19.6	52	24.4
3-4	600	17.1	60	19.9	46	21.6
5-8	1,774	50.6	151	50.2	97	45.5
9-10 (high)	747	21.3	31	10.3	18	8.5
	3,507		301		213	

(N = 4,021)
$p < .001$; $x^2 = 78.94$

Table 14.

	Alcohol service need					
	None		Possible		Probable	
	N	Percent	N	Percent	N	Percent
Ladder 5 years from now						
0-2 (low)	86	2.9	9	3.3	10	5.1
3-4	63	2.1	4	1.5	8	4.1
5-8	1,035	34.8	111	40.7	83	42.3
9-10 (high)	1,793	60.2	149	54.6	95	48.5
	2,977		273		196	

(N = 3,446)
$p < .05$; $x^2 = 17.34$

B. Residential and Occupational Stability and Alcohol Service Needs

	Alcohol service need					
	None		Possible		Probable	
	N	Percent	N	Percent	N	Percent

Table 1.

Times moved in last year

	N	Percent	N	Percent	N	Percent
0 times	2,870	79.4	195	63.3	128	58.4
1 time	517	14.3	65	21.1	50	22.8
2 times	119	3.3	28	9.1	15	6.8
3 or more times	229	3.0	48	6.5	41	12.0
	3,616		308		219	

(N = 4,143)
p < .001; X^2 = 116.08

Table 2.

Times moved in last 5 years

	N	Percent	N	Percent	N	Percent
0 times	1,866	51.7	104	33.7	59	26.8
1-3 times	1,388	38.4	143	46.3	96	43.6
4-5 times	215	6.0	37	12.0	34	15.5
6 or more times	143	4.0	25	8.1	31	14.1
	3,612		309		220	

(N = 4,141)
p < .001; X^2 = 139.06

Table 3.

How long at present place of employment

	N	Percent	N	Percent	N	Percent
Less than 1 year	364	21.3	48	28.4	38	32.5
1-3 years	454	26.6	54	32.0	37	31.6
4-5 years	208	12.2	15	8.9	7	6.0
6 or more years	681	39.9	52	30.8	35	29.9
	1,707		169		117	

(N = 1,993)
n.s.

	Alcohol service need					
	None		Possible		Probable	
	N	Percent	N	Percent	N	Percent

Table 4.

Present employment status

	N	Percent	N	Percent	N	Percent
Full-time	1,521	43.4	157	59.7	117	63.2
Part-time	313	8.9	38	14.4	18	9.7
Housewife	1,010	28.8	39	14.8	20	10.8
Unemployed	93	2.7	7	2.7	12	6.5
Retired	447	12.7	13	4.9	9	4.9
Disabled	122	3.5	9	3.4	9	4.9
	3,506		263		185	

(N = 3,954)
$p < .001$; $x^2 = 103.25$

Table 5.

Current job steady?

	N	Percent	N	Percent	N	Percent
Steady	1,498	87.8	147	87.0	109	91.6
Layoffs	46	2.7	4	2.4	4	3.4
Seasonal	132	7.7	12	7.1	6	5.0
Voluntary layoff	25	1.5	4	2.4	0	0.0
Other	6	0.4	2	1.2	0	0.0
	1,707		169		119	

(N = 1,995)
n.s.

Table 6.

Times unemployed in past 3 years (1 month or more)

	N	Percent	N	Percent	N	Percent
No times	1,349	82.2	120	71.9	86	74.8
1 time	170	10.4	18	10.8	18	15.7
2-3 times	99	6.0	23	13.8	9	7.9
4 or more times	23	1.4	6	3.6	2	1.7
	1,641		167		115	

(N = 1,923)
$p < .001$; $x^2 = 23.42$

C. Interpersonal Characteristics and Alcohol Service Need

	Alcohol service need					
	None		Possible		Probable	
	N	Percent	N	Percent	N	Percent

Table 1.

Marital status

Single	374	10.2	79	25.6	74	33.8
Married	2,478	67.8	185	59.9	102	46.6
Widowed	508	13.9	16	5.2	11	5.0
Separated	103	2.8	13	4.2	14	6.4
Divorced	192	5.3	16	5.2	18	8.2
	3,655		309		219	

(N = 4,183)
$p < .001$; $x^2 = 192.61$

Table 2.

Close relatives nearby

Yes	2,590	70.6	211	68.1	150	67.9
No	1,076	29.4	99	31.9	71	32.1
	3,666		310		221	

(N = 4,197)
n.s.

Table 3.

How often see relatives who live nearby?

Almost daily	1,151	44.9	85	40.3	41	27.7
Several times a week	656	25.6	49	23.2	48	32.4
Several times a month	527	20.6	58	27.5	38	25.7
Several times a year	162	6.3	14	6.6	17	11.5
Seldom	49	1.9	5	2.4	4	2.7
Never	17	0.7	0	0.0	0	0.0
	2,562		211		148	

(N = 2,921)
$p < .005$; $x^2 = 27.61$

	Alcohol service need					
	None		Possible		Probable	
	N	Percent	N	Percent	N	Percent

Table 4.

Could ask nearby relative for help

	N	Percent	N	Percent	N	Percent
Yes	2,250	87.9	177	85.5	123	83.1
No	309	12.1	30	14.5	25	16.9
	2,559		207		148	

(N = 2,914)
n.s.

Table 5.

Close friends nearby to help with real problems

	N	Percent	N	Percent	N	Percent
Yes	2,764	77.9	230	76.2	163	74.8
No	782	22.1	72	23.8	55	25.2
	3,546		302		218	

(N = 4,066)
n.s.

Table 6.

	N	Percent	N	Percent	N	Percent

Close friends nearby to help with personal problems, fears, and hopes

	N	Percent	N	Percent	N	Percent
Yes	2,418	68.0	206	67.5	144	65.8
No	1,137	32.0	99	32.5	75	34.2
	3,555		305		219	

(N = 4,079)
n.s.

D. Family and Interpersonal Problems and
Alcohol Service Needs

	Alcohol service need					
	None		Possible		Probable	
	N	Percent	N	Percent	N	Percent

Table 1.

Married: feel helpless to deal with family problems

	N	Percent	N	Percent	N	Percent
Never	1,432	59.0	104	56.5	42	40.8
Seldom	474	19.5	41	22.3	20	19.4
Sometimes	385	15.9	31	16.8	26	25.2
Often	91	3.7	6	3.3	11	10.7
All the time	47	1.9	2	1.1	4	3.9
	2,429		184		103	

(N = 2,716)
$p < .001$; $x^2 = 26.65$

Table 2.

Unmarried: dealing with problems causes pressure/tension

	N	Percent	N	Percent	N	Percent
Never	349	34.9	38	33.9	24	22.2
Seldom	231	23.1	33	29.5	17	15.7
Sometimes	308	30.8	29	25.9	49	45.4
Often	80	8.0	7	6.3	11	10.2
All the time	31	3.1	5	4.5	7	6.5
	999		112		108	

(N = 1,219)
$p < .01$; $x^2 = 21.51$

Table 3.

Unmarried: helpless to deal with problems

	N	Percent	N	Percent	N	Percent
Never	533	48.6	54	46.2	45	40.5
Seldom	227	20.7	33	28.2	27	24.3
Sometimes	236	21.5	19	16.2	28	25.2
Often	64	5.8	10	8.5	9	8.1
All the time	36	3.3	1	0.9	2	1.8
	1,096		117		111	

(N = 1,324)
n.s.

Table 4.

	Alcohol service need					
	None		Possible		Probable	
	N	Percent	N	Percent	N	Percent
Immediate family member disabled or seriously ill						
Yes	799	22.0	70	22.6	46	20.9
No	2,834	78.0	240	77.4	174	79.1
	3,633		310		220	

($\underline{N}$ = 4,163)
n.s.

E. Health Perceptions and Behaviors and
Alcohol Service Needs

	Alcohol service need					
	None		Possible		Probable	
	N	Percent	N	Percent	N	Percent

Table 1.

Visits to medical doctor in last year

0-2 times	2,197	60.4	205	66.3	144	66.1
3-5	711	19.6	73	23.6	47	21.6
6-9	400	11.0	18	5.8	11	5.0
10 or more	328	9.0	13	4.2	16	7.3
	3,636		309		218	

(N = 4,163)
$p < .001$; $x^2 = 26.03$

Table 2.

Physical health at present

Excellent	1,434	39.1	138	44.5	75	33.9
Good	1,435	39.1	126	40.6	87	39.4
Fair	609	16.6	36	11.6	45	20.4
Poor	148	4.0	8	2.6	12	5.4
Very bad	41	1.1	2	0.6	2	0.9
	3,667		310		221	

(N = 4,198)
n.s.

Table 3.

Mental health at present

Excellent	1,151	31.6	97	31.5	40	18.2
Good	1,805	49.6	159	51.6	111	50.5
Fair	583	16.0	42	13.6	52	23.6
Poor	83	2.3	7	2.3	13	5.9
Very bad	19	0.5	3	1.0	4	1.8
	3,641		308		220	

(N = 4,169)
$p < .001$; $x^2 = 38.59$

	Alcohol service need					
	None		Possible		Probable	
	N	Percent	N	Percent	N	Percent

Table 4.

Visited Vocational Rehabilitation in past year

	N	Percent	N	Percent	N	Percent
No	3,598	98.3	304	98.1	211	95.5
Yes	62	1.7	6	1.9	10	4.5
	3,660		310		221	

(N = 4,191)
$p < .05$; $x^2 = 9.15$

Table 5.

Visited welfare in past year

	N	Percent	N	Percent	N	Percent
No	3,418	93.4	291	93.9	199	90.0
Yes	242	6.6	19	6.1	22	10.0
	3,660		310		221	

(N = 4,191)
n.s.

Table 6.

Visited VA in last year

	N	Percent	N	Percent	N	Percent
No	3,511	96.4	298	96.1	203	91.9
Yes	133	3.6	12	3.9	18	8.1
	3,644		310		221	

(N = 4,175)
$p < .05$; $x^2 = 11.22$

Table 7.

	N	Percent	N	Percent	N	Percent

Gone to minister for problem in past year

	N	Percent	N	Percent	N	Percent
Yes	418	11.5	44	14.3	23	10.6
No	3,226	88.5	264	85.7	195	89.4
	3,644		308		218	

(N = 4,170)
n.s.

	Alcohol service need					
	None		Possible		Probable	
	N	Percent	N	Percent	N	Percent

Table 8.

How often use sleeping pills (prescribed)?

	N	Percent	N	Percent	N	Percent
Never	2,917	80.3	248	80.5	159	72.9
Seldom	379	10.4	37	12.0	27	12.4
Sometimes	214	5.9	14	4.5	17	7.8
Often/all the time	123	3.4	9	2.9	15	6.9
	3,633		308		218	

(N = 4,159)
$p < .05$; $X^2 = 12.48$

Table 9.

Ever use nerve medicine, tranquilizers, or anti-depressants (Rx)?

	N	Percent	N	Percent	N	Percent
Yes	1,217	33.5	117	38.0	93	42.3
No	2,418	66.5	191	62.0	127	57.7
	3,635		308		220	

(N = 4,163)
$p < .01$; $X^2 = 9.15$

Table 10.

Present physical or health problems

	N	Percent	N	Percent	N	Percent
Yes	1,573	42.9	114	36.8	97	44.3
No	2,090	57.1	196	63.2	122	55.7
	3,663		310		219	

(N = 4,192)
n.s.

Table 11.

Health now vs. 1 year ago

	N	Percent	N	Percent	N	Percent
Better	769	21.0	58	18.7	55	24.9
Same	2,485	67.9	217	70.0	131	59.3
Worse	407	11.1	35	11.3	35	15.8
	3,661		310		221	

(N = 4,192)
n.s.

	\<u>Alcohol service need\</u>					
	None		Possible		Probable	
	N	Percent	N	Percent	N	Percent

Table 12.

Health now vs. 5 years ago
Better	847	23.4	71	23.4	58	26.6
Same	1,939	53.5	167	55.1	101	46.3
Worse	836	23.1	65	21.5	59	27.1
	3,622		303		218	

(N = 4,143)
n.s.

Table 13.

Times in hospital as patient in last 3 years
None	2,422	66.1	223	71.9	141	63.8
1-2 times	1,091	29.8	75	24.2	64	29.0
3-5 times	129	3.5	10	3.2	13	5.9
6 or more	24	0.7	2	0.6	3	1.4
	3,666		310		221	

(N = 4,197)
$p < .05$; $X^2 = 9.61$

Table 14.

Ever tried to commit suicide?
Yes	76	2.1	8	2.6	19	8.6
No	3,587	97.9	302	97.4	202	91.4
	3,663		310		221	

(N = 4,194)
$p < .001$; $X^2 = 37.04$

PREDICTORS AND CORRELATES OF RECOVERY IN OLDER VERSUS YOUNGER ALCOHOLICS*

John E. Helzer, M.D., Kristin E. Carey, B.A., and Richard H. Miller, Ph.D.

ABSTRACT

This is a report of the results of a 5- to 8-year followup study of treated alcoholics identified in four inpatient and outpatient treatment facilities. We reviewed treatment records of all persons with a discharge diagnosis suggestive of alcoholism who had been admitted to the medical/surgical inpatient unit, the inpatient psychiatric unit, or the outpatient psychiatric clinic of Barnes Hospital between January 1, 1973, and December 31, 1975. We also reviewed records of all the women and three-fifths of the men admitted to the alcohol unit of a state-run community mental health center during this same period. Over 2,000 records were reviewed, and 1,289 had sufficient record evidence to substantiate a diagnosis of alcoholism, survived the admission, and lived within a 50-mile radius of St. Louis.

After identifying this sample, we searched for evidence of continued alcohol problems or treatment after January 1, 1977. For this latter review, records from the original treatment facility, other treatment facilities in the St. Louis area, and police records were used. We also reviewed vital statistics records for Missouri and Illinois from 1975 forward to identify those who had died. On the basis of the subsequent record review, we divided survivors into two groups—those who had record evidence of continued alcohol treatment or problems after January 1, 1977, and those with no such record evidence. Approximately 600 subjects fell into each sample. We then attempted to locate and personally interview a random sample of 100 of those with record evidence, and all of those with no record evidence, of continued alcoholism. The interview focused on the lifetime history of drinking, a variety of

---

*This work was supported in part by United States Public Health Service Grants AA-03852 and AA-03539.

psychiatric diagnoses, personal and social history, family history, and a detailed history of drinking level and problems in the past 3 years.

We contrast that portion of the sample who were 60 years or older as of the start of the followup period (January 1977) with younger subjects. In these two groups, we describe outcomes, i.e., proportions who became abstinent, who were continued alcoholics, and who were able to continue to drink at a moderate level without relapse to excessive or problem drinking. We found that mortality rates were considerably higher among older alcoholics, but for those who survived, remission to abstinence or problem-free drinking was higher. We discuss the history of alcohol problems, demographic characteristics, other psychiatric disorders, and life situations as predictors of outcome for elderly, as compared with younger, alcoholics.

INTRODUCTION

The present study was undertaken to examine the outcome of persons discharged with a diagnosis of alcoholism from the inpatient and outpatient psychiatric services and inpatient medical services of the Washington University hospitals between 1973 and 1975. The principal objective was to ascertain the rate of recovery to stable, moderate drinking in this sample and, if moderate drinking did occur in a significant number of cases, to search for predictors of this outcome.

The interviewed sample ranged in age from 21 to 81. The mean age was 47 years, and 19 percent of the cohort was 60 years or older at the time of interview. The study thus provides an opportunity to compare both outcome and predictors and correlates of outcome in older vs. younger alcoholics who are serious enough to have come to medical or psychiatric treatment for the illness or its consequences.

Such studies are desirable because of the uncertainties in the published literature regarding the prevalence and natural history of alcoholism in older populations (Dunham 1981). For example, Cahalan (1970) in his national survey of drinking problems reports that in men problems do taper off after the age of 50 but continue at a fairly high level until age 70. But in a separate analysis of the same sample, Cahalan and Room (1972) conclude that drinking problems diminish rapidly after age 50. Zimberg (1979) acknowledges that there is some evidence of a falloff in alcohol problems in older ages but suggests also that alcoholism is underdiagnosed and underreported in older persons. If alcoholism is less prevalent among the elderly, it is not clear if this represents a diminution of alcohol problems with age or whether it might represent differential excess mortality among more serious drinkers as they get older. If there is a natural history effect of a decrease in problems with age, understanding more about this might provide clues to the treatment of young alcoholics.

METHODS

Treatment records of patients admitted to four treatment facilities between 1973 and 1975 were reviewed. The four facilities were the inpatient medical and psychiatric services and the psychiatric outpatient clinic of Barnes Hospital, a privately run university hospital, and the alcohol inpatient unit of a state-run psychiatric hospital in the inner city of St. Louis. The hospital or clinic charts of all patients with a discharge diagnosis of alcoholism or a medical complication of alcoholism were pulled for a case-by-case review of the index admission. Patients were selected as study subjects only if the chart documented current alcohol problems and if the patient survived the index admission, remained in the hospital at least 24 hours, and lived within a 50-mile radius of St. Louis. At the inner city hospital, only three-fifths of the male admissions were randomly sampled since this group was so large and so uniformly alcoholic. In all, we reviewed over 2,000 charts and selected or sampled 1,282 index cases who met the above criteria.

After identifying the index sample, we sought to identify those subjects who had continued alcohol problems after January 1, 1977. To do so, we reviewed all treatment records of the index hospitals, other local treatment facilities, and police and other records after that date. We also reviewed vital statistics records to identify those who had died. We divided the initial sample into two groups: those who had survived until January 1, 1977, and had no retrievable record evidence of continued alcohol problems, and all others. We then attempted to locate and interview all of those in the first group who remained living in the St. Louis area, and a random sample of 100 of those who survived but had record evidence of continued alcoholism. The interview asked for detailed information concerning the subjects' drinking practices, any drinking problems over the previous 3 years (roughly 1978-1980 for most respondents), a lifetime history of drinking patterns and problems, lifetime occurrence of other pertinent psychiatric disorders, a social and employment history, a family history of alcoholism, and the occurrence of significant life events and how they may have influenced alcohol consumption. The interviewed sample was weighted so that each demographic subgroup interviewed represented the same proportion it did in the original sample. Table 1 shows the N's of the various subsamples and the interview success rates.

Table 1.—Moderate Drinking Study

Study sample

Hospital records reviewed............................2,116
Subjects in sampling frame but records not reviewed... 316
Alcoholism tentatively confirmed by record review.....1,289
Died before 1/1/77.................................... 142
Known treatment or alcohol problems after 1/1/77
    Alive.. 449
    Died after 1/1/77.................................... 32

	No known treatment or alcohol problems after 1/1/77 (N = 659*)	Random sample of known alcoholics (N = 100)
Ineligible for interview		
Moved out of interview range	99	5
Dead, with no record documentation of alcohol problems after 1/1/77	69	0
Dead, with record documentation of alcohol problems after 1/1/77	34	10
Forced abstention	8	0
Total	210 (32 percent)	15
Interviewed	324 (49 percent)	69
Total interviewed or ineligible	534 (80 percent)	84 (84 percent)
Subjects not located	58 (9 percent)	12 (12 percent)
Subjects refused interview	67 (10 percent)	4 (4 percent)

Table 1.--Moderate Drinking Study (cont'd.)

Locating efforts

Died before period of risk (1/1/77)...........	142
Known treatment or alcohol problems..........	481
No known treatment or problems	
Ineligible for interview...................	210
Interviewed...............................	324
	1,157 (90 percent of 1,282)

---

*Seven subjects were omitted because they failed to meet DSM-III criteria for alcoholism.

For the present examination, we will dichotomize the weighted sample on the basis of age--60 or more years vs. 59 or less. We will compare these two groups in terms of mortality rates, illness outcome, and predictors and correlates of outcome. Our principal outcome variable is the subject's drinking status over the 3 years prior to interview. This is a four-level variable: 1) abstinence for all of the previous 36 months; 2) drinking moderately without any recurrence of alcohol problems for all 36 months; 3) alternating abstinence and moderate drinking with no alcohol problems; and 4) continued alcohol problems. For most analyses this variable will be dichotomized, with the first three levels constituting a good outcome and the fourth level a poor one. Results for the interviewed sample will be presented using unweighted $\underline{N}$'s and weighted percentages. All statistical tests are performed on unweighted data.

RESULTS

OUTCOME BY AGE

Table 2 shows outcome and interview status by age of the 1,282 index cases. The sample is divided into those with no documented problems (on the basis of all sources of information) and those with continued problems. Percentages can be summed across these two groups. As can be seen, the proportion who died during the approximately 8-year followup that this table represents is about half as great in the younger as compared with the older sample (19

Table 2.—Eight-Year Outcome of Alcoholics
(N = 1,282)

Outcome	Percentages in those aged under and over 60			
	Under 60 at interview or at midpoint of field period (N = 1,048)		60 or more at interview or at midpoint of field period (N = 234)	
	(N)	(Percent)	(N)	(Percent)
No evidence of continuing alcohol problems				
Interviewed	93	9	30	13
Refused interview, not located, or moved out of interview range	198	19	26	11
Dead	93	9	57	24
Forced abstention	4	*	4	2
Total	388	37	117	50
Continued alcohol problems, documented by interview or available records				
Interviewed	229	22	41	18
Refused interview, not located or moved out of interview range	20	2	1	*
Dead	101	10	36	15
Not selected for interview	310	30	39	17
Total	660	64	117	50
Totals with bad outcome, as defined by death, record documentation, or problems at interview	753	73	174	74

*Less than 5 percent.

vs. 39 percent). But among the survivors, the proportion with record or interview evidence of continued alcohol problems is higher in the younger group (64 vs. 50 percent). The excess mortality in the older sample essentially balances the greater proportion of continuing alcoholics in the younger group; the two outcomes together account for 73 percent of those under age 60 at followup and 74 percent of those age 60 and older. It could be argued that the older sample would be more likely to die of natural causes, and thus it is not reasonable to combine death with record or interview evidence of poor outcome as we have done. However, while we do not have extensive data on cause of death, we do have death certificates for most of those who died. We know from previous work by ourselves (Taylor at al. 1982) and others (Petersson et al. 1982) that death certificates give a gross underestimate of death due to alcohol. But assuming that the underestimate is not biased according to age, we can use death certificate data to see if the proportion who have died of alcohol-related causes is similar in younger and older alcoholics. In fact, the proportions were very similar. Among the three causes of death listed on death certificates, alcohol-related causes were listed at least once in 40 percent of the under 60 group and in 37 percent of those 60 or older.

Table 3 illustrates outcome in the interviewed sample ($\underline{N}$ = 393) after appropriate weighting. The most striking finding here is the low rate at which treated alcoholics were able to achieve a pattern of stable and persistent (3 years) moderate drinking. The older alcoholics were more successful in this regard than the younger alcoholics, but for both groups, it was clearly the rare exception. A greater proportion alternated between moderation and abstention during the 3-year period, but in fact, this was largely abstention with only occasional alcohol use. Viewing this variable dichotomously, with the first three levels being considered good outcome, we find that a slightly higher proportion of the older group achieved a good outcome, but the difference was not statistically significant.

It is important to note that, at least on the basis of a lifetime count of alcohol problems, the younger alcoholics appear to have more problems. The lifetime problem count, which included a total of 25 social, legal, and medical problems, was trichotomized into less than 6, 6 to 10, and 11 or more. Despite the fact that the older group obviously had more years over which to accumulate problems, their mean count was nine problems, and 20 percent and 27 percent were at the lowest and highest problem levels respectively. This compares to a mean of 12 problems and 9 percent and 63 percent respectively for the younger group. Other indicators of severity such as mean age of the first alcohol problem, age first met DSM-III criteria for alcohol abuse or dependence, and

Table 3.—Self-Report of Outcome in Interviewed Alcoholics at 6 to 10-Year Followup, by Age

(Sample $\underline{N}$ = 393)*

Outcome in last 3 years	Weighted percentages	
	60 years< ($\underline{N}$ = 314) (Percent)	60+ years ($\underline{N}$ = 73) (Percent)
Abstained all 36 months	14**	18
Drank moderately	1	3
Mixed moderation and abstention	5	3
Continued alcoholic	80	76
Total with good outcome	20	24

*Insufficient information to determine outcome, $\underline{N}$ = 6.
**Includes two subjects for whom there is record evidence to the contrary.

number of years between the first drink and the development of heavy drinking were suggestive of more severe alcoholism in the younger group. One likely explanation of this is that the higher mortality rate already shown for the older sample is differentially concentrated in the more serious alcoholics, so that the survivors are the less severe cases.

THE IMPACT OF DEMOGRAPHY

It has been claimed that the differential outcome by sex, which is true for all age levels, is greater for older persons than for younger ones. There was some evidence of that in our weighted interview sample. The male/female ratio for a poor (continued alcoholic) outcome in the younger group was 3.6, and this same ratio was 11.7 in the older group. The phi coefficient for all levels of outcome by sex was .16 in the younger sample and .41 in the older group, indicating a stronger association between outcome and sex in the latter.

So far, we have seen that in this sample of treated, presumably serious alcoholics, the mortality rate is high and strikingly so for those 60 and older. However, despite the fact that the surviving older alcoholics appear somewhat less severely ill than the younger group, their outcome in terms of how many continue to have drinking problems is not very different. We are also interested in looking at predictors and correlates of outcome to see if these differ in the two age groups. Table 4 examines several demographic variables. The proportion of cases with good outcome (abstainers, moderate drinkers, or a combination of these for all of the past 3 years) is shown for the total sample and then for the age-segregated samples. The statistical significance of the degree of association of each variable with outcome in that particular sample is indicated with asterisks, but for comparisons across samples, the phi coefficient is a more appropriate measure of association since it is independent of sample size.

Sex is a significant predictor of outcome in the total group and in the younger group but not in the older group. That lack of significance is probably a sample size effect, since the phi coefficient for the older cases is the same as for the full sample and only slightly less than for the younger group. The demographic variable with the most interesting relationship to outcome is marital status. Being currently married or cohabiting is associated with a good outcome in the total sample. The association is significant, and the phi is the same as it was for sex. But in the age-segregated samples, the phi is hardly above zero for the younger group and is much larger in those 60 and over. Despite the smaller numbers, the relationship between marital status and outcome is highly significant in the older group. This association is consistent with another that is suggestive of social isolation, i.e., whether or not others are living in the proband's household. Again, living alone shows no association with outcome in the younger alcoholics group (phi = .01) but a significant association with poor outcome in the older group ($p < .01$, phi = .31). Unemployment for 6 or more months is also more strongly associated with poor outcome in older vs. younger persons (phi = .28 and .12 respectively). Thus, it would appear that various kinds of social isolation are more strongly correlated with poor outcome in older alcoholics.

PSYCHIATRIC DIAGNOSES

Table 5 explores the association between other psychiatric diagnoses and remission from alcoholism. The other DSM-III diagnoses asked about in the personal interview were major depression, dysthymia, antisocial personality disorder, panic disorder, drug abuse and dependence, and cognitive impairment. Except

Table 4.--Demographic Predictors and Correlates of Outcome in Interviewed Alcoholics

Demographic variables	Total interviewed sample (N = 387)		Age under 60 years at interview (N = 314)			Age 60+ years at interview (N = 73)		
	Weighted percent with good outcome		N	Weighted percent with good outcome		N	Weighted percent with good outcome	
Sex								
Women	33		102	31		13	45	
Men	18	(*phi = .12)	212	17	(*phi = .14)	60	21	(phi = .12)
Race								
Non-black	23		163	21		50	27	
Black	20	(phi = .06)	151	20	(phi = .02)	23	17	(phi = .15)
Marital status								
Married or cohabiting	28		149	24		38	47	
Neither	15	(*phi = .12)	164	18	(phi = .04)	35	9	(***phi = .41)
Job Level								
Above median	37		142	30		39	19	
Median or below	19	(**phi = .09)	172	16	(*phi = .11)	34	29	(phi < .01)

Significance level

* = p < .05
** = p < .01
*** = p < .001

Table 5.—Diagnostic Predictors and Correlates of Outcome in Interviewed Alcoholics

Diagnostic variables	Total interviewed sample (N = 387) Weighted percent with good outcome	Age under 60 years at interview (N = 314) N	Age under 60 years at interview (N = 314) Weighted percent with good outcome	Age 60+ years at interview (N = 73) N	Age 60+ years at interview (N = 73) Weighted percent with good outcome
Alcoholism and other psychiatric diagnoses					
Alcoholism alone	19	71	22	28	14
Any other psychiatric diagnosis	17 (phi = .10)	188	14 (**phi = .19)	24	39 (**phi = .38)
Depression					
No history of depression	25	180	26	55	20
History of depression	15 (**phi = .14)	127	12 (**phi = .17)	10	50 (phi = .16)
Antisocial personality					
No history of definite ASP	26	217	26	58	27
History of definite ASP	10 (***phi = .23)	86	10 (***phi = .24)	4	6 (phi = .09)
Cognitive impairment					
Absent	20	261	21	48	20
Present	28 (phi = .03)	40	19 (phi = .04)	14	61 (phi = .25)

Significant level
* = p < .05
** = p < .01
*** = p < .001

for a diagnosis of cognitive impairment, which was based on a mini mental status examination given at the time of interview, all of the diagnoses were made on the basis of questions about the lifetime occurrence of pertinent symptoms.

The lifetime occurrence of any other psychiatric disorder in addition to alcoholism is significantly associated with drinking outcome in both age groups, but the association is in opposite directions and thus in the total sample is not significant. The presence of another psychiatric diagnosis is associated with a worse outcome in the younger group and a better outcome in the older group. This appears to be at least partially due to the differential association of depression and outcome in the two age groups. Here, the association is significant only for the younger sample, but the phi is nearly equal in the two groups. Depression seems to be about as strongly associated with a worse outcome in the younger group as it is with a better outcome in the older group.

Because of the frequent intercorrelation of antisocial personality and drug use with depression, we looked at depression alone as a predictor of outcome. This did not alter the differential effect shown in the table. Depression continued to be associated with a poor outcome in the younger group and a better outcome in the older group, and the phi coefficients in each case were higher than before. Antisocial personality is associated with a poor outcome in both groups, although the association is clearly stronger in the younger sample. Cognitive impairment showed essentially no association with outcome in the younger group but a moderate association with good outcome in the older. None of the older subjects had a history of drug problems, so the differential association could not be tested. Panic disorder was only weakly related to outcome in both samples.

OTHER PREDICTORS

Table 6 displays some other variables tested. The recent occurrence of medical problems unrelated to alcoholism was weakly associated with better outcome in both groups, as was the respondent's self-estimate of health. The same was true of medical problems at index admission that contraindicated continued drinking. This seemingly serious state of affairs had a trivial effect on outcome, at least among survivors at followup.

Not surprisingly, more of the older group were raised in a rural setting, and this showed a positive association with outcome but not a significant one. The attitude of the childhood family toward alcohol showed little association with outcome. Having had grandparents born outside the United States, again a more common

Table 6.--Other Predictors and Correlates of Outcome in Interviewed Alcoholics

Other variables	Total interviewed sample (N = 387) Weighted percent with good outcome	Age under 60 years at interview (N = 314)		Age 60+ years at interview (N = 73)	
		N	Weighted percent with good outcome	N	Weighted percent with good outcome
Medical history					
Medical problems un-related to alcoholism	28 percent	62	27 percent	35	29 percent
No such problems	20 (phi = .07)	252	20 (phi = .04)	38	21 (phi = .09)
Factors in childhood					
Rural upbringing	30	36	20	19	49
Nonrural upbringing	20 (phi = .07)	276	20 (phi = .01)	54	17 (phi = .20)
Family attitude tolerant toward alcohol	21	209	22	52	19
Family intolerant	21 (phi = .03)	94	18 (phi = .07)	18	43 (phi =.15)
Grandparents born in U.S.	22	260	21	49	30
Grandparents born outside U.S.	18 (phi = .01)	44	21 (phi = .06)	22	13 (*phi = .27)
Educational status					
No high school diploma or G.E.D.	23	129	22	34	27
High school diploma or G.E.D.	25	115	24	19	26
Education beyond high school	36 (**phi = .16)	67	38 (**phi = .19)	19	25 (phi = .07)
Recent exposure to alcoholic beverages					
Alcohol usually kept in home during last 3 years	17	238	16	52	23
No alcohol in home	34 (***phi = .18)	74	36 (***phi = .22)	19	28 (phi < .01)

Significance level   * = $p < .05$ ** = $p < .01$ *** = $p < .001$

finding in the older sample, showed a weakly significant relationship with a worse outcome in the older group. We tried to see if this might be accounted for by any particular nationality, but there were too few cases to be certain. One variable not shown in the table is childhood religious affiliation of the proband. This showed no association at all with outcome, but we did not have consistent enough information on this variable to segregate cases reliably on the basis of religions that proscribe drinking, and this may be the reason we found no effect. Educational status showed no relationship to outcome in the older group. There was a significant association in the younger group, but it was not monotonic. Those with the least education had the best outcome and those with the most education, the next best. For this entire set of predictors, the strongest one in the younger group is whether alcohol was kept in the home. This showed hardly any association at all with outcome in the older group.

DISCUSSION

In this sample of treated and presumably relatively severe alcoholics, similarities between age groups seem more apparent than differences. First, in terms of outcome, there is some evidence that among the survivors in the original record cohort, older alcoholics have a smaller proportion with continuing alcohol problems. But it is also clear that their mortality rate is much higher and, while we cannot absolutely ascertain what proportion of the deaths were alcohol related, it appears from the death certificate data that the alcohol-related mortality rate is similar in the two groups. When we add the deceased to those with other evidence of poor outcome, there is essentially no difference in overall outcome between the two age groups. Doing this does not require that we assume all deaths to be alcohol related but only that risk of death attributable to alcohol is similar in both age groups. As shown above, it probably is. Furthermore, the interview data show the recent drinking status to be similar in the two groups. This similarity obtains not only for the overall categories of good vs. bad outcome, but also extends to specific outcomes of abstention, moderate drinking, etc., which differ by no more than 4 percentage points between the younger and the older alcoholics.

In addition to outcome, we have examined predictors and correlates of outcome. In our search for differential predictors in the two age groups, we tested a large number of variables. In fact, since we did test so many, the few we found to be differentially predictive might be suspect due to chance. Thus, in our sample, predictors and correlates may differ very little between these age groups. However, assuming the few differences we found are real and not due to chance, let's examine these more closely.

One interesting group of variables are those suggestive of social isolation, which seem to correlate more strongly with continued alcoholism in the older group. The question arises: In what direction might the influence be? Does social isolation lead to continued alcoholism in older persons, or does the tendency for family breakup and job instability in more serious alcoholics begin to express itself more consistently as the alcoholic ages? To examine this, we compared the lifetime number of alcohol problems in the two age groups by cohabitation status. In the younger group, those who were neither married nor cohabiting did have a slightly higher mean lifetime problem count than those who were attached, but the difference was not significant (t-test for independent samples). In the older group, the difference in the mean lifetime problem rate is in the same direction and is significant at the .05 level. Another way of looking at this is to compare the number of times married in these two groups. If the number of marriages is greater among those who are not currently married or cohabiting, it might suggest a preexisting tendency toward marital instability that could partially account for their current cohabitation status. In the younger group, despite one fickle soul who had been through 12 marriages, the currently married (or cohabiting) had been married more times than those who were not living with someone (2.1 vs. 1.6). In the older group, this was reversed. Those not currently married or cohabiting had a mean of 1.8 marriages vs. 1.2 for the others. Both of these analyses suggest that alcohol problems influence social isolation rather than the reverse, but unfortunately there is no definitive way to test this.

The DSM-III diagnoses are another interesting set of differential predictors of outcome. Here, depression was the most striking: It predicted opposite outcomes at about the same level of significance. To examine this predictor more carefully, we divided depressions into those that antedated or had the same onset age as alcoholism and those that postdated the onset of alcoholism. Antedating depression accounted for the largest difference in outcome. Eight percent of such cases in the younger sample had a good outcome, whereas 73 percent of the older cases did. The findings are difficult to interpret, however, because of the small number of such cases (N = 6) in the older sample. Organic brain syndrome was also interesting because it showed almost no association with outcome in the younger sample and a relatively strong association with good outcome in the older group. The differential association between age groups was in the same direction for both mild and severe organic disturbance, but the largest absolute effect was for those with severe organic brain syndrome. Sixty-seven percent of such cases in the older group had a good outcome. Again, however, we are working with very small numbers, particularly in the mild group. The other specific diagnosis we examined is antisocial personality. Here, the most striking finding was the relative infrequence of antisocial personality in the older sample. Twenty-eight percent of the younger group received this diagnosis, but only 6 percent of the older group did. This would be consistent with a differentially high mortality rate among antisocial drinkers who, of course, have two disorders associated with early and nonnatural death.

Among the other variables we examined, the one which is most strikingly predictive of outcome is whether alcoholic beverages were kept in the home. Our assumption is that this merely reflects the large proportion of abstainers in the good outcome group. To account for the large difference in predictive power between the younger and older groups, we considered the possibility that younger subjects might more often be heads of household, and hence more often decide whether to keep alcohol in the home. This did not turn out to be the case--80 percent of the younger probands were heads of household (defined as the main wage earner), and 83 percent of the older probands were.

To summarize, in this sample of treated alcoholics followed for 6 to 10 years, there was evidence of good outcome in a larger proportion of the older subjects. But there was also a much higher mortality rate in the older group, and this approximately balanced the difference in outcome. Among the interviewed sample, outcome was nearly identical. Considering the number of predictors and correlates tested, relatively few were differentially associated with outcome in the two age groups. This record and interview study of a treated population seems to demonstrate considerable similarity between older and younger age groups rather than any marked contrast.

REFERENCES

Cahalan, D. *Problem Drinkers*. San Francisco: Jossey-Bass, 1970.

Cahalan, D., and Room, R. Problem drinking among American men age 21 to 59. *American Journal of Public Health* 62:1473-1482, 1972.

Dunham, R.G. Aging and changing patterns of alcohol use. *Journal of Psychoactive Drugs* 13:143-151, 1981.

Petersson, B.; Krantz, S.J.; Kristensson, H.; Trell, E.; and Sternby, N.H. Alcohol related death: A major contributor to mortality in urban middle-aged men. *Lancet* 2:1088-1090, 1982.

Taylor, J.R.; Holmes, S.J.; Combs-Orme, T.; and Scott, E.B. Alcohol and death certificates. *Journal of the American Medical Association* 248:3096, 1982.

Zimberg, S. Alcohol and the elderly. In: Petersen, D.M.; Whittington, F.J.; and Payne, B.P., eds. *Drugs and the Elderly: Social and Pharmacological Issues*. Springfield, Ill.: Charles C. Thomas, 1979.

CHANGES IN ALCOHOL CONSUMPTION BEHAVIORS AMONG MEN IN THE NORMATIVE AGING STUDY*

Robert J. Glynn, Ph.D., Glen R. Bouchard, S.M.
Joseph S. LoCastro, Ph.D., and John A. Hermos, M.D.

ABSTRACT

This study describes changes over 9 years in the alcohol consumption behaviors of volunteers in the Normative Aging Study, a longitudinal study of human aging. In June 1973, 1,864 men, aged 28 to 87, responded to a mailed drinking survey. In September 1982, 1,570 of these men responded to a followup questionnaire. Respondents to the first survey who were dead in 1982 were more likely to be nondrinkers or drinking two or more drinks per day in 1973. Nonrespondents to the 1982 survey also tended to be from the extreme drinking groups and were far more likely to be in the youngest or oldest age groups. These characteristics of attrition indicate the selection bias inherent in cross-sectional studies of aging and drinking behaviors. Among respondents to both surveys, there was almost no change in mean alcohol consumption levels from 1973 to 1982. This was true in spite of the fact that among men whose consumption levels changed, more men decreased than increased their drinking. Rates of problems with drinking also showed no declines over time within age groups. Men in their forties and fifties in 1973 were particularly consistent in their drinking habits over time. Longitudinal data from the current study do not support the finding from previous cross-sectional studies that aging modifies drinking behaviors. The trend towards increased per capita consumption in the United States during the period of followup influences these results. There are potentially serious public health implications if older men today are drinking more than men the same age drank a decade ago.

---

*Supported by the Medical Research Service of the Veterans Administration and by a grant from the Distilled Spirits Council of the United States.

Alcohol abuse and alcoholism constitute a serious public health problem among the elderly. National and local surveys have found between 2 and 10 percent of older men to be alcoholics or problem drinkers (Cahalan et al. 1969; Clark and Midanik 1982; Bailey et al. 1965; Barnes 1979). Studies in nursing homes have estimated the prevalence of alcoholism among inhabitants to range from 25 percent to as high as 60 percent (Mishara and Kastenbaum 1980; Blose 1978). Reviews of alcohol problems among older patients both in general medical and in psychiatric hospitals (Gomberg 1980) have found rates of alcohol problems among older people admitted to both types of hospital to range from 15 to 49 percent. It is estimated that, of the elderly with alcohol-related problems who are admitted to the hospital, about half are actively drinking at the time of admission (Schuckit and Miller 1976; Gomberg 1975). Finally, of all people aged 65 and above who were arrested in the United States in 1975, 58.4 percent were arrested for either drunkenness or driving under the influence (McCreary 1979).

Although alcohol-related problems are substantial among the elderly, there is some evidence that the elderly have relatively fewer problems than the young. Indeed, national surveys of community-dwelling individuals have consistently found more non-drinkers and fewer heavier and problem drinkers among the elderly than among the young (Clark and Midanik 1982). Prevalences of problem drinking in national surveys (Cahalan et al. 1969; Clark and Midanik 1982) are highest among men aged 21 to 34, with rates about 2.5 to 3.0 times those of men over 65. From a clinical perspective, age-specific prevalences of patients at treatment facilities because of alcoholism are highest in the age group 40 to 49 with a rate 3 to 4 times greater than those aged 61 to 70 (Drew 1968). Gomberg (1980) noted the precipitous drop in heavy drinking rates at age 65 among men in the national survey of Cahalan et al. (1969) (from 24 percent heavy drinkers in the age group 60 to 64 to 7 percent in the age group 65 and older) and proposed that 65 is about the age at which men markedly moderate their drinking behaviors.

Suggestions, drawn from cross-sectional surveys, that aging modifies drinking behaviors are limited because of potential generational effects and survivor bias (Mishara and Kastenbaum 1980). Generational differences, which in cross-sectional studies are inseparable from age differences, occur when one generation consistently drinks less (or more) than a preceding generation. Living through Prohibition is a potential source of a generational effect on drinking behaviors. Survivor bias clouds the interpretation of age differences found in cross-sectional studies because alcoholics are more likely to die at younger ages. In addition, older problem drinkers are more likely to be cognitively impaired and perhaps institutionalized; hence they are less likely to be available for participation in a community survey. A longitudinal study allows for a clearer description of the effects of aging on alcohol consumption behaviors.

This report describes changes in the drinking habits of a population of men who described their drinking habits in 1973 and again in 1982. As well as changes in consumption level, we consider variability in self-reported problems with drinking. A large percentage of these men were initially over age 50, and emphasis is placed on examination of the hypothesis that older men in particular modify their drinking habits.

METHODS

POPULATION

The population for this study consisted of the 1,864 male volunteers in the Normative Aging Study who gave consistent responses to a drinking questionnaire mailed to them in June 1973. The Normative Aging Study is a longitudinal study of human aging initiated in 1963 and located at the Veterans Administration Outpatient Clinic in Boston (Bell et al. 1972). Volunteers were screened according to health criteria at entry in order to provide a population initially free of any serious medical conditions (Glynn et al. 1982). Alcoholism was not a screening criterion, but men with medical complications of alcoholism were excluded. In particular, volunteers were disqualified if they had cirrhosis, pancreatitis, or elevated serum transaminase (SGOT) levels. Many alcoholics have no such medical complications and thus would not have been excluded. The initial population consisted of 2,280 men aged 21 to 81, with a mean age of 42.

DRINKING QUESTIONNAIRES

In June 1973 the Normative Aging Study mailed to its participants a 15-page drinking questionnaire adapted from the instruments of Cahalan et al. (1969). Of the 2,025 men active in the study at the time, 1,897 returned the questionnaire. The questionnaire assessed alcoholic beverage consumption by three different scales: (1) the usual number of drinks of beer, wine, and spirits currently consumed reported in drinks per day, week, month, or year; (2) the number of drinks of beer, wine, and spirits consumed the day before completing the questionnaire; and (3) the regularity of alcohol consumption on specific days of the week. Scale (1), quantified in total drinks/year, was utilized to measure alcohol consumption for each respondent, with scales (2) and (3) used to crosscheck the respondent's consistency. Thirty-three men gave contradictory responses across the three scales, and they were excluded from analyses. Thus, 1,864 men (92 percent of the target population) returned questionnaires with consistent quantity responses. Men who reported that alcohol had recently affected their physical health or psychological or social functioning were classified as drinkers with problems. This is not to be construed as a diagnosis of alcoholism but is rather an indication that drinking has some significant negative consequences. The alcohol consumption levels and rates of problems with drinking found in this first questionnaire have previously been described (Glynn et al. 1983). In particular, alcohol consumption levels in this population were comparable to the levels found in other national surveys as well as in surveys of men from the Boston area.

In September 1982 the Normative Aging Study mailed a revised drinking questionnaire to its currently active participants. Questions assessing alcohol consumption levels and problems with drinking were identical to those in the earlier questionnaire. Of the men returning consistent questionnaires in 1973, 85 were dead in September 1982. Of the remaining 1,779 initial respondents, 1,570 (88 percent) returned consistent questionnaires in 1982. Characteristics of the decedents and nonrespondents will be described below.

STATISTICAL ANALYSIS

The relationship of nonresponse and death to initial age and alcohol consumption levels was examined by multiple logistic regression (Cox 1977). Stepwise multiple linear regression was used to assess changes in alcohol consumption levels. Alcohol consumption levels were transformed by the natural logarithm to normalize the distribution for use in regression analyses. Changes in alcohol consumption categories were examined by tests of symmetry based on loglinear models (Bishop et al. 1978). Logistic regression models were used to consider changes in rates of problems with drinking.

RESULTS

DECEDENTS AND NONRESPONDENTS

As pointed out in the introduction, death and selective nonresponse can lead to bias in describing the association between aging and alcohol consumption behaviors. Table 1 shows the numbers

Table 1.--Decedents at the Time of the Second Survey, by Age and Alcohol Consumption Groups

Age in 1973	Alcoholic drinks/year					
	None	1-29	30-181	182-729	730+	Total
28-39	0/9 0 percent	0/12 0 percent	0/59 0 percent	0/110 0 percent	1/71 1 percent	1/261 0 percent
40-49	1/63 2 percent	2/45 4 percent	3/182 2 percent	5/292 2 percent	11/193 6 percent	22/775 3 percent
50-59	3/51 6 percent	1/49 2 percent	12/166 7 percent	10/188 5 percent	8/145 6 percent	34/599 6 percent
60-87	8/31 26 percent	8/26 31 percent	3/59 5 percent	5/71 7 percent	4/42 10 percent	28/229 12 percent
Total	12/154 8 percent	11/132 8 percent	18/466 4 percent	20/661 3 percent	24/451 5 percent	85/1,864 5 percent

Considering 1,864 men who responded to first survey.

of men in each age group and consumption category who responded consistently to the first drinking questionnaire and were dead at the time of the second questionnaire. Death rates among men initially under age 50 were highest among men drinking on the average two or more drinks per day. In each age group, men drinking on the average between one drink every other day and two drinks per day had the lowest or the second lowest death rate. Older nondrinkers and infrequent drinkers had excessively high death rates, but it is unclear to what extent these men may have given up drinking because of previous illness. The statistical significance of these trends was examined using logistic regression. Controlling for age, men drinking between 30 and 729 drinks per year had a lower probability of dying than both men drinking less (p = .037) and men drinking more (p = .046). Compared with this group, the estimate of the age-adjusted relative risk of dying for men drinking less than 30 drinks per year was 1.81, and for men drinking more than 729 drinks per year, it was 1.72. These results support the U-shaped curve relating alcohol consumption to mortality that has been found by other researchers (Klatsky et al. 1981; Marmot et al. 1981).

Table 2 shows the numbers of men in each age group and consumption category who responded consistently to the first questionnaire and were alive at the time of the second survey but did not respond consistently to it. These data show a slight tendency for men who were in the middle drinking categories at the time of the first survey to be more likely to respond to the second survey. More striking is the nonresponse rate for men initially in their fifties, which is about half of the nonresponse rate for men in other age groups. Possible differences in response rates between age and alcohol consumption level groups were evaluated by logistic regression. In these analyses, age was considered in four categories because the relationship between age and response might not be monotonic. There were no significant differences between consumption groups in response rates. However, men in their fifties were more likely to respond than both younger men (p < .001) and older men (p = .001). Compared with men in their fifties, the estimated relative response rate for younger men was .52; for older men it was .44.

CHANGES IN CONSUMPTION LEVELS

Mean alcohol consumption levels within age groups for the 1,570 respondents to both surveys are shown in table 3. In both 1973 and 1982, older men drank markedly less than younger men. However, there were no significant longitudinal declines in drinking levels. Changes in mean levels ranged from a decline of 59.1 drinks per year among the men initially under 40 to an increase of 8.5 drinks per year among men initially in their fifties. As these

Table 2.—Nonrespondents to Second Survey, by Age and Alcohol Consumption Groups

Age in 1973	Alcoholic drinks/year					
	None	1-29	30-181	182-729	730+	Total
28-39	0/9 0 percent	2/12 17 percent	8/59 14 percent	17/110 15 percent	10/70 14 percent	37/260 14 percent
40-49	11/62 18 percent	5/43 12 percent	13/179 7 percent	41/287 14 percent	29/182 16 percent	99/753 13 percent
50-59	6/48 13 percent	3/48 6 percent	10/154 6 percent	10/178 6 percent	13/137 9 percent	42/565 7 percent
60-84	4/23 17 percent	4/18 22 percent	11/56 20 percent	5/66 8 percent	7/38 18 percent	31/201 15 percent
Total	21/142 15 percent	14/121 12 percent	42/448 9 percent	73/641 11 percent	59/427 14 percent	209/1,779 12 percent

Considering 1,779 men who responded to the first survey and were alive at the second survey.

men in their fifties moved into their sixties, they did not reduce their alcohol consumption to amounts similar to the amounts consumed by men over 60 in the 1973 survey.

Table 3.--Mean Number of Alcoholic Drinks/Year Within Age Groups

Age in 1973	N	Mean (s.d.) drinks in 1973	Mean (s.d.) drinks in 1982	Paired T difference=0	p value
28-39	223	485.7(527.3)	426.6(502.4)	1.73	0.084
40-49	654	436.3(525.2)	435.4(528.6)	0.05	0.963
50-59	523	418.3(548.4)	426.8(629.6)	0.41	0.683
60-84	170	360.7(478.3)	342.4(513.1)	0.54	0.591
Total	1,570	429.1(529.0)	421.2(559.5)	0.64	0.521

Stepwise linear regression was used to better describe changes in alcohol consumption levels between 1973 and 1982. Results are shown in table 4. By far the best predictor of a change in consumption was the amount consumed in 1973; it accounted for 14.3 percent of the variance in consumption change. The negative sign of the regression coefficient of the 1973 consumption level indicates that higher 1973 levels were associated with declines in consumption. This may be attributed to regression to the mean. After controlling for the 1973 consumption level, no other variable was significantly associated with a change in consumption. The estimated effect of age was for older men to decline slightly in consumption, but this effect was small and not significantly different from 0. Marital, retirement, and socioeconomic status in 1982, together with age, could only increase by .003 the variance in consumption change explained by initial level alone.

Results of consumption changes presented until now have considered mean changes or used linear models. A nonparametric tabular analysis may give a better assessment of the variability in alcohol consumption levels over time. Table 5 presents a cross tabulation of 1973 by 1982 consumption levels. Large numbers of men (894 or 56.9 percent) fell in the diagonal of this table, indicating stability over time in their consumption levels. The cells below the diagonal count men whose consumption decreased over time, while the cells above the diagonal count men with consumption increases. A test of the symmetry of this table has a chi square value of 57.8 with 10 degrees of freedom. This is highly significant, indicating that the table is asymmetric. Indeed, it is

Table 4.--Stepwise Linear Regression: Change in Alcohol Consumption Level, Initial Consumption, and Demographic Variables

Variable*	Regression coefficient	Standard error	p value	Model R square
Log (1+ drinks/day at survey #1)	-0.318	0.0196	0.0001	0.143
Age	-0.0025	0.0016	0.104	0.145
Socioeconomic status (Duncan index)	0.00067	0.00054	0.217	0.146
Never married	0.057	0.064	0.375	0.146
Retired	-0.019	0.028	0.489	0.146
Separated or divorced	-0.022	0.044	0.624	0.146
Widowed	-0.021	0.059	0.726	0.146

*Variables are listed in the order in which they entered the regression model.

Change assessed as log(1+ drinks/day, survey #2) - log(1+ drinks/day, survey #1)

Table 5.—Classification of Consumption Levels
at Surveys 1 and 2

Survey #1 Drinks/year	Survey #2 Drinks/year					
	None	1-29	30-181	182-729	730+	Total
None	100	5	7	6	3	121
1-29	28	41	31	6	1	107
30-181	23	42	212	114	15	406
182-729	25	14	107	311	111	568
730+	17	6	25	90	230	368
Total	193	108	382	527	360	1,570

clear that there are many more nondrinkers in 1982 than in 1973. A McNemar type test (Bishop et al. 1978), which compares the number of men below the diagonal to the number of men above the diagonal, has a chi square value of 9.0 with 1 degree of freedom. This is highly significant, indicating that, given that a man changes his consumption level, consumption is more likely to decrease than increase.

Considering each of the four age groups separately, large numbers of men in each age group remained consistent in their consumption groups from 1973 to 1982. The percentage in the same consumption group in both 1973 and 1982 ranged from 53.5 percent of the men initially aged 60 to 84 to 59.3 percent of the men initially aged 50 to 59. Given that a man changes his consumption level, men under age 40 or over age 59 were significantly more likely to decrease their level than to increase. Men aged 40 to 59 were about equally likely to increase as to decrease their consumption. This gives further evidence of the stability of consumption levels among men in these middle age groups.

PROBLEMS WITH DRINKING

The numbers of men reporting problems with drinking at each of the two surveys are shown in table 6. There was a clear trend for older men to report fewer problems at both times. Among men reporting no problems in 1973, problems in 1982 were reported by 12 percent of men initially under age 40, by 8 percent of men 40 to

Table 6.—Numbers of Men Reporting Problems with Drinking

Age in 1973	No problems at either survey	Problems at survey 1 only	Problems at survey 2 only	Problems at both surveys	Total
28-39	161 72 percent	18 10 percent	22 8 percent	22 10 percent	223 100 percent
40-49	528 81 percent	47 7 percent	47 7 percent	32 5 percent	654 100 percent
50-59	449 86 percent	25 5 percent	30 6 percent	19 4 percent	523 100 percent
60-84	161 95 percent	3 2 percent	3 2 percent	3 2 percent	170 100 percent
Total	1,299 83 percent	93 6 percent	102 6 percent	76 5 percent	1,570 100 percent

49, by 6 percent of men 50 to 59, and by 2 percent of men initially over 60. In spite of these pronounced cross-sectional differences between age groups in rates of problems, there was a remarkable consistency within age groups in the number of problems reported in 1973 and 1982. No age group showed a longitudinal decline in the number of drinkers with problems.

Multiple logistic regression was used to determine the probability of reporting problems in 1982 among men free of problems in 1973. Results are summarized in table 7. A positive logistic coefficient indicates that higher levels of a variable are associated with the development of new problems in 1983. Quantity consumed in 1973 and being separated or divorced were positively associated with the development of problems. Controlling for these variables, older age was significantly but negatively associated with new problems in 1982. Thus, older men drinking without consequences in 1973 were more likely to maintain this healthy drinking in 1982 than were younger men. None of the other variables considered were significantly associated with the development of problems.

Table 7.—Multiple Logistic Regression Predicting Problems with Drinking in 1982 Among Men Free of Problems in 1973

Variable	Logistic coefficient	Standard error	Chi square	p value
Log (1 + drinks/day at survey 1)	2.11	0.21	97.4	0.001
Age	-0.070	0.018	15.8	0.001
Separated or divorced	0.99	0.42	5.5	0.019
Retired	-0.44	0.31	1.9	0.164
Widowed	-0.56	0.79	0.5	0.481
Never married	0.23	0.66	0.1	0.726
Socioeconomic status (Duncan index)	0.0013	0.0061	0.0	0.836

DISCUSSION

The drinking habits of men in the Normative Aging Study remained quite stable over time. Cross-sectional studies of the drinking habits of American men have generally found higher percentages of nondrinkers and lower percentages of heavier drinkers among older men as compared with younger men (Clark and Midanik 1982). However, male volunteers in the Normative Aging Study had almost no change in their mean alcohol consumption levels from 1973 to 1982. This was true in spite of the fact that among men whose consumption levels changed, more men decreased than increased their drinking. Rates of problems with drinking also showed no declines over time within age groups. Men in their forties and fifties in 1973 were particularly consistent in their drinking habits over time.

Selection and nonresponse can severely bias the results of drinking surveys. Respondents to the current surveys were volunteer participants in a study of aging and were health conscious, community-dwelling men. Compared with many other drinking surveys, nonresponse rates were low. Analysis of respondents to the 1973 Normative Aging Study drinking survey who did not respond to the 1982 survey suggest the extent to which selection can bias the interpretation of cross-sectional studies. There were differences in 1973 consumption level and age between respondents, decedents, and other nonrespondents in 1982. Thus, for example, cross-sectional studies may find fewer heavier drinkers among older men, not because men decrease their drinking with age, but because heavier drinkers die at a younger age. Of course, nonresponse can affect the results of longitudinal studies, and it is impossible to determine whether nonrespondents to the 1982 survey had changed their drinking habits.

It is natural to hypothesize that the biological, psychological, and social changes that accompany aging have an effect on drinking behaviors. The data presented here cannot be construed as proof that age does not tend to modify drinking behaviors. Glenn (1981) has pointed out the difficulty in drawing inferences about age effects on drinking behaviors. For example, it may be that a natural tendency for aging to reduce consumption levels has been counterbalanced by current social forces encouraging greater consumption. Whatever the underlying causes, however, there was little change in the drinking behaviors of this population over 9 years.

Gordon and Kannel (1983) have recently reported the changes in average alcohol intake from 1952 to 1972 among participants in the Framingham Study. During these 20 years the average amount of alcohol consumed rose 63 percent. The increase was greater for women, but the increase for men was 49 percent. Younger men increased relatively more than older men. It is important to note that per capita alcohol consumption in the United States increased substantially in the 1960s. Per capita consumption increased much more slowly in the 1970s. The large increases in consumption in the Framingham population observed in the 1950s and 1960s are consistent with the stability in consumption of the Normative Aging Study population during the 1970s if these national trends are kept in mind.

There are potentially serious public health implications if older men today are drinking more than men the same age a decade ago. The elderly are particularly vulnerable to the effects of alcohol for three reasons. First, older people tend to weigh less and have, proportionally, even less lean tissue. This is important because alcohol is not fat soluble; this results in higher blood levels relative to intake. Second, aging itself, frequently complicated by disease, further slows alcohol metabolism. Finally, an older person is more likely to be taking medication and is thus more liable to potent drug-alcohol interactions (Lee 1978). Thus, a relatively small amount of alcohol can adversely affect an older person. The elderly have traditionally had lower rates of problems with alcohol than younger men. Relatively increased consumption by older men might jeopardize this advantage.

REFERENCES

Bailey, M.P.; Haberman, P.W.; and Alksne, H. The epidemiology of alcoholism in an urban residential area. Quarterly Journal of Studies on Alcohol 26:19-40, 1965.

Barnes, G. Alcohol use among older persons: Findings from a western New York State general population survey. Journal of the American Geriatrics Society 27:244-250, 1979.

Bell, B.; Rose, C.L.; and Damon, A. The Normative Aging Study: An interdisciplinary and longitudinal study of health and aging. Aging and Human Development 3:5-17, 1972.

Bishop, Y.M.M.; Fienberg, S.E.; and Holland, P.W. Discrete ultivariate Analysis: Theory and Practice. Cambridge, Mass.: MIT, 1978.

Blose, I.L. The relationship of alcohol to aging and the elderly. Alcoholism 2:17-21, 1978.

Cahalan, D.; Cisin, I.H.; and Crossley, H.M. American Drinking Practices: A National Study of Drinking Behavior and Attitudes. Monograph No. 6. New Brunswick, N.J.: Rutgers Center of Alcohol Studies, 1969.

Clark, W.B., and Midanik, L. Alcohol use and alcohol problems among U.S. adults. In: National Institute on Alcohol Abuse and Alcoholism. Alcohol and Health Monograph No. 1: Alcohol Consumption and Related Problems. DHHS Pub. No. (ADM)82-1190, Washington, D.C.: U.S. Government Printing Office, 1982.

Cox, D.R. Analysis of Binary Data, 2d ed. London: Chapman and Hall, 1977.

Drew, L.R.H. Alcoholism as a self-limiting disease. Quarterly Journal of Studies on Alcohol 29:956-967, 1968.

Glenn, N.D. Age, birth cohorts, and drinking: An illustration of the hazards of inferring effects from cohort data. Journal of Gerontology 36:362-369, 1981.

Glynn, R.J.; LoCastro, J.S.; Hermos, J.A.; and Bosse, R. Social contexts and motives for drinking in adult men. Journal of Studies on Alcohol 44:1011-1025, 1983.

Glynn, R.J.; Rosner, B.; and Silbert, J.E. Changes in cholesterol and triglyceride as predictors of ischemic heart disease in men. Circulation 66:724-731, 1982.

Gomberg, E.L. Prevalence of alcoholism among ward patients in a Veterans Administration hospital. *Quarterly Journal of Studies on Alcohol* 36:1458-1467, 1975.

Gomberg, E.L. *Drinking and Problem Drinking Among the Elderly*. Ann Arbor: University of Michigan, Institute of Gerontology, 1980.

Gordon, T., and Kannel, W.B. Drinking and its relation to smoking, BP, blood lipids, and uric acid: The Framingham Study. *Archives of Internal Medicine* 143:1366-1374, 1983.

Klatsky, A.L.; Friedman, G.D.; and Siegelaub, A.B. Alcohol and mortality: A ten-year Kaiser-Permanente experience. *Annals of Internal Medicine* 95:139-145, 1981.

Lee, P.V. Drug therapy in the elderly: The clinical pharmacology of aging. *Alcoholism* 2:31-38, 1978.

Marmot, M.G.; Rose, G.; Shipley, M.J.; and Thomas, B.J. Alcohol and mortality: A U-shaped curve. *Lancet* 1:580-583, 1981.

McCreary, C.P. Criminality and the aging. In: Kaplan, O.J., ed. *Psychopathology of Aging*. New York: Harper and Row, 1979.

Mishara, B.L., and Kastenbaum, R. *Alcohol and Old Age*. New York: Grune and Stratton, 1980.

Schuckit, M.A., and Miller, P.L. Alcoholism in elderly men: A survey of a general medical ward. *Annals of the New York Academy of Sciences* 273:558-571, 1976.

INFLUENCE OF CARDIOVASCULAR DISEASE ON ALCOHOL CONSUMPTION AMONG MEN IN THE NORMATIVE AGING STUDY*

John A. Hermos, M.D., Joseph S. LoCastro, Ph.D.
Glen R. Bouchard, S.M., and Robert J. Glynn, Ph.D.

ABSTRACT

Physical health problems are commonly cited as reasons for decreasing alcohol consumption, particularly by heavier drinkers with well-defined alcohol-related illnesses. It is not known, however, to what extent reductions in drinking because of impaired health occur in the general population or whether health factors are important moderators of drinking with aging. As part of a longitudinal study of drinking in a population of community-dwelling men enrolled in the Veterans Administration Normative Aging Study (NAS), we sought to determine if newly diagnosed hypertension or ischemic heart disease (angina pectoris or myocardial infarction) influenced alcohol consumption and alcohol problems over time.

Alcohol consumption data were available for 1,570 men from both Time 1 (1973) and Time 2 (1982) surveys of NAS participants. By means of periodic NAS medical examinations and review of supplementary medical data, 258 (16.4 percent) men were newly diagnosed as having hypertension and 84 (5.3 percent) as having ischemic heart disease in the 9-year interval. Hypertensive men had higher mean alcohol consumption at Time 1 compared with nonhypertensive (513.1 $\pm$ 591.1 and 412.6 $\pm$ 514.6 dr/yr respectively, p = 0.005), and over time reduced consumption compared with controls (-69.4 $\pm$ 558.2 and +4.2 $\pm$ 472.6 dr/yr respectively, p = 0.03). However, using regression models and controlling for initial alcohol consumption, age, socioeconomic, marital, and work status, only the quantity consumed at Time 1 predicted reductions at Time 2. The subjects with intervening ischemic heart disease also drank more at Time 1 and reduced alcohol consumption between Times 1 and 2,

---

*Supported by the Medical Research Service of the Veterans Administration.

but differences were not statistically significant when compared with controls. However, those with ischemic heart disease were more likely than controls to revert over time from having problems with drinking (81.8 percent and 53.2 percent respectively, $p < 0.025$).

The decrease in problems with drinking reported by the men with ischemic heart disease suggests that reduced episodes of intoxication or changes in lifestyle occurred. Relations among alcohol use, cardiovascular diseases, and widespread use of medications for these diseases, which might interact with alcohol, are only now being clarified. It is important to undertake detailed studies of changes in drinking behaviors in patients with cardiovascular problems and, in particular, to investigate the influence of medical advice on drinking behaviors.

INTRODUCTION

The extent to which physical health problems, whether related or unrelated to alcohol use, influence changes in drinking behaviors is not known. This question has importance in two areas of alcohol studies: (1) clinically, where alcohol-related diseases are often primary manifestations of excessive drinking, and (2) epidemiologically, where health factors may contribute to reductions or stabilization in drinking that occur with increasing age. Evidence of this kind from clinical and epidemiological investigations, however, is scanty, so that physicans and public health officials have little basis upon which to predict that their advice or warnings about the adverse health effects of excessive drinking will be heeded.

Knupfer (1972) and Tuchfeld (1981), in extensive analyses of former spontaneously remitting problem drinkers and alcoholics found that personal health concerns were common motivating factors. Barchha et al. (1968) and Gomberg (1975), in surveys of hospitalized alcoholics, found that alcohol abuse had abated in one-third to one-half of the patients, and that these long-term remissions were often attributed to prior alcohol-health problems. Among outpatients recovered from decompensated alcoholic cirrhosis, Patek and Hermos (1981) reported that extended remissions from heavy drinking were almost entirely attributed to the patients' liver disease and continued medical care, and that these patients rarely used formal alcoholism treatment. Hermos (1983) has subsequently found, from a literature survey of 11 studies with 1,039 alcoholic cirrhotic patients under medical care, that approximately 20 to 50 percent achieve abstinence and 20 to 35 percent reduce consumption over long clinical followup periods. Although all of these survey data suggest that alcohol-related illnesses and medical care have at least a modest beneficial impact on drinking behaviors, such conclusions are weakened by the absence of prospective studies with adequate controls.

There is even less support for the notion that health factors influence the changes in drinking behaviors that occur with aging. National and urban cross-sectional surveys of drinking practices have fairly consistently shown less heavy and problematic drinking in older age groups (Cahalan et al. 1969; Wechsler et al. 1978; Clark and Midanik, 1982), although cohort and survivor differences may affect these findings (Glynn et al. this volume). However, neither cross-sectional nor longitudinal studies of selected or general populations have directly tested whether age-related changes in drinking are influenced by health factors.

In the present study, using a large, volunteer population of community-dwelling men enrolled in a longitudinal study of aging (Bell et al. 1972), we have used the new onset of hypertension and ischemic heart disease to determine (1) if men who have developed these conditions change alcohol consumption habits; (2) if changes in drinking do occur, to what extent are they explained by intervening cardiovascular disorders; and (3) whether intervening cardiovascular diseases are associated with fewer drinking problems.

During the period of longitudinal observation, 1973 to 1982, the epidemiological and pathophysiological associations between alcohol use and hypertension or ischemic heart disease were just beginning to be elucidated (Friedman et al. 1983; Barboriak et al. 1983). It is unlikely that subjects who developed these conditions received either uniform or intensive medical advice about their drinking. Therefore, we expected that the intervening cardiovascular diseases, by themselves, would be only weakly predictive of changes in drinking over time.

METHODS

POPULATION

The study population consisted of 1,570 male participants in the Normative Aging Study who (1) submitted complete and internally consistent responses to two detailed drinking questionnaires mailed in 1973 (Time 1 survey) and 1982 (Time 2 survey), and (2) had either one, two, or three complete medical examinations during the 9-year interval according to the NAS longitudinal protocol. On entry into the study (between 1963 and 1970), volunteers were screened according to laboratory, clinical, radiologic, and electrocardiographic criteria to provide a population free of serious, chronic medical conditions. Specifically, men with a history or evidence of heart disease, diabetes, cancer, cirrhosis, bronchitis, or gout were not admitted into the study. Also disqualified were men with either systolic blood pressure greater than 140 mm Hg or diastolic blood pressure greater than 90 mm Hg. Although alcoholism was not an excluding criterion per se, men with specific medical complications of alcoholism or longstanding excessive drinking were differentially excluded by the presence of certain of these chronic conditions. Enrollment of the initial population of 2,280 men, aged 21 to 81, was completed by 1970. Descriptions of the NAS populaton are published elsewhere (Bell et al. 1972; Glynn et al. this volume).

DRINKING SURVEYS

In June 1973 and in September 1982, NAS participants were mailed drinking questionnaires, which assessed in detail a variety of drinking parameters. From the responses, alcoholic beverage consumption was determined on scales quantified in total drinks/year. One drink was defined as 12 oz of beer, 4 oz of wine, or 1.5 oz of distilled spirits, each containing approximately equal amounts of absolute alcohol. Within this population, higher level drinkers were defined as those consuming 730 or more drinks/yr (on the average, 2 or more drinks/day). Drinkers with problems were categorized on the basis of their responses to items that indicated that alcohol had regularly and adversely affected physical health or psychological or social functioning. The 1,570 respondents to the 1982 (Time 2) drinking questionnaire represented 84 percent of the 1,864 respondents to the 1973 (Time 1) survey and 88 percent of the 1,779 respondents to the 1973 questionnaire who were known to be alive in 1982. Detailed descriptions of the drinking surveys and alcohol consumption categories are published elsewhere (Glynn et al. 1983; Glynn et al. this volume).

CARDIOVASCULAR DISEASE DIAGNOSES

NAS participants who are younger than 52 years have complete medical examinations at 5-year intervals; those 52 years or older are examined at 3-year intervals. Therefore, in the 9 years, approximately one-fifth of participants under age 52 by 1982 had only one NAS medical examination; all other participants in the study had either two or three examinations between 1973 and 1982.

At the periodic NAS examinations, participants were designated as having newly diagnosed hypertension, angina pectoris, or myocardial infarction as follows: Hypertension was diagnosed on the basis of systolic readings (average of both arms) greater than 159 mm Hg or diastolic readings (average of both arms) greater than 94 mm Hg. (Blood pressure was measured at each physical examination, in each arm, with the subject seated, with no systematic methodologic differences from one examination to another.) The clinical diagnosis of hypertension was made by the examining physician (cardiologist consultants to NAS) on the basis of these readings, associated clinical findings, or confirmation of a clinical diagnosis of hypertension made in other medical settings (Sparrow et al. 1982); Angina Pectoris was diagnosed from clinical histories, when the patient reported recurrent symptoms of chest discomfort lasting up to 15 minutes, related to exertion or excitement and relieved by rest or nitroglycerin. This clinical diagnosis was rejected if other explanations were more likely (Glynn et al. 1982); Myocardial infarction was diagnosed in accordance with the criteria of the Framingham Heart Study (Shurtleff 1974), required unequivocal electrocardiographic changes, ST-segment elevations, terminal inversion of T waves, and loss of initial QRS potentials (Q waves of at least 0.04 seconds) followed by reversion toward normal (Glynn et al. 1982; Sparrow et al. 1983).

For the purposes of this study, men with diagnoses of either angina pectoris, myocardial infarction, or both were included together in a category of ischemic heart disease. Eighty-four men were included in this category, 46 with angina pectoris alone, 23 with myocardial infarction alone, and 15 with both diagnoses. Of the 258 men newly diagnosed with hypertension, 237 had this diagnosis alone, and 21 also had clinical evidence of either angina pectoris or myocardial infarction. Therefore, in the two cardiovascular disease groups, hypertension (N = 258) and ischemic heart disease (N = 84), 21 men appear within both diagnostic categories.

STATISTICAL ANALYSES

The relationships between intervening cardiovascular diseases and changes in alcohol consumption were examined by t-tests; relationships between these conditions and changes in higher level drinking as well as changes in drinking with problem status were examined by chi-square analyses. Multiple stepwise linear regression (Seber 1977) was used to assess the relationships between changes in alcohol consumption and intervening cardiovascular diseases, age, and other demographic variables. Multiple stepwise logistic regression (Cox 1977) was used to assess the relationships between categorical changes in drinking status and these same variables. Socioeconomic status was measured by the Duncan Index (Riess et al. 1961).

RESULTS

The numbers of men with newly diagnosed hypertension and ischemic heart disease over the 9-year period 1973 to 1982 in four age groups are shown in table 1. As expected, these conditions were detected more frequently in men 50 years or older in 1973, but this may have resulted, in part, from older men having had more periodic NAS medical examinations (see methods). That the incidence of these conditions was no higher in men 60 to 84 years than in men 50 to 60 years at Time 1 may be a reflection, in part, of the higher intervening death rate in the oldest age group and of a possible selection bias when the oldest men were accepted into the NAS protocol.

Table 1.--Newly Diagnosed Cardiovascular Diseases, by Age Groups Between 1973 (Time 1) and 1982 (Time 2)

Age group at disease Time 1	Total $\underline{N}$	Cardiovascular Disease			
		Hypertension		Ischemic heart disease	
		$\underline{N}$	Percent	$\underline{N}$	Percent
28-39	223	24	(10.8)	7	(3.1)
40-49	654	95	(14.5)	22	(3.3)
50-59	523	107	(20.5)	41	(7.8)
60-84	170	32	(18.8)	14	(8.2)
Total	1,570	258	(16.4)	84	(5.3)

In table 2 alcohol consumption expressed in the mean number of drinks/yr is presented. The modest elevation in Time 1 alcohol consumption for participants subsequently diagnosed as hypertensive is statistically significant ($\underline{p}$ = .005), and is consistent with observations in other populations (Klatsky et al. 1977; Gordon and Kannel, 1983). The change in consumption for the hypertensive men compared with the change for nonhypertensive men (-69 and +4 drinks/yr respectively, $\underline{p}$ < .03) suggests that the intervening diagnosis influenced reduced drinking over time. However, using multiple stepwise linear regression (table 3), only Time 1 quantity appreciably predicted change, accounting for 15.8 percent of the variance in reduced alcohol consumption. Intervening hypertension entered third into the regression model, but because of the large standard error, its contribution to reduced consumption after controlling for initial quantity was minimal. The influence of hypertension in predicting a large categorical decrease in consumption (a mean reduction of one-half drink or more/day or 182 or more drinks/yr) was assessed using multiple stepwise logistic regression (table 4). Again, only Time 1 quantity predicted this level of reduction in alcohol consumption. In this logistic regression, older age was weakly predictive of change (p = 0.08), and intervening hypertension, by itself, was not predictive of change (p = 0.21). However, because of the close association of heavier alcohol consumption and elevated blood pressure, these analyses do not rule out the possibility that, for some heavier drinkers, hypertension and initial high quantity may interact in the reductions in drinking seen over the 9-year interval.

Table 2.—Mean Alcohol Consumption at Time 1 (1973) and Time 2 (1982) for Respondents with Intervening Cardiovascular Disease

Cardiovascular disease	N	Time 1 Drinks/yr (s.d.)	Time 2 Drinks/yr (s.d.)	Time 1 - Time 2 Drinks/yr (s.d.)
Hypertension				
Present	258	513.1 (591.1)	443.6 (586.5)	-69.4 (558.2)
Absent	1,312	412.6 (514.6)	416.8 (554.1)	+4.2 (472.6)
		(p = .005)	(p < .50)	(p < .03)
Ischemic heart disease				
Present	84	500.0 (775.9)	422.2 (561.9)	-77.8 (609.5)
Absent	1,486	425.1 (511.6)	421.2 (518.0)	-4.0 (480.6)
		(p = .20)	(p = .98)	(p < .20)

Table 3.—Stepwise Linear Regression: Change in Alcohol Consumption Between Time 1 and Time 2

Variable	Regression coefficient	Standard error	p value	Model R square
Quantity at Time 1	-0.37	0.02	<0.001	0.158
Never married	112.36	70.24	0.109	0.159
Intervening hypertension	-37.18	30.78	0.214	0.160
Retired	-35.36	30.16	0.272	0.161
Separated or divorced	-50.99	48.55	0.311	0.161
Age	-2.51	1.71	0.333	0.162
Socioeconomic status	0.51	0.59	0.393	0.162
Widowed	4.80	64.70	0.940	0.162

Table 4.—Multiple Stepwise Logistic Regression: Predicting the Probability of Reducing Alcohol Consumption by One-Half or More Drinks/Day (182 or More Drinks/Yr)

Variable*	Logistic coefficient	Standard error	Chi square	p value
Quantity at Time 1	0.0023	0.00015	245.82	<0.001
Age	0.015	0.0087	3.07	0.08
Intervening hypertension	0.23	0.19	1.57	0.21

*Other variables entered (socioeconomic status, work status, and marital status) had no predictive value.

Although the mean levels of alcohol consumed and the mean reductions over time for participants with ischemic heart diseases were generally similar to those with hypertension, statistical significance was not reached (table 2); in both the linear and logistic regression analyses predicting reduction, intervening ischemic heart diseases had no predictive effects. The relatively few cases and the large variability in alcohol consumption levels in the ischemic heart disease group contributed to these findings.

We sought to determine if subjects with cardiovascular disorders drinking 2 or more drinks/day or 730 or more drinks/yr, designated in this population as higher level drinkers, were more likely to reduce drinking between Time 1 and Time 2 surveys (table 5). In this analysis we were looking for reductions from drinking levels that might be clinically relevant in the etiology of hypertension to levels that might be considered clinically safer (Klatsky et al. 1977).

For the hypertensive men there is a slight reduction in the proportion of higher level drinkers at Time 2, but turnover from and into higher level drinking for hypertensive and nonhypertensive men are virtually identical. An unexpected finding was the lack of turnover from the higher level drinking group for men with ischemic heart diseases, with only 2 of 19 (10.5 percent) leaving this category compared with 39 percent for the control group. The small numbers, however, preclude speculations as to whether these differences can be generalized and whether they have any clinical significance.

In a similar manner, we examined whether intervening cardiovascular diseases influenced turnover from and into a drinking with problems status (table 6). Here, hypertensive men demonstrated no differences compared with their controls. For men with ischemic heart diseases, the proportion of men with drinking problems at Time 2 was half that at Time 1, and there was an increased turnover from the drinking with problems category when compared with controls (81.8 percent and 53.2 percent respectively, $p < .025$). Logistic regression analysis (table 7) showed that although Time 1 quantity and being separated or divorced were negatively associated with change, intervening ischemic heart disease was weakly predictive of change out of the drinking with problems status.

Table 5.—Higher Level Drinking Status and Turnover
for Respondents with Intervening Cardiovascular Disease

Cardiovascular disease	N	Higher level drinkers[1]		Time 1 - Time 2 turnover			
		Time 1 (Percent)	Time 2 (Percent)	Yes - No[2]		No - Yes[3]	
				N	(Percent)	N	(Percent)
Hypertension							
Present	258	(29.5)	(23.6)	31	(40.8)	16	(8.9)
Absent	1,312	(22.3)	(22.8)	107	(36.6)	114	(11.2)
Ischemic heart disease							
Present	84	(22.6)	(27.4)	2	(10.5)	6	(9.2)
Absent	1,486	(23.5)	(22.7)	136	(39.0)*	124	(10.9)

* $p < 0.02$
[1] Higher level drinking: average consumption of 730 or more drinks/yr.
[2] Yes - No: drinking with problems at Time 1 but not at Time 2.
[3] No - Yes: drinking with problems at Time 2 but not at Time 1.

Table 6.—Drinking with Problems Status and Turnover
for Respondents With Intervening Cardiovascular Disease

Cardiovascular disease	N	Drinking with Problems		Time 1 - Time 2 turnover			
		Time 1 (Percent)	Time 2 (Percent)	Yes - No[1]		No - Yes[2]	
				N	(Percent)	N	(Percent)
Hypertension							
Present	258	(13.6)	(12.0)	20	(57.1)	16	(7.2)
Absent	1,312	(10.0)	(11.2)	73	(54.5)	86	(7.3)
Ischemic heart disease							
Present	84	(13.1)	(6.0)	9	(81.8)	3	(4.1)
Absent	1,486	(10.6)	(11.6)	84	(53.2)*	99	(7.5)

* $p < 0.025$
[1] Yes - No: drinking with problems at Time 1 but not at Time 2.
[2] No - Yes: drinking with problems at Time 2 but not at Time 1.

Table 7.—Multiple Stepwise Logistic Regression: Predicting Change from Time 1 Drinking with Problems Status

Variable*	Logistic coefficient	Standard error	Chi square	p value
Quantity at Time 1	-0.0010	0.00027	14.26	0.0002
Separated/divorced	-1.1	0.46	5.70	0.017
Intervening ischemic heart disease	1.72	0.85	4.09	0.043

*Other variables entered (age, socioeconomic status, work status, marital status, and intervening hypertension) had no predictive value.

DISCUSSION

The relationships between alcohol consumption and the development of hypertension and coronary artery disease and mortality are far from clearly understood. Although it is not within the scope of this report to describe progress in these areas of research, several consistent trends are emerging. There is an epidemiologic and clinical association between heavier drinking and high blood pressure, in both alcoholic (Saunders et al. 1981) and general populations (Klatsky et al. 1977; Gordon and Kannel 1983). Regular use of alcohol, through its effects of increasing high density lipoprotein cholesterol, may impair the development of coronary artery disease (Barboriak et al. 1983); light and moderate drinking may be associated with overall lower mortality rates than abstinent or heavy drinking (Blackwelder et al. 1980; Marmot et al. 1981; Klatsky et al. 1981). The clinical applicability of these findings is not at all clear, however, and there are no data indicating that changing drinking habits alter the course of the conditions or mortality rates.

The extensive use of ß-adrenoceptor antagonists (beta-blockers) as the primary drugs in the management of hypertension, angina pectoris, and postmyocardial infarction (Frishman 1981) adds another dimension to the clinical significance of excessive or even moderate alcohol use in middle-aged and older populations. Alcohol is known to enhance the blood pressure lowering action of a variety of antihypertensive drugs, and beta-blockers can ameliorate the peripheral manifestations of alcohol and CNS depressant withdrawal (Sellers and Kalant 1976; Tyrer et al. 1981). It is highly conceivable, although presently untested, that patients taking beta-blocker agents and drinking moderate to large amounts of alcohol could develop symptoms attributable to hypertension. Such complications could be especially common in the elderly, among whom the prevalence of chronic cardiovascular diseases and medication use is high and whose drug and alcohol metabolism is altered or impaired (Lee 1978).

From this study there is some evidence, albeit slight, that the occurrence of cardiovascular disorders influences changes in drinking. Specifically, the participants with hypertension reduced their drinking significantly between 1973 and 1982, but we were unable to detect the factors predicting that reduction, other than the initial higher consumption levels. Further, we found no evidence that hypertensive patients were more likely than controls to decrease consumption from levels of two or more drinks/day or to abate from drinking with problems. Curiously, the patients with ischemic heart disease who drank on average two or more drinks/day were likely to remain drinking above that level; these men also were less likely to have problems with drinking at the second survey. Although we have previously found quantity consumed to be strongly correlated with drinking problems in this population (Glynn et al. 1983), it is likely that impaired physical health both reduced episodes of intoxication and discouraged behaviors that would result in drinking problems. Adequate testing of these notions requires a more focused examination of changes in drinking behaviors of the men with ischemic heart disease.

The design of the study reported here had certain deficiencies that may have weakened the findings and precluded attempts to find cause and effect relationships. With the 9-year interval between drinking surveys, short-term variations in drinking may have occurred that were influenced by intervening cardiovascular disorders and other events not tested for. We have not determined the severity of the cardiovascular disorders, whether the men received continued medical care for these problems, whether they received medications, or what psychological impact, if any, these conditions had. A further consideration is to what extent we overlooked substantial changes in drinking patterns (i.e., from sporadic intoxication to daily drinking) or contexts (i.e., from barroom to home) by determining only yearly alcohol consumption. These drinking parameters were examined in depth from the 1973 drinking survey (Glynn et al. 1983) and will provide the basis for subsequent analyses of the impact of health factors on longitudinal changes in drinking.

The number of patients with alcohol-related health problems treated in medical settings is sizable, and is probably as large as any other group receiving treatment for alcohol problems (Kissen 1977; Room 1980). This medical population is by no means restricted to alcohol-dependent persons or alcohol abusers, but includes those whose primary and only overt manifestations of relatively heavy drinking are medical conditions (Straus 1983). With the increased awareness of the epidemiologic association between high blood pressure and heavier drinking and the widespread use of medications for cardiovascular disorders with which alcohol may interfere or enhance, physicians are managing an even larger number of patients who have, broadly speaking, alcohol-related health problems. There is a need, then, not only to continue to investigate how much alcohol is safe, and for whom it is safe, but to study the effectiveness of medical advice, health education, and other measures in achieving reductions or moderation in alcohol consumption in medical populations.

REFERENCES

Barboriak, J.J.; Gruchow, H.W.; and Anderson, A.J. Alcohol consumption and the diet-heart controversy. Alcoholism 7:31-34, 1983.

Barchha, R.; Stewart, M.A.; and Guze, S.B. The prevalence of alcoholism among general hospital ward patients. American Journal of Psychiatry 125:681-684, 1968.

Bell, B.; Rose, C.L.; and Damon, A. The Normative Aging Study: An interdisciplinary and longitudinal study of health and aging. Aging and Human Development 3:5-17, 1972.

Blackwelder, W.C.; Yano, K.; Rhoads, G.G.; Kagan, A.; Gordon, T.; and Palesch, Y. Alcohol and mortality: The Honolulu Heart Study. American Journal of Medicine 68:164-169, 1980.

Cahalan, D.; Cisin, I.H.; and Crossley, H.M. American Drinking Practices: A National Study of Drinking Behavior and Attitudes. Monograph No. 6. New Brunswick, N.J.: Rutgers Center of Alcohol Studies, 1969.

Clark, W.B., and Midanik, L. Alcohol use and alcohol problems among U.S. adults. In: National Institute on Alcohol Abuse and Alcoholism. Alcohol and Health Monograph No. 1: Alcohol Consumption and Related Problems. DHHS Pub. No. ADM(82-1190). Washington, D.C.: U.S. Government Printing Office, 1982.

Cox, D.R. Analysis of Binary Data. London: Chapman and Hall, 1977.

Friedman, G.D.; Klatsky, A.L.; and Siegelaub, A.B. Alcohol intake and hypertension. Annals of Internal Medicine 98:846-849, 1983.

Frishman, W.H. ß-adrenoceptor antagonists: New drugs and new indications. New England Journal of Medicine 305:500-506, 1981.

Glynn, R.J.; Bouchard, G.R.; LoCastro, J.S.; and Hermos, J.A. Changes in alcohol consumption behaviors among men in The Normative Aging Study. (in this volume)

Glynn, R.J.; LoCastro, J.S.; Hermos, J.A.; and Bosse, R. Social contexts and motives for drinking in adult men. Journal of Studies on Alcohol 44:1011-1025, 1983.

Glynn, R.J.; Rosner, B.; and Silbert, J.E. Changes in cholesterol and triglyceride as predictors of ischemic heart disease in men. Circulation 66:724-731, 1982.

Gomberg, E.S. Prevalence of alcoholism among ward patients in a Veterans Administration hospital. Quarterly Journal of Studies on Alcohol 36:1458-1468, 1975.

Gordon, T., and Kannel, W.B. Drinking and its relation to smoking, BP, blood lipids and uric acid: The Framingham Study. Archives of Internal Medicine 143:1366-1374, 1983.

Hermos, J.A. Drinking by alcoholic cirrhotic patients under medical care. Alcoholism, 1983.

Kissen, B. Medical management of the alcoholic patient. In: Kissen, B., and Begleiter, H., eds. The Biology of Alcoholism. Vol. 5: Treatment and Rehabilitation of the Chronic Alcoholic. New York: Plenum Press, 1977. pp. 53-103.

Klatsky, A.L.; Friedman, G.D.; and Siegelaub, A.B. Alcohol and mortality: A ten-year Kaiser Permanente experience. Annals of Internal Medicine 95:139-145, 1981.

Klatsky, A.L.; Friedman, G.D.; Siegelaub, A.B.; and Gerard, M.J. Alcohol consumption and blood pressure: Kaiser Permanente multiphasic health examination data. New England Journal of Medicine 296:1194-2000, 1977.

Knupfer, G. Ex-problem drinkers. In Roff, M.; Robins, L.; and Pollack, M., eds. Life History Research in Psychopathology. Vol. 2. New York: Plenum Press, 1972. pp. 256-280.

Lee, N. Drug therapy in the elderly: The clinical pharmacology of aging. Alcoholism 2:39-42, 1978.

Marmot, M.G.; Rose, G.; Shipley, M.J.; and Thomas, B.J. Alcohol and mortality: A U-shaped curve. Lancet 1:580-583, 1981.

Patek, A.J., and Hermos, J.A. Recovery from alcoholism in cirrhotic patients: A study of 45 cases. American Journal of Medicine 70:782-785, 1981.

Riess, A.; Duncan, O.; Hatt, P.; and North, C. Occupations and Their Social Status. New York: Free Press of Glencoe, 1961.

Room, R. Treatment-seeking populations and larger realities. In: Edwards, G., and Grand, M., eds. Alcoholism Treatment in Transition. London: Croom Helm, 1980. pp. 105-224.

Saunders, J.B.; Beevers, D.G.; and Paton, A. Alcohol-induced hypertension. Lancet 2:653-656, 1981.

Seber, G.A.F. Linear Regression Analysis. New York: John Wiley and Sons, 1977. p. 376.

Sellers, E.M., and Kalant, H. Medical intelligence: Drug therapy, alcohol intoxication and withdrawal. New England Journal of Medicine 294:757-762, 1976.

Shurtleff, D. Some Characteristics Related to the Incidence of Cardiovascular Disease and Death: Framingham Study, 18 Year Follow Up. DHEW Pub. No. (NIH)74-519. Bethesda, Md.: National Institutes of Health, 1974. Section 30.

Sparrow, D.; Weiss, S.T.; Thomas, H.E.; Rosner, B.; and Baden, L. The relationship of the U wave to the 10-year incidence of myocardial infarction. American Journal of Epidemiology 117:729-734, 1983.

Straus, R. Types of alcohol dependence. In: Kissen, B., and Begleiter, H., eds. The Biology of Alcoholism. Vol. 6: The Pathogenesis of Alcoholism, Psychosocial Factors. New York: Plenum Press, 1983.

Tuchfeld, B. Spontaneous remission in alcoholics: Empirical observations and theoretical implications. Journal of Studies on Alcohol 42:626-641, 1981..

Tyrer, P.; Rutherford, D.; and Huggett, T. Benzodiazepine withdrawal symptoms and propranolol. Lancet 1:520-522, 1981.

Wechsler, H.; Demone, H.W.; and Gottlieb, N. Drinking patterns of Greater Boston adults: Subgroup differences on the QFV index. Journal of Studies on Alcohol 39:1158-1165, 1978.

DISCUSSION: SESSION I

George Maddox

The keynote address and the first four papers have summarized and focused our attention on some key issues illustrated in a growing literature that are relevant for an understanding of alcohol abuse and aging. Two themes in these presentations warrant special attention. First, a variety of disciplines has contributed to our understanding of aging, alcohol abuse, and the relationship between alcohol use and abuse in the later years of life. The perspectives of biomedical, behavioral, and social scientific disciplines will be essential in advancing knowledge about the complex interrelationship between aging and alcohol use--incidence, prevalence, etiology, therapeutic management, and prevention.

Second, a number of methodological issues are particularly important in the development of the research likely to provide definitive information on alcohol abuse in later life. These methodological issues include the reliability of measurement techniques, the adequacy of sampling procedures, and the possibility of cohort differences in alcohol abuse among older adults. In pursuing these issues, we can learn a great deal from scientific investigators working on other topics who have dealt with similar methodological problems.

The Framingham Study of Heart Disease was hardly designed to make a significant contribution to drinking behavior. Yet, an article by one of the Framingham investigators, which was brought to our attention, addresses some basic issues relevant for this workshop. So, both in the role of giving us insight into the Framingham study and the kind of incidental information we get about drinking, and for general commentary on the initial papers presented in the workshop, we are pleased to hear from Tavia Gordon, Research Professor of Statistics, Biostatistics Center, George Washington University.

Tavia Gordon, Research Professor of Statistics, Biostatistics Center, George Washington University, Washington, D.C.

I will comment first on the papers that report the Normative Aging Study, because those are, in methodology, closer to the Framingham Study and other longitudinal studies with which I have been associated.

The first comment, as Dr. Glynn pointed out, is that there are some differences quantitatively between the Framingham findings and some of the findings reported in their paper, a copy of which you either have or can get. He also points out, quite correctly I think, that these differences are historical in origin. That is to say, the Framingham Study covers a somewhat different time period than the Normative Aging Study, and different things were happening in that time period. I view all such observations made by the three previous speakers as very much rooted in historical specificity. That is to say, I think of some research findings as being peculiar, not necessarily unique, but perhaps different from what you would find at some other time and at some other place and conceivably in some other context. We had, when I was with the National Heart, Lung, and Blood Institute, five different prospective studies in process, one of them in Yugoslavia, one in Puerto Rico, one in Honolulu, the Framingham Study, and an Israeli study. Within each of those populations, particularly the Slavic and Israeli populations, there were subgroups within the populations that differed substantially, one from the other. Under those circumstances, you become very conscious of the differentials that are associated with different contexts, and conceivably with different times.

It is important, I think, to remember that the associations of variables one observes in a given study are in fact a function of the particular time and place. While I am sure that all of us would immediately disclaim that the associations we report are ordinarily causative-type associations, I think there is a tendency to think of them that way. It is always a corrective to stop for a moment and say, "Would it be the same in some different context?"

One of the things pointed out in the Normative Aging Study was the U-shaped curve in mortaliy. Nondrinkers have higher mortality than persons who drink lightly, but at some point, the curve turns upward as drinking increases. The explanation for that—and by the way, although it is not reported in all studies, a surprisingly large number of studies do report this finding—may be twofold.

One is the fact that in typical studies you find an inverse relationship between the amount people drink and the risk of coronary heart disease. The more people drink, the less likely they

DISCUSSION: SESSION I

are to develop or to die from coronary heart disease. Since coronary heart disease is, in most populations, a substantial cause of death, the impact on the shape of the overall mortality curve will sometimes wind up with excess mortality among nondrinkers as well as excess mortality (from other causes) among heavy drinkers.

Another factor, however--and I feel more and more strongly about this--is the possible selective factor involved in nondrinking. I will not try to define what that selective factor is, because I don't know what it is. But, I will say that I think one has to be very careful, when dealing with a habit, to be clear that one is talking about what people choose to do. Now, they may choose to act under social compulsion or under some psychological pressures. You know this as well as I do. But, the fact is, they make a choice, and that choice will not necessarily lead to observations similar to those one would obtain from an experiment in which one assigns varying doses to a homogeneous population on a random basis.

There are to me two clues to possible selection effects. One is the data that is reported in our paper and alluded to by Dr. Maddox. The data for blood pressure in relation to drinking exhibits a U-shape. Nondrinkers have higher blood pressures on average than persons who drink small amounts. Among drinkers, there appears to be an increasing dose-response relationship. I use the word "response" without understanding its precise meaning. Nobody has really ever explained the mechanism by which a rise in blood pressure should follow an increasing amount of alcohol consumption. But my guess is that a selective factor is involved, in part.

Another clue is in the paper presented here this morning by Dr. Warheit in which he indicated a similar kind of U-shaped curve. That is to say, abstainers had more of certain kinds of problems that he used as outcomes than did problem drinkers. Again, I suggest this finding may very well reflect a selective factor. Again, I don't want to define the nature of the selective factor.

Another question raised is whether among the nondrinkers there are people who previously drank, perhaps drank a lot, and have quit. These may be the people who account for the excess mortality among nondrinkers. It may be true. One of the Chicago prospective studies did report that among previous drinkers who are currently not drinking there was a distinct excess of mortality. Among persons who had never drunk, mortality was relatively low. All I can say is that in the Framingham Study that isn't what we find. We find that people who previously drank and who were no longer drinking had about the same mortality as people who had never reported drinking.

Questions were raised about the large standard deviations observed. Take a look at the distribution of the amount people drink. You have a substantial number of people who report that they don't drink at all, and then a larger number of people who drink very small amounts. Then the curve drops off, and there is a long tail to the right, representing increasing rates of consumption. Typically, such curves will yield a standard deviation that is larger than the mean for the curve, and, in fact, this is the basis for attempting a log transformation in order to equalize variances.

Incidentally, I have never been enthusiastic about log transformation, although I have used it. I have become more and more sensitive to the fact that in a distribution there is a zero category--that is, the group of people who don't drink at all--who may be different from people who do drink. And, the assumption that we are dealing with a single distribution may not be justified. We want to normalize this distribution because there are a lot of useful tools available to cope with normal distributions. The statistical theory of normal distributions is such that if anybody can appeal to it for justification, no matter how far they want to stretch the data to do it, they will do so, because it is just convenient to do so. I think you will find, if you search your hearts, that maybe some of the things you do in connection with some of your methodologies are dictated by convenience rather than by the presumption that this is necessarily the most accurate way of thinking about the data with which you are dealing.

Problems associated with the analysis of data with respect to changes in drinking in the Normative Aging Study are similar to those we encountered in the Framingham Study. We took four different readings of how much people drank over a period of something like 22 years. Most people shifted relatively small amounts; they moved from one category to the next in most instances. Relatively few made large changes. This suggests that, by and large, there are not major changes in drinking habits over time. We did report average changes and they are nontrivial, but my feeling is that a large amount of the change that we saw in the Framingham Study population was in fact a historical change. That is, they were riding along with the general increase of drinking in the population.

Historical change makes it very difficult when one does prospective studies. If one characterizes a group of people at baseline, one may argue that they remain, relative to their peers, in about the same position. But, since there is presumably a dose-response relationship, if everybody is moving, then the dose for everybody is changing. It becomes a little tricky then to be sure what the dose-response relationship is on an absolute scale. It becomes particularly difficult if the end point of interest is mortality because, when somebody has died, you can't get too much information about subsequent drinking habits.

We did not find the same kind of relationship reported in the Normative Aging Study for drinkers who develop ischemic heart disease. What we found was that drinkers who developed ischemic heart disease in the Framingham Study actually drank a little bit more afterwards than they did before. On the other hand, our study occurred in a period when the average consumption of alcohol was going up. The consumption of persons who did not develop coronary heart disease increased also; but they increased their consumption even more than the persons who did develop coronary heart disease. So conceivably the conclusions from both studies are qualitatively similar.

I would like to say something about what are called alcohol-related diseases. We all use that phrase, and I think we can assign a well-defined meaning to it. What we mean is that a regression relationship exists between the amount and frequency people drink and morbidity or mortality. The regression relationship between that drinking behavior and subsequent development of disease or death is a positive relationship and may be fairly strong. Where one gets into trouble, at least from where I sit, is when one begins to infer too much.

As you know, there are in the literature several different formulas for estimating the number of alcoholics from mortality statistics. Changes in the level of prevalence of alcoholism are inferred from changes in mortality. Such inferences should make us uncomfortable. I object to taking data with respect to apparent changes in consumption of alcohol in the population of the United States and relating these changes to changes in mortality for cirrhosis of the liver. Cirrhosis of the liver is a cause of death that, outside of accidents, provides the largest number of deaths assigned to any particular cause. I would suggest with respect to cirrhosis of the liver (or, for that matter, any cause of death) that what one is dealing with is multifactorial causation. By and large, we cannot really define in a comprehensive way what all the causes of a particular outcome are that completely explain the death involved. Various factors may exist in the different balance from one population to another.

Consider also the incidence of stroke. If a person has developed coronary heart disease, the chances of having a stroke are substantially greater. The incidence of coronary heart disease varies markedly from one population to another. So, the importance of coronary heart disease as a causative factor is obviously going to vary from one population to another. I suggest that this is equally true with respect to cirrhosis of the liver or any of the causes that one normally thinks of as alcohol related.

There is one German study that concluded that a sizable proportion of cirrhosis of the liver could be explained by hepatitis. About the same proportion of variance could be explained by alcohol use or alcoholism. For those of you who are interested in cirrhosis of the liver, I think this is a subject worthy of a great deal more serious study. There is available an easy test that can be applied to a general population to determine whether somebody has in fact been exposed to hepatitis. The prevalence of elevated titers to type A or type B hepatitis is quite high. It is conceivable that the infection constitutes a predisposing factor toward the development of cirrhosis of the liver, and I think it would be interesting for somebody to attempt to study this subject since it seems to me relatively easy to do so.

From the Normative Aging Study, there were some data presented with respect to the relationship of drinking to hypertension or blood pressure and hypertension. I just want to make a technical point worth considering. If one examines the correlation between blood pressure among people who are normotensive and persons who develop hypertension, the correlation will be fairly high for an obvious reason: That is, people who are normotensive but at the high end of normotensive are more likely on the next measurement to have a blood pressure measurement on the other side of the cut point. That correlation is going to appear when one puts both of these variables into the regression equation. The initial measurement is the one that gives the most information for the obvious reason that it is, in fact, the one that is the more stable of the two measurements. If changes seem to be less stable than initial measurement, as was pointed out quite correctly, our finding in the Framingham Study was that when we studied changes in drinking related to changes in blood pressure, we found a very weak positive relationship. But, it was a positive relationship.

George Maddox

Tomorrow Ben Locke's paper will present the promise of the ECA program for answering some questions about aging and alcohol abuse that have not been adequately answered to date. One of the reasons we spent so much time discussing background issues today is to provide the kind of backdrop against which we can assess the promise of the ECA program. Some of the questions raised today can be raised again tomorrow. To what extent will the kinds of issues we discussed this afternoon be resolved by ECA data?

DISCUSSION: SESSION I

Our formal discussion today will conclude with a reaction paper by Rudolf Moos that discusses the initial papers from the perspective of social ecology. General discussion will follow.

REACTION PAPER

<u>Rudolf Moos, Ph.D., Research Career Scientist, Palo Alto Veterans Administration, Department of Psychiatry and Behavioral Sciences, Stanford University, Stanford, California</u>

Note: An expanded version of these remarks appears at the end of this section.

When George Maddox called to ask me to be a discussant, I demurred at first and resisted because I didn't know very much about the area. He persuaded me that lack of knowledge about the specific area might be an asset. He persuaded me that I was the ideal discussant. Although I have not actually worked on problem drinking among older people, I have worked a little bit in the alcoholism field, mainly with regard to treatment evaluation. I have, of course, over the last decade or so worked with older people, mainly in research on residential and sheltered care settings. This work is related to understanding distressful living circumstances, to lack of choice and control in such settings, and to stressful events such as residential relocation. One more word of background. I have worked over many years on stress and coping theory in a variety of populations including alcohol abusers, depressed patients, and patients with medical illnesses and have a strong interest in the role of contextual and environmental factors in each of these areas.

My experience in this work leads me to emphasize somewhat the value of developing a general model or perspective in an area of research. At the most general level, I basically endorse Robert Straus' call for biobehavioral approach. I have a slight preference, I don't know whether he would agree with me or not, for the term "psychosomatic," or in the new terms, possibly, "biopsychosocial." The latter form may be preferable because it includes specifically an emphasis on cognitive factors as well as on social and environmental factors. I highlight this emphasis. I know that behavioral medicine is moving in this direction currently. From my perspective, the medical model is biopsychosocial. It is the biomedical model that takes a narrower view of human interaction.

I also endorse very strongly, as you might suspect, Robert Straus' emphasis on both <u>intra</u>- and <u>inter</u>-individual variations and his recommendation for developing models that allow us to do this.

Finally, from his overview, I underscore the emphasis on the social and environmental factors that he mentioned and stress the importance of understanding:

- How the general social contexts, such as, perhaps, environments fostering more leisure and recreation time, are related to general patterns of changes in drinking;

- How a great reliance on technology makes drinking problems somewhat more likely and somewhat more noticeable;

- And how different types of alcohol problems are related to situational dependency and social dependency.

We have done some studies on the context of drinking among college students. We found, for example, in terms of social dependency, that the amount of drinking within a dormitory was related to social cohesion in that dormitory; high social cohesion tended to increase the amount of drinking among the freshmen students who lived in the dorm. A social resource, cohesion in this case, may have possibly negative effects.

I want now to turn to the other papers and highlight in those papers what I saw as the main findings, how I see them in relation to prior literature in the area, and the models I think we need to develop for further work in this area. I will also emphasize how work outside the area of this workshop (specifically how advances in evaluation research, on the one hand, and stress and coping theory on the other) can help expand the models we are using and improve the research on aging and alcohol abuse. My basic ideas are very consistent or consonant with George Warheit's call for a broad systems perspective and also with Matilda White Riley's comment about looking at aging as a social process. Processes are involved in the development of problem drinking, and we need to understand these processes in order to change them.

Because I am a bit more familiar with the treatment research, the paper by John Helzer will be considered first. Basically, older problem drinkers (or, in this case, I think, alcoholics is probably more accurate) were the patients being studied. "Are they differentially responsive to treatment?" is the first question. And secondly, "What are the predictors of recovery among younger and older alcoholics?"

Consider the magnitude of the problem. In this particular study, as I read the data, 234 of the 1,280 alcoholic patients (18 percent) were 60 or older. That figure is based on interviews at the midpoint of the field period; so it is a few years after the index admission. But still, 18 percent is a little higher than what one would find in most studies (e.g., more likely around 10 percent or 12 percent). Nevertheless, we get an idea of the magnitude of the problem.

The findings in that study were as follows:

- Essentially no difference in outcome between older and younger patients was found;

- Outcome was relatively poor, if one can put it that way, in that only 20 to 24 percent became abstainers or nonproblem drinkers; and

- Some prognostic factors were identified. For example, married patients did better, socially isolated patients did somewhat worse, and cognitively impaired patients did slightly better.

How do these findings relate to the literature and the few existing studies? What do we learn about the kind of future studies we need?

In terms of other studies, as I see it, earlier studies did suggest that older patients might do somewhat better. Three recent studies I have seen don't seem to support that conclusion. One study included in the background materials for the workshop (Art Wiens, on the Raleigh Hills Aversion Conditioning Study) reported that 65 percent of patients over 65 showed continuous sobriety over 12 months with the aversion conditioning treatment. Overall, for all patients reported in another paper, 63 percent responded favorably. In that study no age differences were found either. The Norburger Study, you probably know, was done in a different Raleigh Hills hospital. The same treatment was used but with a different mix of patients. This study reported 52 percent sobriety for a year among patients over 61 years of age vs. 59 percent for other patients. The study having the most patients involved was done by Yenna Gandunom, published recently in an NIAAA report on alcohol treatment centers. The study compared treated patients 60 and over (about 2,000) with a similar sample of younger (21 to 59) patients. Six month followup data were routinely collected at the alcohol treatment centers. No differences in outcome between younger and older patients were found.

The proportion of older patients who improve with treatment varies tremendously from study to study. The same is true for treatment outcome studies of younger populations. In various studies, a variation of from 20 to 65 percent is observed in reported favorable outcomes (that is, continuous sobriety for a year). Now clearly, the patients in Dr. Helzer's study were, one would say, seriously impaired alcoholics; three of the treatment settings that were described were inpatient settings, and one was a medical treatment setting. The followup interval was far longer than usual (6 to 10 years rather than 1 year). In any case, the failure to find age differences in outcome is not surprising.

In terms of other work on prognostic factors, Dr. Helzer's results are largely as expected. Married status generally is related to positive outcome, although Dr. Helzer notes the interesting finding that married status seemed to be a more important prognostic factor for positive outcome among men than it was among women. In our own studies among younger groups of alcoholics, we found that marital status conferred, if I can put it this way, an advantage on men, but did not confer a similar advantage on women. In a very general way, this finding is consistent with George Warheit's finding that widowers exhibit increased depression and widows do not. It will be ironic if we find a cohort effect over the next 10 or 20 years suggesting that marriage might become more of an advantage for women than men as women become more emancipated from it. In that sense, I was glad to hear Dr. Riley's comment that, in the year 2000 when there are likely to be 150 or 200 or 250 women for every 100 men, this outcome might cause some women to become depressed.

In future studies of aging and alcohol abuse, particularly in studies of patients, we need to expand the general model or framework that is being used in treatment outcome studies. Some of you who have read some of our work know the model we have used. Our model is basically this. One focuses on client characteristics at intake (e.g., sociodemographic factors and perhaps personal functioning). Then one introduces treatment. As often as not, treatment is the proverbial "black box" because one frequently has very little, if any, information about the treatment that was actually administered. Then one focuses on client outcome, typically in terms of global and distant outcome factors. This is the standard, simplified treatment evaluation research model that many people are using.

Our feeling is that in future studies of aging, alcohol abuse, and treatment, one needs to expand that model at least in two ways and probably in more. First, one clearly needs much more specific emphasis and information on the treatment itself--on quantity of treatment, on treatment components, and on quality of treatment. And second, much more emphasis is needed on extratreatment or life context factors that intervene between the end of treatment and the time of followup. Obviously these intervening factors can have strong effects on the recovery-relapse process.

Let me illustrate. A lot of the treatment outcome literature was provoked by the second Rand study of outcome 4 years after treatment of alcohol abuse problems. We haven't heard very much about the average amount and the kind of treatment provided. Six sessions of outpatient treatment were noted with followup 4 years later. To bring the point home, review your own assumptions about the probable effect of six sessions of outpatient treatment on problem drinking or alcoholism as assessed 4 years later. I think one would probably not expect a large effect.

Attention also needs to be directed in the future to process analysis that links specific aspects of treatment to specific indices of treatment outcome. Again, for example, consider the Raleigh Hills studies. Aversion conditioning sessions may be important, but they may not be the only active treatment component in an aversion conditioning program. For instance, in our own studies we found that AA attendance was as predictive of abstinence and low alcohol consumption as was the number of aversion conditioning sessions in which a patient participated.

I have repeatedly stressed the quality of treatment as a variable in treatment evaluation research. Factors in a residential treatment setting such as cohesion and organization and the degree of independence and self-understanding that is emphasized in the program are also important. Our studies show that factors such as these are independently related to treatment outcome. By independently, I mean over and above intake symptoms or quantity of treatment. This is a very important issue.

Extratreatment or life context factors warrant additional comment. I have in mind the characteristics of an individual's family; the extent to which patients are working; work settings; life stress events; and social resources. Again, in our own work, we found that having information on these life context factors, which occur between the end of treatment and followup, will predict as much of the variance in the recovery-relapse process as all of the other factors combined. One often hears that the best prediction one can make about what a patient will be doing after treatment is what a patient did before the problem that required treatment occurred. That basically is usually the case, but this best prediction is not very good and is not good enough. A very small proportion of the variance can be accounted for in this way, say roughly 5 to 20 percent, depending on the outcome criterion one uses. In fact, abstinence is particularly difficult to predict.

Intervention programs ought to be studied as open systems and related to the context of an individual's life. Clearly, if a treatment program is an environmental intervention that can change drinking, then we can imagine the beneficial effects of changing community settings. If community settings can affect drinking patterns, so can treatment programs. Clearly, one would expect their effects to be reciprocal.

The importance of matching older patients with treatment interventions should be noted. There is an enormous amount of work that needs to be done here. One needs to match the cognitive demands of treatment with the cognitive abilities of the patients to understand treatment outcomes. This is particularly important for the more behavioral treatments of the skills-learning type. We would hypothesize that older, more cognitively impaired patients (not all older patients are necessarily more cognitively impaired) are likely to benefit more from cognitively simpler treatments. The behavior of less competent or more impaired persons may be molded relatively more than the behavior of others by environmental factors. Powell Lawton's environmental facility hypothesis suggests that this is the case. Cognitively limited patients, for example, may do better than others in more structured treatment settings, which is consistent, as I see it, with the evidence on younger, more disturbed patients. The effects of matching patients and treatment programs are ripe for investigation.

The finding of no differences between older and younger patients in treatment outcome in the NIAAA studies has invited the conclusion that one need not have specialized treatment programs for older people. I do not agree. The available evidence simply shows that the treatment we are using now has about the same effect on older and younger patients. Whether there should be specialized programs for older people with alcohol abuse problems remains to be determined.

Several basic issues in the Normative Aging Study warrant comments. For example, how much change in drinking patterns was observed among men as they grew older? What were the predictors of change? Did new episodes of cardiovascular disease predict change in consumption levels or problems? One point was mentioned in both papers reporting this study. The followup rates in this longitudinal study were impressively high. The investigator deserves some credit for that. Having been involved in studies of this sort, I know that it is not easy to get such high followup rates. While the reported mean drinking levels in the various age groups stayed roughly the same, we learn very little about the factors that predict stability and change. High consumption at Time 1, as you heard, was the best predictor of change. This is a familiar finding, one found frequently in the treatment literature; but only 14 percent of the variance in change was accounted for. So, Time 1 drinking was the best predictor of change but was not a very good predictor.

In terms of drinking problems, older men tended to report slightly fewer problems, although there was no actual decline in problems with age. What interests me most about this work is that two potentially stressful events had at least minor relationships to changes in drinking status. Men who developed new cardiovascular disease consumed more alcohol at Time 1 in the 1973 survey and reduced their drinking (at least as indicated by mean levels; see table 2 in the paper). That wasn't shown so well in the regression analysis. Look at the actual tabulations in trying to understand the issue. Once you control for Time 1 drinking levels (since they were higher for the men who developed the heart disease in the first place), you would be less likely to expect heart disease to have an additional, statistically significant explanatory effect. My interpretation is something like this. There is a small effect attributable to separation and divorce predicting additional drinking problems. New cardiovascular disease, on the other hand, tends to be slightly predictive of a decrease in drinking problems. Of course, the standard deviations that have been mentioned by Tavia Gordon are as interesting as anything else because they are huge. These large standard deviations, by the way, are found also for the change scores, not only of the Time 1 and Time 2 variables. The variance that is most interesting involves individual differences in changes over time. In terms of the literature in this area, the link between life stress and problem drinking has been known for a long time, particularly in the case of reactive alcoholics.

A distinction has been made between early onset and late onset problem drinking, and it warrants at least a brief comment. Initially there was some debate, and I guess there is still some debate, about the number of older drinkers who are late onset problem drinkers. In a review to be published soon, a colleague and I concluded that about one-third of people who are identified as problem drinkers or alcoholics at 50, 55, 60 or so and over are probably late onset. We are not too confident about that conclusion, however. In the Normative Aging Study, among people aged 40 to 49 in 1973, 47 of the 126 who had problems in drinking were new entrants to this category. That is, at Time 2, 37 percent reported problems for the first time. At age 50 to 59, 30 of the 74 (40 percent) were new to the category. I think this suggests, consistent with our review, that there may be a somewhat higher proportion of late onset drinkers than has been thought previously.

Work on life stress and problem drinking and on factors in general that cause changes in problem drinking among older people suggests that life context problems are very important potential factors in explaining changes in drinking as people age. If contextual factors in an individual's life at ages of 55 or 60 do not predict changes in drinking habits, what is a better hypothesis?

The model we need to relate life stress work to drinking behavior in later life is very similar to the treatment model discussed earlier. Life stress is an intervening variable between the behavior of individuals at a Time 1 and their subsequent behavior at a Time 2.

The idea that life stress such as physical illnesses might have positive consequences fits very well with the work on spontaneous recovery in younger problem drinkers. This is a somewhat novel idea, however, in the context of the stress and coping literature generally. Perhaps some of the future work in alcohol abuse and aging can help to advance our understanding of stress and coping. There has been very little work on potentially positive consequences of stressful events. This is an important issue.

Life stress, whether it is separation/divorce or a new physical illness, is unlikely to be either a necessary or a sufficient condition for increased or decreased problem drinking. But stress is clearly going to be one nonredundant part of a composite sufficient condition. I like McKay's concept, although it is a little complicated, of an INUS condition. That is, life stress is insufficient (I) in and of itself, but nonredundant (N); that is, it probably has an independent contribution to make. It is part of an unnecessary (U) condition in the sense that other combinations of factors can also result in changes in problem drinking, but is part, in the overall framework, of a sufficient (S) set of composite conditions. I think that is a useful way to think about stress as a predictor of drinking problems. A concrete example a clinician might offer is that the death of a spouse "caused" a survivor's drinking problem. Naturally, one doesn't mean it that way. One really means that typically the death of a spouse might be a condition that would transform normal social drinking of the survivor into problem drinking. Death of a spouse might be an INUS condition; if you will, the most active of a combination of factors comprising sufficient condition.

In work on life stress and problem drinking, I think we need to go beyond stress and coping theory to crisis theory. Crisis theory, as formulated early on by Linderman and Kaplan, has always made it very clear that a life crisis is a turning point and that the changes that can occur can be either for better or for worse. This is an obvious point, but the model we use typically doesn't recognize this.

In expanding our model on life stress, we need to consider, as much work in the aging field is doing now, vulnerability and resistance factors. Personal resources such as self-efficacy are clearly important in the coping strategies people use to deal with events like separation and divorce or a physician's announcement that one has cardiovascular disease. And, social network resources are important. We need to know more about the moderators or mediators of stressors.

What is important for future work on aging and alcohol abuse--both on the treatment side and on the life stress side--are factors that predict problem drinking and predict ameliorative changes in problem drinking. There are certain similarities in the somewhat simplified model we have proposed to examine both the effects of treatment and the effects of stress. I have argued for an expansion of work in each of these areas to consider advances in research outside of aging and alcoholism, advances in evaluation research, and advances in stress and coping research. Those general ideas, in fact, are being used now in research on recovery and relapse, depression, and other areas of substance abuse, e.g., drug abuse and cigarette smoking; and in research on normal stress and the coping process. To end on a positive and hopeful note, which is generally my predilection, I hope that some advances of the kinds discussed can help to combat the specialism that is inherent in alcoholism research and that could develop in aging and alcoholism research unless we are careful. I stress the need to integrate the work we are going to be doing in these areas with advances in other areas to the benefit of each of the areas.

GENERAL DISCUSSION

Tavia Gordon

I just want to make a methodological comment that may concern some of you. The term "proportional variance explained" is commonly used. That is a well-defined statistical concept when one is dealing with multiple variance in normal distributions. When one deviates from that use, the concept becomes hazier and hazier, particularly when one is dealing with an outcome that is a zero-one variable: In this case, the concept is not very well defined. There is literature on this problem, and an article that we published about a year ago in the Journal of Chronic Diseases deals with this question. I do not have the exact reference, but could provide it on request.

George Maddox

This is a point worth making, because it came up several times in the presentations. Should we be apologetic or describe as "not very significant" a small amount of variance accounted for in our research?

Jacob Brody, M.D., Associate Director for Epidemiology, Demography and Biometry Program, National Institute on Aging, Bethesda, Maryland

Note: A paper on aging and alcohol abuse prepared by Dr. Brody for the 1981 White House Conference on Aging appears at the end of this section.

I would like to bring up some issues that have been touched upon, but that relate more specifically to the problems of aging in relationship to alcohol, rather than to the concept of treatment of alcohol-related problems in general. I believe most of the discussion has been related to alcohol treatment at younger ages rather than to treatment of those who are 65 and older. The issue of whether there is a decrease in alcohol consumption by the average drinker or whether there is simply an increase in the total number of abstainers with age has not been clarified during these discussions. I believe, however, that the bulk of the evidence suggests that both phenomena occur. There is an overall diminution in the amount drunk by the average individual as he or she ages and as the number of total abstainers increases with age.

Another subject that has come up relates to the articles by Rosenblatt and Zimberg, who claim that it is relatively easy to treat elderly alcoholics. Dr. Moos has referred to these early studies, and I believe he shares the same concern as I. These studies have not been repeated for 15 years. If the elderly are indeed treated more easily than younger people, then we should establish this as a fact and determine which of the simple methods available we should use. Another critical observation relates to the issue of late onset vs. early onset alcoholism. By late onset alcoholism we usually mean a person who has been drinking moderately all his life, but because of situation events later in life, he begins to drink more heavily and becomes an alcohol abuser. While, undoubtedly, such people do exist, I know of no systematic survey of true late onset alcoholics. The group of late onset alcoholics, or more especially the late onset alcohol abusers, is potentially very large and needs definition. Most of the reports of elderly alcoholics involve sturdy older folk who have been drinking all their lives and have superior constitutions, in the sense that the alcohol has not yet carried them off.

An extremely important observation made by several prominent investigators is that from 15 to 25 percent of people age 65 and older who seek health care either through hospitalization or other health care givers have some alcohol-related component to their complaint. This observation begs to be corroborated. If it is true, an enormous number of people over age 65 have an alcohol-related component to their illness. If one considers that

DISCUSSION: SESSION I

17 percent of people over age 65 are hospitalized at least once per year, we can get some notion of the number of people we are discussing. If indeed a significant percentage of these people do have an alcohol-related problem, then it becomes very important to educate all the health care givers, from surgeons to social workers, to be on the alert for alcohol-related problems. The amount of good that could be done by very early detection of an alcohol component in these elderly people seeking health care is of major public health importance.

George Maddox

Thank you. That is a very helpful statement. What do the numbers and research classifications mean? What do we propose to do with the information we produce? Presumably, gathering information is supposed to inform somebody about something, supposed to answer questions that they want answered. What Dr. Brody is saying is that by giving a statistic or an average, we are not being helpful. When we relate a high probability of hospitalization and a high probability that some of those people hospitalized will have an alcohol problem, we may be saying something useful, alerting professionals who are likely to encounter these individuals. Late onset is frequently discussed. But how certain are we that their classification is valid and useful? Why are we bothering to make the distinction? Is it really an important distinction? I would like to ask Dr. Glynn, if I might, a question. Rudy Moos made the observation that your information about time of onset was not altogether convincing. Would you care to comment?

Robert Glynn

There is a very important qualification. There is a tremendous amount of moving in and out of the problem-drinking category. The literature quite clearly supports this. The issue of when problem drinking begins is a very important one as noted in the comment just made. There doesn't seem to be any solid answer.

George Maddox

We agree that the determination of time of onset of alcohol abuse is important but also agree that the evidence is weak. What do we conclude from this?

John Helzer

In the study I presented, it was interesting to look at the age of onset of first drinking problem and age at which the two samples met criteria for prealcohol abuse or addiction. In the older age sample, the mean age of onset of the first drinking problem was about age 31. The mean age of first meeting the criteria of alcoholism was the early 40s. Obviously, this is a highly selected sample of very seriously ill people and not necessarily generalizable, but the late onset of this group was very impressive.

George Maddox

The late onset we were talking about was later than that. We were considering whether or not there is a category of individuals who have been essentially nondrinkers or asymptomatic drinkers for a long period of time in adulthood who, as a result of experiencing some age-related events (like death of a spouse) would be transformed into a person with a significant drinking problem. That is the lateness of interest.

John Helzer

But my estimate from the data was just a mean, so obviously some were later than that.

John Hermos

I think one of the problems seems to be no correlation or lack of fit between what population studies have shown and what clinical studies have shown. My understanding is that the epidemiologic survey data present real difficulties in identifying the progressive alcoholism problems that clinicians recognize. I think the failure to find late onset alcoholics or problem drinkers in clinical populations is indeed because late onset is a population survey finding; perhaps the two findings just haven't meshed, probably because of the composition of the two population samples.

REACTION PAPER

A SYSTEMS PERSPECTIVE ON PROBLEM DRINKING AMONG OLDER ADULTS*

Rudolf H. Moos and John W. Finney

New systems perspectives in the behavioral and social sciences can deepen our understanding of how environmental and contextual processes affect problem drinking among older adults. Such perspectives enable clinicians and researchers to locate their work within a broad conceptual framework, to apprehend the value of complementary or competing orientations, and to identify productive areas for collaborative endeavor. In addition, they can combat the specialism that besets alcoholism research and encourage a more general view of health and well-being and the personal and contextual factors that maintain them (see also Straus, this volume, and Warheit and Auth, this volume). More specifically, conceptual advances in stress and coping theory and evaluation research can help to address some fundamental issues involved in understanding problem drinking among older persons.

In regard to stress and coping, recent research has identified the presence of a complex process underlying the relationship between stress and a personal dysfunction such as problem drinking. This process encompasses sociodemographic factors such as social status, personal resources such as self-esteem and coping skills, and contextual factors such as social network resources, as well as stressful life circumstances. Current studies are examining the protective role of personal resources and the extent to which social resources and coping processes moderate or amplify the association between stress and illness (Dohrenwend and Dohrenwend 1981). The concepts developed in this body of work can clarify the mechanisms by which life stressors and coping resources affect the

---

*An expanded version of the informal reaction of Dr. Moos to the papers presented in session 1. The work discussed in this Reaction Paper was supported by NIAAA Grant AA02863, NIMH Grant MH28177, and Veterans Administration Medical Research Funds.

onset, maintenance, and cessation of problem drinking among older adults.

Turning to evaluation research, we note that advances in this area have sparked new ideas about the nature of problem drinking and the role of treatment and life context factors in the recovery-relapse process. Combined with current trends toward a holistic, biopsychosocial view of health and illness, these ideas are promoting a conceptually based approach to treatment evaluation. This approach can help to integrate seemingly disparate factors about alcohol abuse, to incorporate information on extratreatment factors in treatment planning, and ultimately, to develop a clearer understanding of the nature of alcohol problems (Moos and Finney 1983).

An Integrated Conceptual Framework

A systems approach to problem drinking among older adults provides a guide or road map that helps to identify common issues and place them within an overall perspective. The framework shown in figure 1 depicts the major sets of factors that influence health and health-related behavior, such as problem drinking. In general, the framework follows a biopsychosocial model, though it primarily emphasizes personal and social factors. We posit that personal and environmental factors influence each other, as well as aspects of alcohol consumption and related symptoms and problems, the chance that an individual will seek and utilize health care, and the amount and quality of such care.

Only a small proportion of older persons are in need of formal treatment for problem drinking, but many of those who are, neither seek nor obtain it. For those who do, the treatment they receive acts in conjunction with pretreatment factors to affect the subsequent status of the personal and environmental system and, in turn, drinking and drinking-related outcome criteria. The mainly nonrecursive nature of the model (that is, the bidirectional paths) shows that these processes are transactional and that reciprocal feedback can occur among the panels.

Drinking-Related Factors

The drinking-related factors in the model encompass the history and amount of alcohol consumption, symptoms of alcohol dependence or withdrawal, and the number and kind of alcohol-related adverse consequences or life problems. These three types of indices have been used to estimate the prevalence of problem drinking among older people and to examine the change of prevalence with age. For instance, in a national probability sample of adults, Clark and

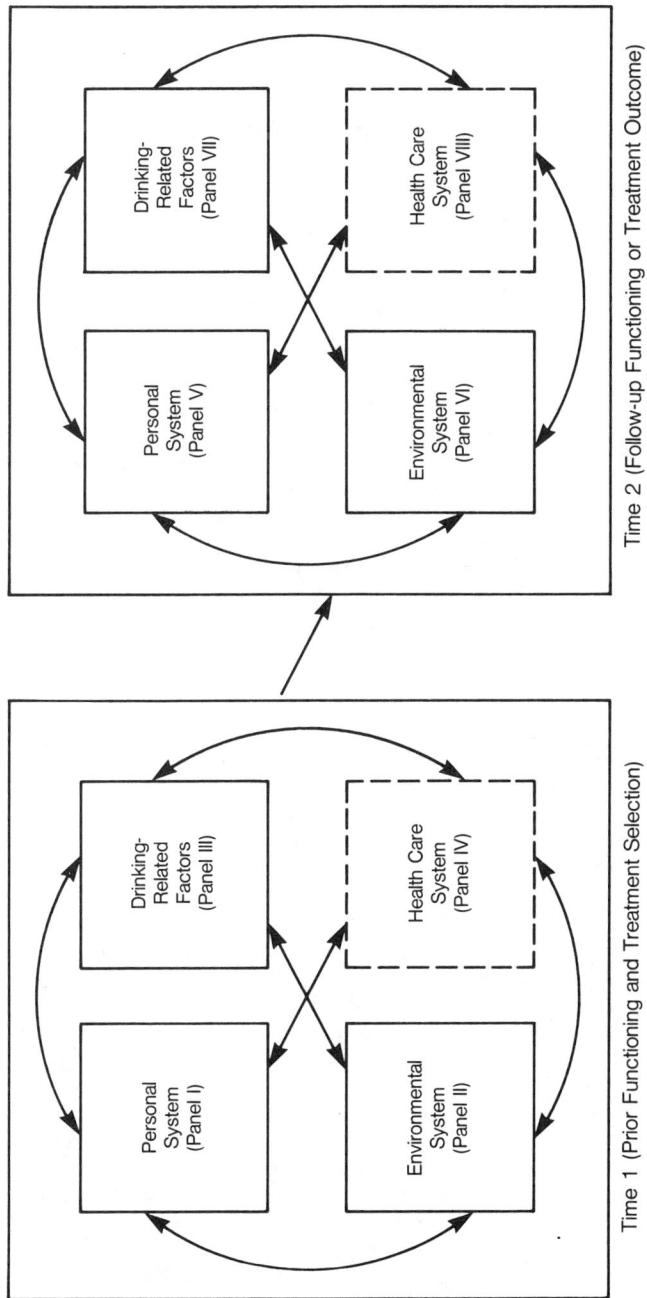

Figure 1.—A Longitudinal Framework that Considers the Role of Personal, Environmental, and Health Care System Factors in Problem Drinking

Midanik (1980) found that men older than 60 were more likely to be heavy drinkers (about 10 percent averaged two or more drinks per day over the past year) and to report some dependence symptoms (about 4 percent) and social consequences (about 4 percent) than were older women (1 percent or less). The "young-old" (ages 61 to 70) tended to report slightly more drinking problems than the "old-old" (over 70).

The VA Normative Aging Study findings are roughly comparable in that about 11 percent of men ages 50 and older reported consuming two or more drinks per day, while about 9 percent of men ages 50 to 59 and 4 percent of men 60 and older reported at least one drinking problem (Glynn et al., this volume). Warheit and Auth (this volume) noted that 4.3 percent of men and 0.8 percent of women ages 50 and older were in a high-risk alcohol group. Preliminary findings from the NIMH Epidemiologic Catchment Area (ECA) projects indicate that the 6-month prevalence rates of alcohol abuse and dependence vary between 1.9 and 4.6 percent among men ages 60 and older and are less than 1 percent among women ages 60 and over (Holzer et al., this volume). These prevalence rates may increase as birth cohorts that have experienced more liberal attitudes toward alcohol reach the age of 60. However, even if prevalence rates remain stable, the rapidly expanding number of elderly persons foreshadows a growing group of older individuals with drinking problems.

The Personal System

Sociodemographic and Personal Factors. Sociodemographic factors, which identify the individual's location in the social structure, include aspects of social status, such as educational and occupational level, as well as such other characteristics as sex, age, marital status, ethnicity, and religious affiliation. Personal factors cover facets of individual functioning such as cognitive ability and problem-solving styles, personal attributes such as self-esteem and sense of mastery, and beliefs about alcohol and its appropriate use such as reasons for drinking or abstaining. Such variables may help to explain the channeling of stress effects, that is, why some vulnerable persons turn to excessive drinking while others become depressed.

Appraisal and Coping Responses. The personal system also encompasses the way in which individuals appraise situations and the coping responses they use to deal with them. Cognitive appraisal processes influence the individual's selection of coping responses and the eventual impact of stressors on individual adaptation. Coping responses refer to a person's attempts to handle stressful life circumstances and can be classified according to method (cognitive and behavioral) and focus (e.g., problem-focused and emotion-focused; for a recent review, see Moos and Billings 1982).

In this regard, McCrae (1982) has noted that older and younger persons show considerable similarity in their coping responses, once type of stress is controlled. He posits that earlier findings of coping deficits among the elderly may have come from groups of sick and disadvantaged people.

The Environmental System

Acute and Chronic Stressors. Most gerontological researchers have examined single, discrete life events, such as bereavement, retirement, or relocation (Chiriboga and Cutler 1980; George 1980). In broader perspective, however, it is useful to consider long-term strains as well as stressful events. Long-term strains exist when an older individual's basic survival needs and personal security are chronically threatened (e.g., living in an unsafe neighborhood, unmet financial need after retirement) or when there are persistent problems in interpersonal relationships with family and friends. Older people also face comparatively minor but frequent irritants that stem from both the physical and social context, such as noise, difficult stairways, and arguments with shopkeepers. These daily hassles may mediate the problematic aspects of life events and strains and thus may instigate intraindividual changes in problem drinking and other dysfunctions.

Social Network Resources. We use the term "social network resources" to refer to measures of social connectedness, based on such factors as membership in social and community groups, and to indices of the quality of relationships with family and friends. Some relevant aspects of social resources, such as quantity, quality, density, and intimacy of relationships, are drawn from social network research, while others, such as satisfaction with contacts in family and work settings and perceptions of meaningful community ties, stem from the literature on social integration (Moos and Mitchell 1982). Indices from these domains have been related to the alcoholism recovery-relapse process (Finney et al. 1980).

The Health Care System

Studies of the use of health services and treatment outcome need to consider the characteristics of intervention programs in conjunction with an individual's personal resources and life context. In this regard, the health care or intervention program lies at the heart of any study of alcoholism treatment. Such programs can be described in terms of the type (aversion conditioning or milieu therapy, lectures and films on alcoholism or AA meetings) and duration (length of inpatient stay, number of outpatient sessions) of treatment, as well as its quality (supportiveness of a residential setting, empathy expressed by a counselor).

Information about the treatment as actually delivered can be used to examine the factors involved in treatment selection and assignment and to conduct process analyses linking treatment components with outcome (Moos and Finney 1983).

With this conceptual framework as a backdrop, we now consider two prominent issues in the literature on problem drinking among older people: the role of life stressors in the onset and perpetuation of problem drinking and the responsiveness of older problem drinkers to treatment. In general, existing research has been guided (perhaps implicitly) by a simplified model that posits a direct link between life stress or treatment experiences and problem drinking. We use our framework to emphasize the value of considering the personal and social resources that may mediate and/or moderate the impact of stress or treatment on drinking behavior.

Life Stress and Alcohol Consumption Among Older Men

Such longitudinal research programs as the VA Normative Aging and Framingham Studies are beginning to develop dependable information on the stability and change in drinking practices over time. Gordon and Kannel's (1983) findings indicate a 40 to 50 percent average increase in alcohol consumption over a 20-year interval (approximately 1952 to 1972) among men initially between 40 and 50 years old. However, men over 50 showed only a small average increase during the subsequent 20 years. In contrast, Glynn and his colleagues (this volume) found that average alcohol consumption remained roughly constant over a 9-year interval (1973 to 1982) among men initially between the ages of 40 and 59. Men who were 60 or older were slightly more likely to decrease than to increase their alcohol consumption in the subsequent 9 years. The differences in the results of these two studies among 40- to 50-year-old men probably are a function of birth cohort and generational factors. However, both studies point to relative stability in the average level of alcohol consumption among men over 50.

Even though group consumption levels may remain stable, there is considerable intraindividual change over time. Stressors have been implicated primarily as contributors to problem drinking, though some recent work has linked stress to decreases in individuals' levels of alcohol consumption. For example, in the VA Normative Aging Study separated or divorced status was significantly linked to the likelihood of developing drinking problems among men who were initially free of such problems (Glynn et al., this volume). Conversely, men who developed a cardiovascular disease (hypertension, angina, or myocardial infarction) tended to reduce their subsequent alcohol consumption (as expected, they also drank more initially). Men with intervening heart disease (angina or myocardial infarction) also showed a tendency to shift out of problem drinking status (Hermos et al., this volume).

Age of Onset and the Role of Life Stress

Most of the limited amount of prior research on life stress has tried to distinguish between two types of elderly problem drinkers. One group is composed of early-onset problem drinkers, or persons whose abuse of alcohol has continued into old age, contrary to a trend observed among some persons to mature out of problem drinking (Hyman 1976). Some of these early-onset drinkers show a pattern of intermittent problem drinking as young and/or middle-aged adults, while others have a history of relatively persistent alcohol abuse. Stressful life circumstances have been implicated in triggering new episodes of alcohol abuse among intermittent early-onset problem drinkers (Hubbard et al. 1979); in addition, the stressors associated with aging are thought to perpetuate excessive drinking among chronic early-onset alcohol abusers (Rosin and Glatt 1971). Beyond these few observations, little is known about how life stressors may aggravate or counter alcohol abuse in the later stages of the life cycle.

The second group consists of late-onset alcohol abusers who begin to drink excessively in their later years, presumably in reaction to a stressful event such as bereavement, retirement, or failing health. Although there is some debate about the existence of late-onset (over age 60) problem drinkers, several clinical reports (e.g., Gaitz and Baer 1971; Merry 1980) and community surveys (e.g., Abrahams and Patterson 1978-79) have identified such individuals among groups of elderly alcohol abusers. In our overview, we estimated that there were 148 (33.6 percent) late-onset individuals among 440 elderly alcohol abusers included in a set of relevant studies (Finney and Moos, in press).

A total of 102 men (6 percent) in the VA study who reported no drinking problems in 1973 did report such problems in 1982 (Glynn et al., this volume). This group constitutes about 38 percent of the total number of men ($\underline{N}$ = 271) who reported drinking problems at either or both intervals. Moreover, the proportion of individuals who report new drinking problems is similar among men of ages 40 to 49, 50 to 59, and 60 and over (but there were only nine problem drinkers in the 60+ group, three of whom were late-onset). Although some of the men with new drinking problems at the 1982 survey may have had such problems prior to the 1973 survey, these findings are consistent with the idea that a sizable proportion of older male problem drinkers may be experiencing troubles with alcohol either for the first time or subsequent to a long trouble-free interval.

The idea that life stressors may trigger late-onset problem drinking stems from a long history of research on essential and reactive alcoholics. Reactive alcoholics have a later onset of drinking problems, are more socially competent, and more often point to life stressors as precipitants of their alcohol abuse. In this regard, Rosin and Glatt (1971) concluded that stressful circumstances were more likely to contribute to late- than to early-onset problem drinking. Of 41 individuals designated as late-onset abusers (37 percent of the total sample of 111), stressful situations such as bereavement and retirement were seen as the precipitating cause of excessive drinking for 29 persons (71 percent). By contrast, such situations were implicated as the precipitating cause among only 16 (23 percent) of the 70 early-onset drinkers. The intraindividual variability in drinking behavior shown by older alcoholic men thus implies that environmental conditions may trigger relapse or promote remission (Schuckit and Miller 1976; Schuckit et al. 1980; for an overview, see Finney and Moos, in press).

A recent study compared men over age 60 who were first time drunken-driving offenders with demographically comparable non-offenders. The prior 1-year period was relatively stressful for the offenders, in that they reported experiencing more illnesses and deaths among their close acquaintances. Moreover, the unmarried offenders--presumably those who had fewer social resources--were more likely to be recidivists. Compared with the nonoffenders, the offenders also reported more drinking problems when they were young (Wells-Parker et al. 1983). These findings are consistent with a triggering role of stress in problem drinking among the elderly.

Marital/Employment Status and Problem Drinking

Conjugal bereavement, separation/divorce, and retirement are prominent loss events among older persons. Thus, a relationship between widowed/divorced or retired status and problem drinking could imply a role of life stress. In their survey of the Washington Heights Health District, Bailey and her colleagues (1965) found a prevalence rate for alcoholism of 2.2 percent among persons 65 to 74 years old and of 1.2 percent for those 75 and older. Among widows, the rate of alcoholism was only 0.5 percent; for widowers, however, the prevalence rate was 10.5 percent--the highest for any of the sociodemographic groups examined (but see Finney and Moos, in press). Preliminary ECA findings also show higher rates (varying from 4.8 to 8.4 percent in three sites) among widowers 60 and over than among their currently married counterparts (1.2 to 2.4 percent), though rates among separated or divorced older men tend to be even higher (4.2 to 20.2 percent; see Holzer et al., this volume).

However, retired persons are no more likely than employed individuals to drink heavily or in a problematic manner (Barnes 1979; Meyers et al. 1982). Men over 60 who were not currently employed showed no higher 6-month prevalence rates of alcohol abuse or dependence in three ECA sites (Holzer et al., this volume). Future analyses should consider age more precisely, since the young-old are more likely to be married and working and to consume larger quantities of alcohol than are the old-old. More generally, probing the link between marital or employment status and drinking behavior may underestimate the role of stress in problem drinking. For many older respondents in a community survey, bereavement or retirement may be temporally distant past events whose effects are mitigated over time by intervening circumstances.

A Systems Analysis of the Causes of Problem Drinking

The studies we have cited provide modest support for the idea that life stressors may be associated with changes in problem drinking among older adults. In that regard, they are consistent with findings from groups of younger problem drinkers. Influenced by these observations, some individuals have adopted a "strong etiology" position (Meehl 1977) on the effects of stress. That is, they assume (sometimes implicitly) that the stresses of aging (panel II in the framework shown in figure 1) have a substantial direct impact on problem drinking, particularly late-onset problem drinking (panel III). However, not all late-onset problem drinkers report that stress precipitated their excessive drinking. Moreover, relatively few of the older persons in community surveys drink excessively, even though many of them have experienced stressors associated with aging. In short, life stressors are neither necessary nor sufficient to produce or impede problem drinking among older (or younger) persons.

Mackie (1974) has outlined a conception of causality that is consistent with these complex relationships between stress and alcohol abuse. Problem drinking is influenced by multiple factors and may be produced in an individual by one or more different combinations of them. Across all individuals, it is the entire set of combinations of factors (some of which are unknown, many of which are only partially specified) that constitutes the necessary and sufficient condition for problem drinking. Stressful life circumstances almost certainly are a component of one or more of the combinations of factors that produce problem drinking among older persons. But such circumstances are neither necessary nor sufficient to cause problem drinking. In this formulation, stress constitutes what Mackie (1974, p. 62) calls an INUS condition--that is, it is an **insufficient** but **nonredundant** (it provides an independent contribution) component of an **unnecessary** (other combinations of factors can also produce problem drinking) but **sufficient** composite condition.

For example, a clinician may conclude that the death of a man's wife caused him to develop a drinking problem. In actuality, however, it was the spouse's death in the context of a history of moderate drinking and relative isolation from social contacts that combined to cause (was the sufficient condition for) the drinking problem. Under most other circumstances the death of a spouse does not lead to alcohol abuse. Moreover, there are causes for problem drinking other than a death in the family; that is, the combination of circumstances just described is not a necessary condition. Thus, the wife's death in this example is an INUS condition. It is the most "active" of a combination of factors that comprise a sufficient condition for alcohol abuse; similarly, stress is often viewed as a provoking agent in other types of individual dysfunction such as depression.

Our task is to specify the combinations of factors that may be sufficient conditions for problem drinking among the elderly. Such sets of conditions will not necessarily involve acute stressful events. For example, Schuckit and Pastor (1978) note that some individuals enter adulthood genetically predisposed toward alcohol abuse. They argue that the "rigid patterns demanded by job and family may provide protection from allowing drinking to get out of hand--a defense that disappears as the family grows or retirement nears or is achieved" (p. 37). In this view, the withdrawal of structure in the individual's life and the concomitant decrease in social control over drinking combines with a genetic predisposition to produce alcohol abuse in some older persons (see also Peck 1979).

The development of serious health problems has been linked to spontaneous recovery among some alcohol abusers (Tuchfeld 1981). Such findings are consistent with the observation that new episodes of cardiovascular disorders can prompt a reduction of problem drinking (Hermos et al., this volume). In this regard, some persons report enhanced personal growth and integration and a transcendental redirection of their lives in the aftermath of an acute health crisis. However, many persons are barely able to resume their former level of adaptation, while others are totally demoralized and may suffer serious psychological consequences. The variability of individual reactions to acute health crises implies that they also can be seen as INUS conditions. Like other stressful events, health crises are potential turning points whose impact on an individual can be for better or for worse.

Specifying Vulnerability and Resistance Factors

The foregoing analysis highlights the need to specify moderators of the link between stress and drinking, i.e., factors that promote vulnerability or increase resistance to the development of excessive drinking in the aftermath of stressful life events. In regard to vulnerability factors, our own research implies that individuals who rely on emotion-focused coping styles are more likely to relapse following treatment for alcoholism (Cronkite and Moos 1980). Cognitive impairment, living alone, and need for specific types of medications that potentiate the effects of alcohol also are risk factors, as are feelings of helplessness and dissatisfaction (Straus, this volume; Warheit and Auth, this volume). Conversely, stress-resistant individuals tend to be more self-confident, to enjoy more social resources, and to be more inclined to use active coping strategies than their more distressed counterparts (Kobasa and Pucetti 1983; Pearlin and Schooler 1978). Such personal resources may lessen the chance that an older person will turn to problem drinking when confronted by a stressful situation or make it more likely that such a situation will lead to a cessation of alcohol abuse. In short, these resources may play a crucial role in both the development and recovery process in alcoholism.

Life stressors may provoke individual dysfunction by loosening social controls and/or reducing the availability of social support. One example is a stressful event, such as the death of one's spouse, that entails a loss of support as well as a change in the regularity of one's social routine. Another example is provided by friends who avoid a man with a serious illness in order to protect themselves from feelings of vulnerability or powerlessness to help him. In this regard, older persons who enjoy more social integration and support seem to be better protected from the adverse impact of life stressors (Pilisuk and Minkler 1980). Future research can identify the extent to which social networks can compensate for decrements in personal resources and functioning associated with aging. For instance, such networks may balance the loss of worker and spouse roles by providing opportunities to expand other roles, such as those of grandparent or volunteer.

The Responsiveness of Older Problem Drinkers to Treatment

Somewhere between 10 and 25 percent of older persons who obtain medical treatment or who are referred to a community outreach program may have an alcohol-related problem (Brody 1982; Reifler et al. 1982). About 10 percent of persons who seek out alcoholism treatment are over 60 (Schuckit and Pastor 1978). In this regard,

Helzer and his colleagues (this volume) found that 234 of the 1,282 alcoholic patients they followed (18 percent) were 60 or older. This is somewhat higher than the percentage shown in other studies, but the reported ages were at or during a followup period that was several years after the index admission. In any case, we need to determine whether older problem drinkers respond differently to treatment than younger patients, as well as to identify the predictors of recovery and relapse among such drinkers.

Helzer and his colleagues (this volume) addressed these issues by following alcoholic patients 6 to 10 years after admission to one of four inpatient and outpatient treatment programs. There were essentially no differences in treatment outcome between younger and older patients. Moreover, only about 20 percent of the patients showed a stable pattern of recovery by becoming abstainers or nonproblem drinkers. In terms of prognostic factors, women and married patients tended to do somewhat better, while patients who were socially isolated showed worse outcomes than those who were not. These factors also have been related to prognoses in other studies of older (Janik and Dunham 1983) and younger alcoholic patients (Moos and Finney 1983), though married status tends to confer more of an advantage on men than on women.

With regard to recovery and relapse, recent empirical studies imply that older and younger alcoholic patients experience comparable treatment outcome. In a followup of a medical-behavioral (aversion conditioning) treatment, Wiens and his colleagues (in press) noted that 65 percent of a group ($\underline{N}$ = 78) of patients 65 years of age and older reported continuous sobriety over a 12-month posttreatment period. This figure is similar to the 12-month sobriety rate of 63 percent identified among patients of all ages treated in the program (Wiens and Menustik 1983). Neuberger et al. (1982) followed patients exposed to aversion conditioning treatment at another facility. They found slightly lower average 1-year abstinence rates (52 percent) among retired (age 62 and older) medicare patients than among non-medicare patients (59 percent). In addition, after controlling for prognostic factors at intake, Janik and Dunham (1983) did not identify any differences in 6-month outcomes between older (ages 60 and over) and younger (ages 21 to 59) patients who were seen in a nationwide sample of NIAAA supported programs. Moreover, the two groups of patients received roughly comparable amounts and types of treatment.

An apparent responsiveness of older alcoholics to socially oriented therapy led Zimberg (1978) to recommend that treatment for such patients be targeted toward the psychosocial stressors associated with aging. This idea is supported by an evaluation of a special older alcohol rehabilitation program that included information on the psychosocial and physical aspects of aging and community resources for the elderly, and that stressed creative socialization and the activity theory of successful aging. Graduates of the special program showed more positive change on multiple outcome dimensions than demographically similar graduates of a traditional VA inpatient alcoholism program (Thomas-Knight 1978). However, since similar results have been obtained in treatment research on younger patients, such findings are not unique to older problem drinkers. For instance, Azrin (1976) reported that an alcoholism program that focused on patients' marital, employment, and other stressors proved more effective than conventional hospital treatment.

Conducting Conceptually Informed Alcoholism Evaluation Research

Evaluation research among older (as well as younger) problem drinkers has been guided by a paradigm in which individuals are assessed on personal and drinking-related factors (panels I and II in the framework), exposed to a treatment (or control) condition (panel IV), and then reevaluated to identify treatment-related changes in their behavior and adaptation (panel VII). The framework we espouse expands this summative paradigm in at least two ways. First, it points to the need to document the implementation and delivery of treatment and assess the quantity and quality of treatment processes. Second, the framework considers life context or extratreatment factors as important determinants of treatment entry, duration, and outcome. These issues are involved in examining the effects of treatments that range from pharmacological interventions (such as disulfiram) to community treatment (such as AA), as well as in identifying factors involved in recovery without treatment.

Implementation Assessment and Process Analyses. An examination of treatment implementation considers the quantity and quality of treatment activity. This assessment can be conducted either by documenting what was done by treatment providers, or by demonstrating that treatment produced in clients intermediate changes presumed to foster the ultimate positive outcome. In either case, evaluators must identify the congruence between the intervention as actually conducted and responded to and the intervention as it was intended to be applied and experienced. Relevant standards for assessing the amount and quality of treatment can be developed from normative information about conditions in other programs and theoretical analysis and expert judgment (Moos and Finney 1983; Sechrest et al. 1979). For example, expert judgment may imply that residential treatment for older problem drinkers be relatively structured and oriented toward ameliorating the social stressors associated with aging (Zimberg 1978). More generally, assessment of treatment implementation can alert providers to differences in the treatment selected by and allocated to older vs. younger problem drinkers.

Treatment process analyses focus on the causal chain between treatment and outcome. One overarching linkage in that chain is the relationship between treatment as actually delivered and outcome. For instance, we found that attendance at Sunday worship services in a Salvation Army program was as strongly related to 6-month abstinence as other treatment components (Bromet et al. 1977). Moreover, conditioning sessions may not be the only active treatment component in an aversion-oriented program; participation in AA meetings is also linked to treatment outcome. In addition, the perceived quality of residential alcoholism programs, based on factors such as cohesion, organization, and an orientation toward independence and self-understanding, is associated with treatment outcome. These findings show the value of considering the quantity and quality of treatment as independent predictors of outcome (Cronkite and Moos 1978). By exploring age and treatment component interactions in process analyses, researchers may be able to isolate components that are especially effective among older patients.

Extratreatment Factors and Treatment Formulations. Although comparatively little is known about the impact of extratreatment or life context factors on alcohol abuse, current evidence points to this as a highly promising area. In this regard, we estimated a conceptual model that considered three domains of extratreatment factors--stressful events and family and coping resources--in conjunction with patient and treatment factors. Information about the contextual factors accounted for an increment of between 7 and 27 percent of the variance in treatment outcome (depending on the specific criterion), compared with between 4 and 20 percent accounted for by patient-related and treatment-related factors (Cronkite and Moos 1980). In short, the inclusion of information about patients' life contexts more than doubled the explained variance in treatment outcome. These findings support the idea that alcoholism treatment may be more effective when oriented toward patients' ongoing life circumstances (Azrin 1976).

Knowledge about the causal mechanisms through which a treatment exerts its effects--including the extratreatment factors that enhance or impede positive outcome--can help to generate new and potentially more effective intervention strategies. Recognizing that stressful or relapse-inducing life situations inevitably occur, researchers have begun to identify coping resources that clients can acquire to help them deal with these situations more effectively. Marlatt (1982) is using a cognitive social learning model to develop individualized intervention strategies that reduce the probability of relapse episodes and help patients to handle them effectively when they occur. Such developments highlight the inadequacy of the model of intensive residential treatment during which the endogenous disease is treated, followed by occasional aftercare or check-up visits. In fact, Litman (1980) has suggested a restructuring of alcoholism treatment in which hospitalization, if necessary, is followed by intensive outpatient treatment (not aftercare) oriented specifically toward the prevention of relapse.

More generally, our perspective affirms the need for a fundamental shift in thinking about intervention programs and their effects. The paradigm we have described explicitly assumes that treatment is part of an open system. An intervention program is but one (indeed, a temporary one) of the multiple microsystems or specific settings that influence problem drinking and other aspects of adaptation. Other powerful current environments also shape individual mood and behavior; subsequently, the initial effects of an intervention can be augmented or nullified by new contextual factors. For instance, community settings can influence treatment settings by inhibiting their effects (as when the family or peer group does not value abstinence as a treatment goal), by augmenting their effects (as when family and social factors reinforce an abstinence-oriented treatment program), or by compensating for their lack of effects (as when AA teaches clients skills--such as how to refuse drinks at social gatherings--that they have not learned in treatment).

Matching Older Patients with Treatments. The heterogeneity in older patients' responses to alcoholism treatment emphasizes the potential value of matching different groups of patients with appropriate forms of treatment. In comparison with younger patients, for example, older alcoholics tend to experience more serious and persistent cognitive impairment, especially in information processing, short-term memory, abstraction, and problem-solving abilities (Goldman 1983). Such cognitive deficits need to be considered in implementing problem-solving or coping skills training approaches. As a case in point, Sanchez-Craig and Walker (1982) taught chronic alcoholic halfway house residents a 5-step problem-solving process to criterion. One month after training, however, only 5 of the 15 residents were able to remember at least 4 of the 5 steps and only 2 residents recalled all 5 steps. Thus, selection of an appropriate treatment method should be determined in part by the match between the cognitive demands of the treatment and a patient's current cognitive ability (Wilkinson and Sanchez-Craig 1981).

Another general perspective assumes that competent people have greater latitude for person-environment congruence and are able to function effectively in a wide range of situations. Conversely, less competent individuals can function adequately in a relatively narrow range of settings (Lawton 1982). Similarly, Hunt's (1975) conceptual level matching model posits that more conceptually able individuals are able to organize their own environments, while those who are less able need the stabilizing effect of a well-structured setting. McLachlan (1974) used this model to identify relevant cognitive capabilities and conceptual styles of alcoholic patients and to characterize the degree of structure to which they were exposed during inpatient treatment and aftercare. Consistent with his hypothesis, McLachlan (1974) found that low conceptual level patients benefited more from structured treatment that compensated for their inability to structure their own experiences. High conceptual level patients did better in a less structured setting that encouraged them to use their own resources (a setting that was thought to create confusion in low conceptual level patients).

These findings are consistent with the idea that less disturbed patients can do well in fairly stimulating high expectation environments, while their more disturbed counterparts need a tolerant and relatively well-organized setting that insulates them from too many demands (Moos, in press a). They suggest that older, impaired patients may do better in somewhat more structured environments, and that clinicians need to be especially thoughtful in selecting appropriate treatment settings for such patients. Such considerations imply that the finding of little or no difference in treatment outcome between younger and older alcoholics may stem from inappropriate treatment allocation. Thus, it is premature to conclude that older alcoholics do not need specialized treatment regimens (Janik and Dunham 1983).

Future Directions

The framework we have described can help to guide and integrate research on what typically are separate lines of empirical work--those on etiology and those on treatment impact. The model can identify commonalities and gaps in our knowledge about the influence of contextual and treatment system factors on older problem drinkers. A critical need in future studies in this area is to identify the risk factors that cause older persons to be vulnerable to excessive drinking. At the same time, such studies should try to clarify the causal mechanisms through which stressful circumstances may activate problem drinking and those (including treatment) that may inhibit it.

The framework also applies to patients being treated for unipolar depression and their families and to persons with serious medical conditions, as well as to representative groups of normal men and women (Moos, in press a, in press b). There is some evidence that the salient factors and processes related to the formation of diagnosable disorders such as alcohol abuse and depression are similar (albeit accentuated) to those involved in normal variations in adaptation among healthy individuals. Thus, a systems perspective can serve to integrate work on problem drinking among the elderly into the mainstream of stress research. As evidence from such studies accumulates, treatment providers should be better able to identify older persons at risk for problem drinking and, ultimately, to intervene more effectively.

REFERENCES

Abrahams, R., and Patterson, P. Psychological distress among the community elderly: Prevalence, characteristics, and implications for service. International Journal of Aging and Human Development 9:1-19, 1978-79.

Azrin, W. Improvements in the community-reinforcement approach to alcoholism. Behavior Research and Therapy 14:339-348, 1976.

Bailey, M.; Haberman, P.; and Alksne, H. The epidemiology of alcoholism in an urban residential area. Quarterly Journal of Studies on Alcohol 26:19-40, 1965.

Barnes, G. Alcohol use among older persons: Findings from a western New York State general population survey. Journal of the American Geriatrics Society 27:244-250, 1979.

Brody, J. Aging and alcohol abuse. Journal of the American Geriatric Society 30:123-126, 1982.

Bromet, E.; Moos, R.; Bliss, F.; and Wuthmann, C. Posttreatment functioning of alcoholic patients: Its relation to program participation. Journal of Consulting and Clinical Psychology 45:829-842, 1977.

Chiriboga, D., and Cutler, L. Stress and adaptation: Life span perspectives. In L. W. Poon (Ed.), Aging in the 1980s. Washington, D.C.: American Psychological Association, 1980.

Clark, W., and Midanik, L. Alcohol use and alcohol problems among U.S. adults: Results of the 1979 national survey. Research Report, Alcohol Research Group, Berkeley, Calif., 1980.

Cronkite, R., and Moos, R. Evaluating alcoholism treatment programs: An integrated approach. Journal of Consulting and Clinical Psychology 46:1105-1119, 1978.

Cronkite, R., and Moos, R. Determinants of the posttreatment functioning of alcoholic patients: A conceptual framework. Journal of Consulting and Clinical Psychology 48:305-316, 1980.

Dohrenwend, B.S., and Dohrenwend, B.P., eds. Stressful Life Events and Their Contexts. New York: Neale Watson, 1981.

Finney, J., and Moos, R. Life stressors and problem drinking among older adults. In: Galanter, M., ed. Recent Developments in Alcoholism. Vol. 2. New York: Plenum, in press.

Finney, J.; Moos, R.; and Mewborn, C.R. Posttreatment experiences and treatment outcome of alcoholic patients six months and two years after hospitalization. Journal of Consulting and Clinical Psychology 48:17-29, 1980.

Gaitz, C., and Baer, P. Characteristics of elderly patients with alcoholism. Archives of General Psychiatry 24:372-378, 1971.

George, L. Role Transitions in Later Life. Monterey, Calif.: Brooks/Cole, 1980.

Glynn, R.; Bouchard, G.; LoCastro, J.; and Hermos, J. Changes in alcohol consumption behaviors among men in the Normative Aging Study. (in this volume)

Goldman, M. Cognitive impairment in chronic alcoholics: Some cause for optimism. American Psychologist 38:1045-1054, 1983.

Gordon, T., and Kannel, W. Drinking and its relation to smoking, BP, blood lipids, and uric acid: The Framingham study. Archives of Internal Medicine 143:1366-1374, 1983.

Helzer, J.; Miller, R.; and Carey, K. Predictors and correlates of recovery in older versus younger alcoholics. (in this volume)

Hermos, J.; LoCastro, J.; Bouchard, G.; and Glynn, R. Influence of cardiovascular disease on alcohol consumption in middle and older aged men. (in this volume)

Holzer, C.; Myers, J.; Weissman, M.; Tischler, G.; and Leaf, P. Antecedents and correlates of alcohol abuse and dependence in the elderly. (in this volume)

Hubbard, R.; Santos, J.; and Santos, M. Alcohol and older adults: Overt and covert influences. Social Casework 60:166-170, 1979.

Hunt, D. Person-environment interaction: A challenge found wanting before it was tried. Review of Educational Research 45:209-230, 1975.

Hyman, M. Alcoholics 15 years later. Annals of the New York Academy of Sciences 273:613-623, 1976.

Janik, S., and Dunham, R. A nationwide examination of the need for specific alcoholism treatment programs for the elderly. Journal of Studies on Alcohol 44:307-317, 1983.

Kobasa, S., and Puccetti, M. Personality and social resources in stress resistance. Journal of Personality and Social Psychology 45:839-850, 1983.

Lawton, M.P. Competence, environmental press, and the adaptation of older people. In: Lawton, M.P.; Windley, P.G.; and Byerts, T.O., eds. Aging and the Environment: Theoretical Approaches. New York: Springer, pp. 33-59.

Litman, G. Relapse in alcoholism: Traditional and current approaches. In: Edwards, G., and Grant, M., eds. Alcohol Treatment in Transition. Baltimore: University Park Press, 1980. pp. 294-303.

Mackie, J. The Cement of the Universe: A Study of Causation. Oxford, England: Clarendon Press, 1974.

Marlatt, G. Relapse prevention: A self-control program for the treatment of addictive behaviors. In: Stuart, R.B., ed. Adherence, Compliance, and Generalization in Behavioral Medicine. New York: Brunner/Mazel, 1982. pp. 329-378.

McCrae, R. Age differences in the use of coping mechanisms. Journal of Gerontology 37:454-460, 1982.

McLachlan, J. Therapy strategies, personality orientation, and recovery from alcoholism. Canadian Psychiatric Association Journal 19:25-30, 1974.

Meehl, P. Specific etiology and other forms of strong inference: Some quantitative meanings. Journal of Medicine and Philosophy 2:33-53, 1977.

Merry, J. Alcoholism in the aged. British Journal of Alcohol and Alcoholism 15:56-57, 1980.

Meyers, A.; Hingson, R.; Mucatel, M.; and Goldman, E. Social and psychologic correlates of problem drinking in old age. Journal of the American Geriatric Society 30:453-456, 1982.

Moos, R. Context and coping: Toward a unifying conceptual framework. American Journal of Community Psychology in press a.

Moos, R. Creating healthy human contexts: Environmental and individual stress. In: Rosen, J., and Solomon, L., eds. Prevention in Health Psychology. New York: Wiley, in press b.

Moos, R., and Billings, A. Conceptualizing and measuring coping resources and processes. In: Goldberger, L., and Breznitz, S., eds. <u>Handbook of Stress: Theoretical and Clinical Aspects</u>. New York: Macmillan, 1982. pp. 212-230.

Moos, R., and Finney J. The expanding scope of alcoholism treatment evaluation. <u>American Psychologist</u> 38:1036-1044, 1983.

Moos, R., and Mitchell, R. Social network resources and adaptation: A conceptual framework. In: Wills, T.A., ed. <u>Basic Processes in Helping Relationships</u>. New York: Academic Press, 1982. pp. 213-232.

Neubuerger, O.; Miller, S.; Schmitz, R.; Matarazzo, J.; Pratt, H.; and Hasha, N. Replicable abstinence rates in an alcoholism treatment program. <u>Journal of the American Medical Association</u> 248:960-963, 1982.

Pearlin, L., and Schooler, C. The structure of coping. <u>Journal of Health and Social Behavior</u> 19:2-21, 1978.

Peck, D. Alcohol abuse and the elderly: Social control and conformity. <u>Journal of Drug Abuse</u> 9:63-71, 1979.

Pilisuk, M., and Minkler, M. Supportive networks: Life ties for the elderly. <u>Journal of Social Issues</u> 36:95-116, 1980.

Reifler, B.; Kethley, A.; O'Neill, P.; Hanley, R.; Lewis, S.; and Stencheuer, D. Five year experience of a community outreach program for the elderly. <u>American Journal of Psychiatry</u> 139:220-223, 1982.

Rosin, A., and Glatt, M. Alcohol excess in the elderly. <u>Quarterly Journal of Studies on Alcohol</u> 32:53-59, 1971.

Sanchez-Craig, M., and Walker, K. Teaching coping skills to chronic alcoholics in a coeducational halfway house. I: Assessment of programme effects. <u>British Journal of Addiction</u> 77:35-50, 1982.

Schuckit, M., and Miller, P. Alcoholism in elderly men: A survey of a general hospital medical ward. <u>Annals of the New York Academy of Sciences</u> 273:558-571, 1976.

Schuckit, M., and Pastor, P. The elderly as a unique population: Alcoholism. <u>Alcoholism</u> 2:31-38, 1978.

Schuckit, M.; Atkinson, J.; Miller, P.; and Berman, J. A three-year follow-up of elderly alcoholics. Journal of Clinical Psychiatry 41:412-416, 1980.

Sechrest, L.; West, S.; Phillips, M.; Redner, R.; and Yeaton, W. Some neglected problems in evaluation research: Strength and integrity of treatments. In: Sechrest, L.; West, W.; Phillips, M.; Redner, R.; and Yeaton, W., eds. Evaluation Studies Review Annual. Vol. 4. Beverly Hills, Calif.: Sage, 1979. pp. 15-35.

Straus, R. Keynote remarks. (in this volume)

Thomas-Knight, R. Treating alcoholism among the aged: The effectiveness of a special treatment program for older problem drinkers. Dissertation Abstracts International 39:3009-B, 1978.

Tuchfeld, B. Spontaneous remission in alcoholics: Empirical observations and theoretical observations. Journal of Studies on Alcohol 42:626-641, 1981.

Warheit, G., and Auth, J. The mental health and social correlates of alcohol use among differing life cycle groups. (in this volume)

Wells-Parker, E.; Miles, S.; and Spencer, B. Stress experiences and drinking histories of elderly drunken driving offenders. Journal of Studies on Alcohol 44:429-437, 1983.

Wiens, A., and Menustik, C. Treatment outcome and patient characteristics in an aversion therapy program for alcoholics. American Psychologist 38:1089-1096, 1983.

Wiens, A.; Menustik, C.; Miller, S.; and Schmitz, R. Medical-behavioral treatment of the older alcoholic patient. American Journal of Drug and Alcohol Abuse, in press.

Wilkinson, D.A., and Sanchez-Craig, M. Relevance of brain dysfunction in treatment objectives: Should alcohol-related cognitive deficits influence the way we think about treatment? Addictive Behaviors 6:253-260, 1981.

Zimberg, S. Diagnosis and treatment of the elderly alcoholic. Alcoholism 2:27-29, 1978.

INTRODUCTION: SESSION II

Lee N. Robins, Chairman

We probably won't quite live up to Dr. Maddox's buildup in terms of solving all the problems you might ever want answered. I notice there are a lot of young people in the audience, and you can be sure we will leave you a little something to do in the alcohol/aging field even after today. We certainly have been busy, and we have thought about the whole conceptual aspect of the program a great deal. I doubt if any program ever has had more people thinking harder about it. One of the architects of that program is Ben Locke. There is no one who can tell you better about how it was conceived and what it was intended to do. Following Ben's presentation, my paper will be presented and then papers from the Epidemiologic Catchment Area sites.

The Epidemiologic Catchment Area Program is a series of five epidemiologic research studies performed by independent research teams in collaboration with staff of the Division of Biometry and Epidemiology (DBE) of the National Institute of Mental Health (NIMH). The NIMH principal collaborators are Darrel A. Regier, Ben Z. Locke, and William W. Eaton; the NIMH Project Officer is Carl A. Taube. The principal investigators and co-investigators from the five sites are: Yale University, U01 MH34224--Jerome K. Myers, Myrna M. Weissman, and Gary L. Tischler; Johns Hopkins University, U01 MH33870--Morton Kramer, Ernest Gruenberg, and Sam Shapiro; Washington University, St. Louis, U01 MH33883--Lee N. Robins and Johns Helzer, Duke University, U01 MH35386--Dan Blazer and Linda George; University of California, Los Angeles, U01 MH35865--Richard L. Hough, Marvin Karno, Javier I. Escobar, M. Audrey Burnam, and Dianne M. Timbers.

THE EPIDEMIOLOGIC CATCHMENT AREA PROGRAM OF NIMH

Ben Z. Locke

ABSTRACT

An overview of the Epidemiologic Catchment Area Program (ECA) of NIMH is presented: its development, objectives, population characteristics, and historical context. The program involved five independent research sites in collaboration with the Division of Biometry and Epidemiology of NIMH. The broad aims of the ECA Program are the historical goals of psychiatric epidemiology: to estimate the incidence and prevalence rates for specific mental disorders, to study factors influencing the development and continuance of these disorders, to estimate rates of health and mental services use and factors influencing such use. Six months prevalence data presented in this report are from the first three sites to complete their field work and analyze the data obtained from the household interviews. The three most common disorders in these three study areas are phobias, alcohol abuse and/or dependence, and major depression. All three sites show that for women the most common diagnoses were phobias and major depression whereas for men the predominant psychiatric disorder was alcohol abuse/or dependence. Less than half of the participants with a recent DIS/DSM III disorder had a visit in the past 6 months to either a mental health specialist or a general medical provider. Other types of data dealing with functioning and activities of daily living are mentioned.

As we all know, epidemiology is the study of the occurrence, distribution, and determinants of states of health in a population. The ultimate goals of epidemiology are to contribute to an understanding of the etiology of these states and to their control. A more immediate use is the planning and/or evaluation of health services and programs (WHO 1960).

In psychiatric epidemiology, we usually have minimal data about persons undergoing psychiatric treatment. Even less is known about those many people in the general population who are so psychiatrically impaired as to meet the diagnostic criteria, yet not be in treatment. There are as yet no accurate estimates of the level of need for treatment and few good estimates of the rates of prevalence of specific psychiatric disorders. The factors that facilitate or obstruct pathways to treatment are unknown. Knowledge about those in high risk groups who successfully cope and avoid treatment is meager. Most important, the incidence of specific mental disorders is not known, and etiologic or associated risk factors are few and not well understood. Inasmuch as the bottom line, indeed the Holy Grail, for all epidemiologists is prevention, it is obvious that in addressing the mental disorders we have a long way to go.

In 1978 the President's Commission on Mental Health (1978) highlighted the dearth of epidemiologic data with which to estimate the need for facilities. The report recommended "immediate efforts to gather reliable data . . . on the incidence of mental health problems and the utilization of mental health services." I had the good fortune of having specified the need for a program like the Epidemiologic Catchment Area (ECA) in the Center's 5-year plan a year earlier. The, then, institute director (Bertram Brown, M.D.) decided to move ahead, and the ECA Program became a major NIMH initiative in response to this and other recommendations of the commission. The next institute director (Herbert Pardes, M.D.) continued to give it his full support.

This paper will present an overview of the ECA program--its development, objectives, population characteristics, and historical context. Such a review is timely since results of the initial survey of the noninstitutionalized population are now available for the first four of five study sites. This presentation follows 6 years of conceptual development, planning, data collection, and data analysis that will help us begin to bridge some of the major epidemiologic and services research gaps identified by the report of the President's Commission on Mental Health (1978). ECA program research advances should be viewed as part of the third generation of mental disorder epidemiologic studies, a generation that will take advantage of recent improvements in mental disorder diagnostic criteria, standardized diagnostic interviews, survey research design, and computerized data processing.

First generation studies are those conducted, in the main, prior to World War II; they relied heavily on institutional records and key informants. Second generation studies, conducted in the early 1950s (e.g., Stirling Co., 1952; Baltimore, 1953-54; Midtown Manhattan, 1954) involved direct interviews of community residents by nonclinician interviewers using structured interview protocols and subsequent ratings by one or more psychiatrists (Dohrenwend and Dohrenwend 1982).

The Epidemiologic Catchment Area (ECA) Program is a developmental series of epidemiologic research studies performed by independent research teams in collaboration with the Center for

Epidemiologic Studies of the National Institute of Mental Health. The broad aims of the ECA Program are the historical goals of psychiatric epidemiology: to estimate the rates of prevalence and incidence of mental disorders; to study factors influencing the development and continuance of these disorders, to estimate rates of health and mental health services use; and to study factors influencing use of services. One might assume that getting to the truth of these issues would be a relatively straightforward methodologic task, but as most researchers know or quickly learn, finding the truth of a matter is a peculiar process in which we aim at the bull's-eye but are lucky if we hit the target. The important thing is to minimize the error inherent in the measurement process. The two principles of control and measurement of error have guided the design of the program's methodology. This methodology is more complex and sophisticated than that in any prior psychiatric general population survey.

In short, although the ECA Program retains the historical goals of mental health epidemiology, the methodologies involved are not in general use. Table 1 illustrates the five methodologic aspects of the ECA Program that together form the basic research design: the emphasis on specific diagnoses; the integration of community and institutional surveys; the collection of prevalence and incidence data; the systematic linkage of service utilization data with other epidemiologic variables; and the multisite comparative-collaborative aspect. None of these aspects is totally new to the field, but they have never been combined in this way, and we feel that data from the ECA Program may address these traditional goals in an innovative fashion. I will now address each of these five aspects.

Table 1.-- Methodologic Aspects of the ECA Program

Specific diagnoses with lay interviewers (DIS)

Coordinated community and institution surveys

Incidence data

Service utilization data linked to diagnoses

Comparative-collaborative aspect

Specific Mental Disorders

A major difference between the ECA Program and many other recent epidemiologic studies is the focus on specific mental disorders instead of on global impairment ratings. Until the early 1950s, the dominant conceptual framework for psychiatric epidemiology was the medical model. After World War II, various developments established community survey research as a practical, accepted technology: the development of multiple-item scaling, accurate and usable survey sampling, and standardized interview training, to name just a few. Researchers also became more aware of the need for assessing the reliability and validity of their measurements. In mental health epidemiology, it became clear that psychiatric diagnoses could not be made with acceptable reliability and validity using existing survey technology, or even, some would say, in standard clinical practice. Therefore, the field switched over to mental health scales that measured overall impairment as the best indicator of need for treatment. This trend began with the famous Midtown-Manhattan Study and the Stirling County, Nova Scotia Study and has continued to the present, with a few exceptions.

The trend toward global mental health ratings satisfied the need of psychiatric epidemiologists to accommodate survey technology, but was in opposition to many changes in the area of psychiatric classification. Increasingly, available epidemiologic evidence suggested that different types of mental disorders were differentially related to demographic variables such as sex, social class, area residence, and so forth (Dohrenwend 1975). Genetic evidence began to suggest that there were different degrees of inheritance for the different specific diagnoses (Weissman and Klerman 1978). Also, new drugs were discovered that had beneficial effects for specific diagnoses and not for others (Berger 1978). In the areas of classification and diagnosis, operational criteria for diagnoses were developed, along with standardized interview questionnaires and standardized interviewer training techniques, to improve the reliability of diagnosis (Endicott and Spitzer 1978; Helzer et al. 1977).

Therefore, one very important contribution of the ECA Program has been its focus on specific mental disorders without sacrificing interest in rigorous survey methodology. The vehicle to accomplish this end is the NIMH Diagnostic Interview Schedule (DIS), which focuses on specific disorders and takes advantage of the recently developed capabilities in diagnostic assessment (Regier et al. 1978). Credit for initiating workshops to discuss the DIS and to contract for its development belongs to Dr. Darrel Regier, Director of the Division of Biometry and Epidemiology, NIMH. Table 2 shows the specific DSM-III disorders addressed by our DIS. The findings

Table 2.—Adequacy of Lay Interviewers in Giving DIS Version II: Lifetime DSM-III Diagnoses Without Exclusion Criteria

	N Positive	Kappa	Sensitivity (percent)	Specificity (percent)
Anorexia nervosa	9	1.00	100	100
Pathological gambling	13	.96	92	100
Alcohol abuse	77	.86	86	98
Alcohol dependence	52	.80	79	97
Organic: mild/severe	20	.79	85	97
Tobacco use disorder	108	.78	89	90
Drug abuse	26	.73	88	94
Drug dependence	23	.77	87	96
Agoraphobia	53	.67	77	91
Simple phobia	39	.47	59	88
Mania	31	.65	65	97
Antisocial personality	16	.63	75	96
Depression	99	.63	80	84
Obsessive compulsive	30	.60	63	95
Schizophrenia	34	.60	65	94
Psychosexual	71	.56	72	84
Somatization	32	.50	41	99
Panic	39	.40	44	93

from a clinical validation study conducted by Robins, its principal developer, have been published, and other clinical concordance studies are nearing completion. The important point is that the DIS converts the methodology of clinical assessment to that of field surveys, for the first time. The implications of this development for the field of psychiatric epidemiology are quite broad: It not only ties the field into diagnostic categories on which much laboratory and clinical research is being done (thus aiding in the search for etiologic clues) but it also ties the field into diagnostic categories used in clinical practice (thus aiding in the planning of mental health facilities and provision of services).

Before going on to the overall ECA Program, one other comment is in order. It is best stated by Robins et al. (1981, p. 385) as follows:

> The DIS also differs from the PSE in providing lifetime as well as current diagnoses and differs from both the PSE and SADS in defining "current" flexibly so that results can be compared with the one-month definition of the PSE or the

one-year definition of the SADS. But the DIS's most important difference from both the PSE and the SADS lies in the degree to which questions and probes have been specified (so that the interviewer is not called on to improvise questions) and the degree to which scoring of symptoms follows automatically from answers to the questions posed (to minimize the clinical judgment required). These features make possible the use of lay interviewers after a fairly brief training period.

Furthermore, the DIS has the advantage of serving more than one diagnostic schema, so that the alternative systems can be compared. It also offers flexibility with respect to using or ignoring diagnostic hierarchies, which makes it possible to compare different methods for established hierarchies.

It should be noted, as will be seen in a figure later on, that not all these diagnoses were obtained at all sites. Because the ECA Program is conducted as a cooperative agreement, it necessitated our obtaining Office of Management and Budget (OMB) clearance. OMB disallowed questions requisite to making a diagnosis of psychosexual dysfunction. I should note, however, that some sites were also not interested in obtaining that diagnosis or a diagnosis of tobacco use disorder or pathological gambling. On the other hand, OMB and our study design did allow each site approximately 30 minutes time to collect data dear to their research interests. Obviously, Lee Robins at Washington University, our St. Louis site, elected to obtain these data.

It should also be noted that the published clinical validation, from which table 2 was derived, is based on lifetime DSM-III diagnoses using DIS version II. Except for wave 1 at Yale University, all sites have used DIS version III. But note, please, that while the kappa for a few diagnoses is of an order not conducive to confidence, it is quite good with regard to alcohol abuse and dependence.

Let me return to the major design and issues at the time the program was initiated. The requirement for data on specific disorders necessitates a larger sample size than is common in psychiatric epidemiologic studies. The sample size for the general population surveys at each site in the ECA Program is set at 4,000 households. Interviewing one member of the household, and allowing for a 75 percent response rate, yields an estimated 3,000 respondents in the general population. The relatively new emphasis on specific mental disorders requires much larger sample sizes than research conducted on global impairment ratings because of the rarity of the specific disorders. Although as many as 10 to 20 percent of the general population may have *some* mental disorder at any given time, fewer than 5 percent will have *any specific* disorder, and for many disorders the point prevalence may be closer to 1 percent or less (Weissman et al. 1978). These low frequencies mean that even with a large sample, the yield in cases of specific mental disorders is relatively small.

Community and Institution Surveys

A second aspect of the methodology implemented by the ECA Program is the integration of data from community surveys with data from institutions. Surveys have been conducted in each of such settings, but it is rare to use both methods simultaneously and rarer still to rigorously integrate the two methods. The aim of the ECA Program is to study the total true prevalence of specific mental disorders--that is, the prevalence of these disorders without regard to treatment status.

A result of the increase in the community surveys and related research after the war was the realization that many persons with bona fide mental disorders never entered a treatment setting. The implication was that epidemiologic data based on admission to treatment were of dubious value for etiologic research and for rational planning of services and facilities. This realization became clear fairly early to epidemiologists and social scientists, and both groups began to study in detail the processes by which individuals with personal problems found their way into the psychiatric treatment system (Hammer 1963; Kadushin 1969; Kitsuse and Cicourel 1963; Scheff 1966). Later on it became apparent that the majority of persons treated for psychiatric problems were treated in the general health care sector, not the psychiatric sector (Locke and Gardner 1969; Regier et al. 1978). But since data on psychiatric problems are not routinely collected in general health care facilities, this fact only emphasized the difficulty of studying the total true prevalence of mental disorders.

The dissatisfaction with treated case data was one reason for shifting to field surveys, but the shift entailed a loss of data on specific mental disorders, as discussed earlier. Dohrenwend and Dohrenwend (1969) are illustrative of those researchers who decided to completely ignore psychiatric epidemiologic research that relied on treated case studies.

The degree to which individuals with psychiatric disorders are treated varies by specific diagnosis. After an intensive search for cases in Detroit, Dunham concluded that "virtually all schizophrenics are eventually hospitalized" (1965). In a study in rural Sweden, 12 psychotics were located through a combination of case-finding techniques, and all 12 had been seen by a physician (Hagnell 1966), 11 by a psychiatrist. Thus, it would appear that most psychotics receive some sort of psychiatric treatment, although there are exceptions in some rural or premodern societies such as the Hutterites (Eaton and Weil 1953). For nonpsychotic disorders, the proportion treated is probably much lower. Data from treatment institutions probably include a higher proportion of the total population of schizophrenics than do community data; but for depressive disorders, probably the majority are not treated, and community data are more accurate. The upshot of these considerations is that data solely from community surveys are also inaccurate because they miss severe cases in treatment. Thus, one requirement of the ECA Program has been the integration of community surveys with surveys of institution residents (see figure 1). For needs assessment research and planning purposes, it would be best to do comprehensive surveys in each setting; for epidemiologic research it was essential to obtain an overall combined picture in these initial sites.

In the ECA Program, the sites for research are previously designated Community Mental Health Center Catchment Areas, from which the name of the program itself comes. These are geographic areas with populations of 75,000 to 250,000, but to insure a large enough population base for the sample survey, the program requires an area with a minimum population size of 200,000.

The sample size for the survey of the institutions had been tentatively set at 500. As well as an increase in precision for the total prevalence rate, the sample size of 500 will yield rough estimates of the overall rate of mental disorders within each of the three major types of institutions (mental hospitals, homes for the aged, and prisons).

Incidence and Prevalence Data

Another aspect of the ECA Program is the emphasis on incidence. Incidence rates are superior to prevalence rates for etiologic studies because differences between groups are uncontaminated by mortality and less contaminated by insidious onset and secondary complications. For diseases that are often fatal (e.g., heart disease or cancer), the first advantage of the incidence rate is most important; for chronic, nonfatal diseases (e.g., diabetes and mental disorders) the second advantage is more important. Mental disorders develop over extended periods of time, sometimes moving from one diagnosis to another or from one level of severity to another, in as yet unknown ways. The incidence rate gives the investigator the least contaminated look at the disorder, and etiologic relationships should be more visible. If there is a precipitating event, the investigator should be able to discern it much more easily than if it occurred in the distant past. Incidence rates and etiologic relationships are relevant to programs of primary prevention. For other planning and services, prevalence

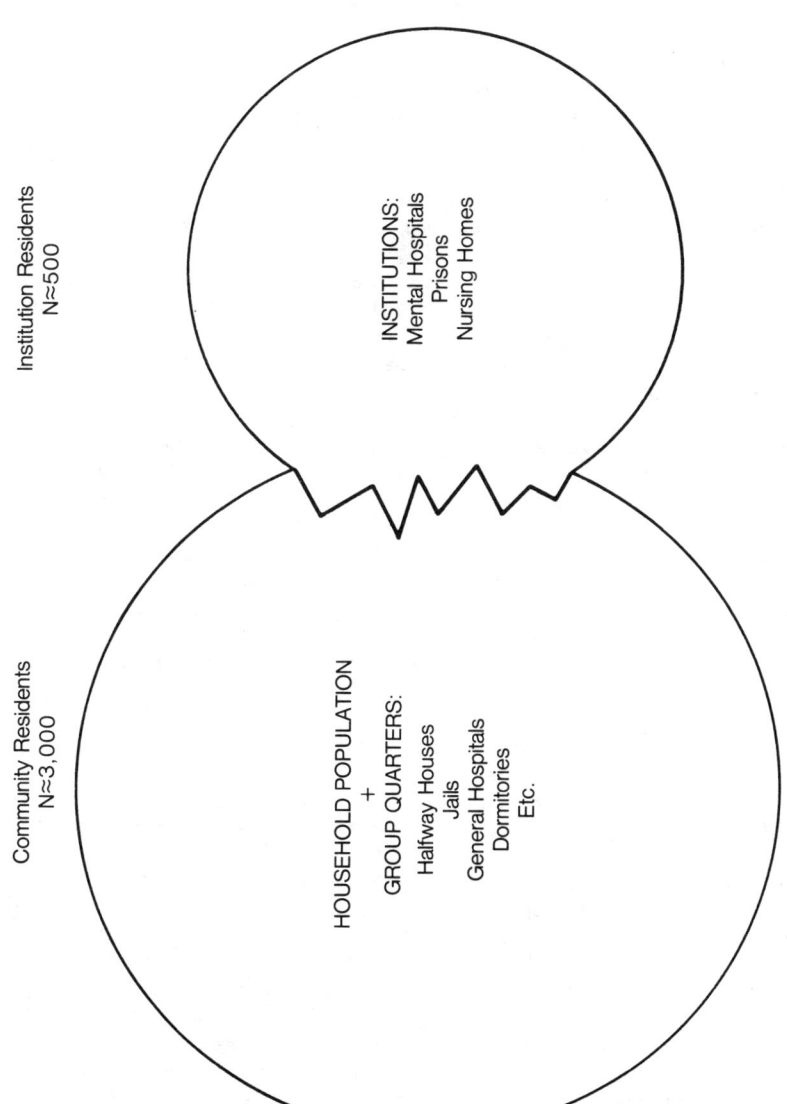

Figure 1.—Coordination of Community and Institution Surveys in ECA Program

rates are superior because they are closer to an estimate of demand for treatment. The familiar epidemiologic equation $P = I \times D$, where P = prevalence, I = incidence, and D = duration, emphasizes the relationships.

The ECA Program requires at least two waves of interviews on the same individuals in both the community and the institution surveys (see figure 2). Two waves are the minimum required for identification of new cases.

Briefly, please note some of the data obtained at each wave and what inferences such information allows. At wave 1, we will obtain lifetime symptom counts, lifetime diagnosis, and lifetime utilization of services. (Yes, we are well aware of problems involving recall!) Also note that prevalence could be for the usual point prevalence (past 2 weeks), but could also be for longer periods of time. That relates to my earlier quote from Robins regarding the 1-month definition used in the PSE and the 1-year definition used by SADS. Wave 2, as shown in figure 2, is 1-year later except at Yale. At Yale, our first ECA site, we conducted the household interview at 6-month intervals. Therefore, 1 year after the initial interview Yale had a wave 3.

Because of cost constraints, we could only conduct household interviews 1 year later at all other sites. It was our intent to conduct telephone interviews obtaining some minimal service utilization data at 3-month intervals at the other four sites, but again due to cost constraints, we only had one telephone interview at the 6-month interval.

Linkage with Service Utilization Data

Another fundamental innovation in the ECA Program is the systematic collection of survey data from individuals on their use of psychiatric, general health, and other human services. Integrating the institutional and general population surveys and studying incidence rates are crucially important for this health services research aspect of the ECA Program. The single most important advantage of the inclusion of the two separate surveys (institutional and general population) is that it gives a clean (though perhaps primitive) measure of unmet need by counting psychiatrically disordered persons who are not being treated. Areas where there are many such persons may be candidates for new treatment facilities or other innovative service programs. Groups including many persons meeting criteria for diagnosis but not in treatment are underserved (President's Commission on Mental Health 1978).

EPIDEMIOLOGIC CATCHMENT AREA PROGRAM OF NIMH 185

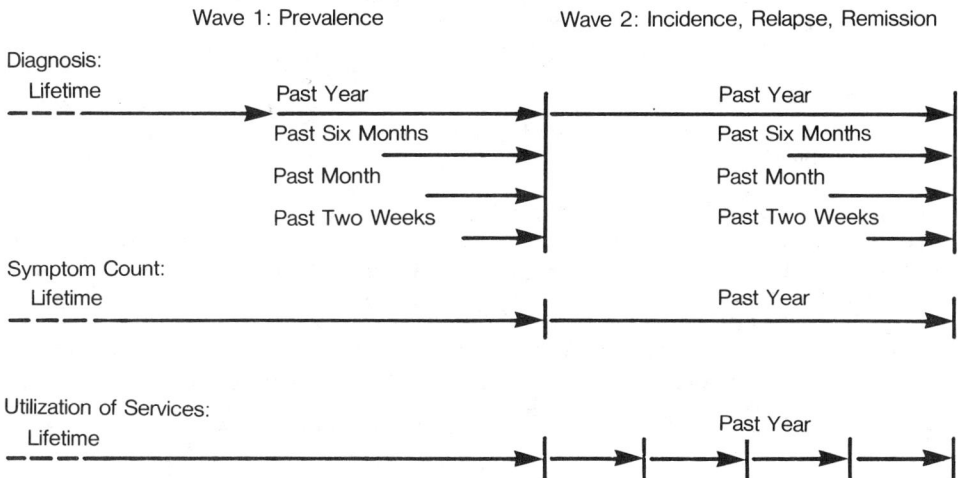

Figure 2.--Diagnostic, Symptom, and Utilization Data Obtained in the ECA Program

One of the goals of the ECA Program is to understand why people use or do not use treatment facilities. Thus, the objective is to ascertain how unmet need is generated and why some groups are underserved. The strategy here is to analyze differences between psychiatrically disordered persons who are in treatment as against those with the same diagnoses who are not in treatment. We suspect two types of factors may be important here: barriers to care, which include aspects of mental health services and programs that hinder treatment, such as long waiting times for appointments, long distances to treatment facilities, inadequate or understaffed facilities, the cost of care, and so forth; and illness behavior, which includes the individual's ability and willingness to identify psychiatric problems, attitudes toward help-seeking in general, and avoidance of psychiatric treatment due to stigma. In the first wave of interviews, factors can be identified in the data analysis that are associated with barriers to care and/or illness behavior; these factors can then be used prospectively to predict utilization over the coming year.

A related goal of the ECA Program is to understand how people choose the specific locus of treatment and to assess the degree to which facilities are used appropriately. Utilization data will include the specialty mental health sector as well as the general health care sector and the nonhealth sector, so that we should be able to understand better the pathways into these various types of services. Covering a broad range of facilities and having diagnostic data available means that we can study issues connected to duplication of services, inappropriate provision of services, multiple facility use for a single clinical episode, and related analyses that have major policy implications for the financing and operation of the mental health service system and, indeed, the entire health care system. This sort of data base is much more powerful than the earlier case registers, which relied solely on treated cases (Bahn 1965).

The Multisite Aspect

The ECA Program was designed to have several different sites of research. The plan is tentative and depends on results from early sites, response from the field, special research opportunities that may present themselves, and availability of funds. This multisite program was designed to complement the psychiatric component of a large-scale national sample survey such as the National Center for Health Statistics Health Examination Surveys. Only a large-scale project such as the Health Examination Survey can provide nationwide estimates of prevalence; but the multisite design has many advantages that the large single-shot survey does not.

The first advantage is the ability to compare results from many sites of research. In the past there has been a disparity in results from different research sites because, it is suspected, of the different orientations (Regier et al. 1978). The divergence in results has led some to despair over the possibility of observing replicable results and the resultant inability to build a scientific foundation for the field of psychiatric epidemiology. Our hope in this project is to demonstrate which results are replicable and which depend on the specific research site. The results that occur repeatedly can contribute to the scientific foundation for the field, but results that are observed in only one or a few sites may provide etiologic leads if methodologic differences are examined and ruled out.

Table 3 shows where the five ECA sites are located and the special nature of their study populations. As mentioned earlier, each site was expected to obtain 3,000 respondents in its household survey. At Yale, because of funding from the National Institute on Aging, we were able to obtain 2,000 interviews from those aged 65 and over. At Hopkins and Duke, the elderly oversample was funded by the Center for Studies of the Mental Health of the Aging. At Hopkins the oversample was slightly more than 400; at Duke approximately 900. The oversample of blacks at St. Louis is within the 3,000 respondents, and the same is true for Hispanics at Los Angeles.

Yale, Johns Hopkins, Washington University (St. Louis), and Duke have completed their wave 1 data collection, and I shall present some preliminary data from those sites. We expect that by this time next year all five sites will be done with their data collection and will be analyzing data.

Table 4 shows some sample characteristics for our first three sites. As you can see, the completion rate ranges from 77 percent to 79 percent (Regier et al., in press).

Table 5 presents data on the 6-month prevalence of psychiatric disorder for areas in New Haven, Baltimore, and St. Louis based on household interviews. It is essential to remember that when we incorporate institutional data, we may well increase these rates. Based on the Mini-Mental State Exam, severe cognitive impairment occurs in about 1.2 percent, and mild cognitive impairment about 5.2 percent. Rates for cognitive impairment will rise when we add data from nursing homes. These data were originally presented at the November 1982 meeting of the American Public Health Association and are now being prepared for publication (Myers et al., in press).

Table 3.—ECA Sites

Site 1
    Jerome K. Myers, Yale University

    Special focus:
      3 waves of interviews
      Oversample of aged population

Site 2
    Morton Kramer, Johns Hopkins University

    Special focus:
      Field validation
      Oversample of aged population

Site 3
    Lee N. Robins, Washington University

    Special focus:
      Field validation
      Oversample of blacks

Site 4
    Dan Blazer, Duke University

    Special focus:
      Rural areas
      Black population

Site 5
    Richard Hough, University of California--Los Angeles

    Special focus:
      Spanish speaking population

Table 4.—NIMH Epidemiological Catchment Area (ECA) Program
First Three Site-Wave 1 Sample Characteristics

	Yale	Hopkins	Washington U. St. Louis
Survey date--wave 1	1980-81	1981	1981-82
Total population size	420,000	268,000	380,000
Sample population size (1980 census)	300,000	175,000	277,000
Sample characteristics	Noninstitutionalized and institutionalized, urban adults	Noninstitutionalized and institutionalized, urban adults	Noninstitutionalized and institutionalized, urban adults
Sample age range	18+	18+	18+
Completed interviews			
Household, wave I	5,035	3,481	3,004
General population	3,058	3,020	3,004
Elderly population over-sample	1,977	461	---
Completion rate	76.6 percent	78 percent	79.1 percent

Table 5.—Six-Month Prevalence of Psychiatric Disorder for
New Haven, Baltimore, and St. Louis: Household Survey

Disorder	New Haven 1980-81 (N = 3,058) (percent)	Baltimore 1981-82 (N = 3,481) (percent)	St. Louis 1981-82 (N = 3,004) (percent)
Major depression	3.5	3.0	3.2
Bipolar	0.8	0.4	0.7
Alcohol abuse/ dependence	4.8	6.1	4.5
Drug abuse/ dependence	1.8	2.3	2.0
Schizophrenia/ schizophreniform	1.1	0.9	0.4
Phobia	5.8	13.4	5.4
Panic	0.6	1.0	0.9
Obsessive compulsive	1.4	2.0	1.3
Somatization	0.1	0.1	0.1
Antisocial	0.6	0.8	1.3

From Yale APHA presentation, Montreal, 11/17/82; revised for publication in Archives of General Psychiatry.

In general, these data contain no major surprises. Even without adjustment for age, sex, and ethnicity, comparison of the raw rates across these three ECA sites shows considerable concordance of results. The three most common disorders in these three study areas are phobias, alcohol abuse and/or dependence, and major depression. All three sites show that for women the most common diagnoses were phobias and major depression, and for men the predominant psychiatric disorder was alcohol abuse and/or dependence.

Figure 3 presents for New Haven and Baltimore the proportion of persons with specific recent DIS disorders who had a mental health visit in the past 6 months. The data are essentially the same at the St. Louis site. These data, also originally presented at the 1982 meeting of the American Public Health Association, are being prepared for publication (Shapiro et al., in press). These data are still being analyzed, but it is doubtful that Shapiro et al. will abandon this overview, namely, that "despite diversity in the characteristics of the areas and quite small frequencies for some measures, the utilization patterns are marked more by similarity than dissimilarity. One of the clearest differences concerns which sector of health services is utilized when people seek care for mental or emotional problems. In New Haven, where the ratio of psychiatrists to population is relatively high, the population more often turns to the speciality mental health sector than to general medical providers; in the other two areas, there is little difference in which sector is used." But more important, less than half of the respondents from our household survey with a recent DIS disorder made a visit in the past 6 months to either a mental health specialist or a general medical provider.

Now, I would like to refer to several figures that show additional types of data collected at all five sites that should prove of interest when we start the more sophisticated analysis of our data.

Figure 4 illustrates the type of questions asked with regard to health. Similar questions are asked about diabetes, heart trouble, high blood pressure, arthritis or rheumatism, emotional or nervous conditions, trouble breathing, stroke, and cancer. Figures 5, 6, and 7 show an extensive list of activities; the respondent is asked about his/her ability to do these things.

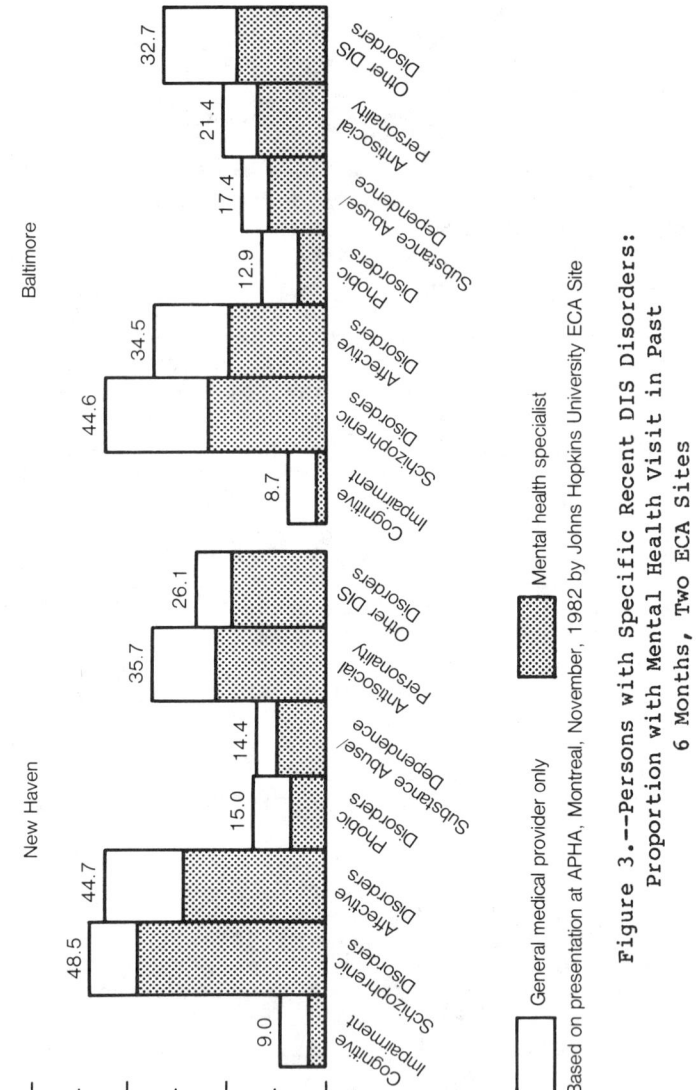

Figure 3.—Persons with Specific Recent DIS Disorders: Proportion with Mental Health Visit in Past 6 Months, Two ECA Sites

ECA Program: Health

Now I'd like to ask you some questions about your health.

At the present time, would you say that your health is excellent, good, fair or poor?

☐ Excellent ☐ Good ☐ Fair ☐ Poor ☐ RF ☐ DK

Compared to other people your age, would you say that your health is better than others, about the same as others, or worse than others

☐ Better ☐ Same ☐ Worse ☐ RF ☐ DK

Now I will read you a list of health problems some people have. Would you tell me if you have **ever** had any of these problems?

Have you **ever** had asthma?

☐ No ☐ Yes ☐ RF ☐ DK

Do you have asthma now?

☐ No ☐ Yes ☐ RF ☐ DK ☐ NA

Are you receiving regular care from a health professional such as a doctor or nurse practitioner for this condition?

☐ No ☐ Yes ☐ RF ☐ DK ☐ NA

Based on Johns Hopkins University Site

Figure 4.--ECA Program: Health

ECA Program: Health (cont.)

Do you have any **other** physical or mental health problems you have had for more than three months or that you were born with?

☐ No ☐ Yes ☐ RF ☐ DK

What is this health problem?
DESCRIBE:

IF MORE THAN 1 PROBLEM GIVEN, RECORD IN Q. 77 AND 79.

Are you receiving regular care from a health professional such as a doctor or nurse practitioner for this condition?

☐ No ☐ Yes ☐ RF ☐ DK ☐ NA

Based on Johns Hopkins University Site

Figure 4.—ECA Program: Health (cont'd.)

ECA Program: Activities 1

Now I'd like to ask you some questions about your ability to do certain activities (HAND CARD E). Would you use this card to select the phrase that best describes your ability to do each of these activities.

Are you usually able to:

	YES	WITH DIFF	WITH HELP	NO	RF	DK
Walk for a distance of a quarter of a mile—about 3 city blocks?........	1	2	3	4	7	8
Walk up and down a flight of stairs without resting?.................	1	2	3	4	7	8
Get around in this building?.........	1	2	3	4	7	8
Get around in this neighborhood?.....	1	2	3	4	7	8
Go out to church or club meetings?...	1	2	3	4	7	8
Go out to movies, restaurants or other entertainments?..............	1	2	3	4	7	8
Use public transportation, such as taxis, buses or trains?............	1	2	3	4	7	8

Based on Johns Hopkins University Site

Figure 5.--ECA Program: Activities 1

ECA Program: Activities 2

For this next group of activities, would you use this card (HAND CARD F) to select the phrase that best describes your ability to do them.

Are you usually able to:

	YES	WITH DIFF	NO	RF	DK
Carry a full bag of groceries across a room?................................	1	2	3	7	8
Are you able, while standing, to bend down and pick up a shoe from the floor?..	1	2	3	7	8
Cut your toenails?......................	1	2	3	7	8
Get in and out of bed by yourself?.......	1	2	3	7	8
Dress and undress yourself?.............	1	2	3	7	8
Take a bath or shower?..................	1	2	3	7	8
Use the toilet, including getting to the bathroom?.........................	1	2	3	7	8
Use a knife and fork to cut up food such as meat and fruit?..................	1	2	3	7	8
Stand for long periods of time?..........	1	2	3	7	8
Sit for long periods of time?..............	1	2	3	7	8
Use your arms to reach?.................	1	2	3	7	8
Use your fingers to grasp or handle?.....	1	2	3	7	8
Keep track of money and bills?..........	1	2	3	7	8

Based on Johns Hopkins University Site

Figure 6.--ECA Program: Activities 2

ECA Program: Activities 3

Are you usually able to:	YES	WITH DIFF	NO	RF	DK
Take care of children?	1	2	3	7	8
Clean house?	1	2	3	7	8
Prepare meals?	1	2	3	7	8
Do yardwork or gardening?	1	2	3	7	8
Fix things around the house?	1	2	3	7	8
Watch television?	1	2	3	7	8
Use the telephone?	1	2	3	7	8
Get together with friends?	1	2	3	7	8
Talk to people?	1	2	3	7	8
Work on hobbies?	1	2	3	7	8
Play games or sports?	1	2	3	7	8
Are you able to hear what is said in a normal conversation with another person (even when using a hearing aid if you usually wear one)?	1	2	3	7	8
Are you able to see the words and letters in ordinary newspaper print even when wearing glasses or contact lenses if you usually wear them?	1	2	3	7	8

Do you find that you have trouble with your memory?
- No 1
- Yes 2
- RF 7
- DK 8

Based on Johns Hopkins University Site

Figure 7.—ECA Program: Activities 3

In summary, it is our expectation that the ECA Program can make a significant contribution to the field of mental health epidemiology, to health services research, and to the measurement of mental illness disability. It is, however, going to take time to analyze the enormous amount of data collected; about 1,000 items per respondent and about 3,500 to 5,500 respondents from each of five sites at wave 1. Then there is a repeat collection 1 year later, and a telephone inquiry about 6 months between the two.

Without getting into details of findings that should flow from this study, it seems to me that the provision of diagnostic specific prevalence data is an important contribution, if only because it will be according to the official (DSM-III) criteria. Furthermore, these prevalence data should be of enormous benefit to those interested in etiology, as well as those interested in health services research. For those interested in etiology, the data can be used to identify high risk groups. For those interested in health services research, the data can serve as a guide to planning health facilities.

The incidence data are a second major contribution the ECA Program will provide. As well as the benefits for the study of the causes and the natural history of disorders, the two-wave design, which permits estimation of incidence, also allows study of the treatment-entry behavior of individuals with mental disorders, an important advantage for health planners.

REFERENCES

Bahn, A.K. Experience and philosophy with regard to case registers in health and welfare. *Community Mental Health Journal* 1:245-250, 1965.

Berger, P.A. Medical treatment of mental disorder. *Science* 200:974-981, 1978.

Dohrenwend, B.P., and Dohrenwend, B.S. Perspectives on the past and future of psychiatric epidemiology (The 1981 Rema Lapouse lecture). *American Journal of Public Health* 72:1271-1279, 1982.

Dohrenwend, B.P. Sociocultural and social-psychological factors in the genesis of mental disorders. *Journal of Health and Social Behavior* 16:365-392, 1975.

Dohrenwend, B.P., and Dohrenwend, B.S. *Social Status and Psychological Disorder: A Causal Inquiry*. New York: Wiley, 1969.

Dunham, H.W. *Community and Schizophrenia: An Epidemiological Analysis*. Detroit: Wayne State University Press, 1965.

Eaton, J.W., and Weil, R.J. The mental health of the Hutterites. *Scientific American* 189:31-37, 1953.

Endicott, J., and Spitzer, R.L. A diagnostic interview. *Archives of General Psychiatry* 35:837-844, 1978.

Hagnell, O. *A Prospective Study of the Incidence of Mental Disorder*. Stockholm: Strenska Bokforlaget, 1966.

Hammer, M. Influences of small social networks as factors on mental hospital admissions. *Human Organization* 22:243-251, 1963.

Helzer, J.; Robins, L.; Taibleson, M., et al. Reliability of psychiatric diagnosis: A methodological review. *Archives of General Psychiatry* 34:129-133, 1977.

Kadushin, C. *Why People Go to Psychiatrists*. New York: Atherton, 1969.

Kitsuse, J., and Cicourel, A. A note on the use of official statistics. *Social Problems* 11:131-159, 1963.

Locke, B.Z., and Gardner, E.A. Psychiatric disorders among the patients of general practitioners and internists. *Public Health Reports* 84:167-173, 1969.

Myers, J.K.; Weissman, M.M.; Tischler, G.L., et al. Six-month prevalence of psychiatric disorders in three communities: 1980-1982. Archives of General Psychiatry (in press).

President's Commission on Mental Health. Report to the President. Washington, D.C.: U.S. Government Printing Office, 1978.

Regier, D; Goldberg, I.; and Taube, C. The de facto mental health system. Archives of General Psychiatry 35:685-693, 1978.

Regier, D.A.; Myers, J.K.; Kramer, M., et al. The NIMH epidemiologic catchment area (ECA) program: Historical context, major objectives, and study population characteristics. Archives of General Psychiatry (in press).

Robins, L.N., et al. National Institute of Mental Health diagnostic interview schedule. Archives of General Psychiatry 38:381-389, 1981.

Scheff, T. Being Mentally Ill: A Sociological Theory. Chicago: Aldine, 1966.

Shapiro, S.; Skinner, E.A.; VonKorff, M., et al. Utilization of health services, three epidemiologic catchment area sites. Archives of General Psychiatry (in press).

Weissman, M.M.; Klerman, G.L. The epidemiology of mental disorder: Emerging trends. Archives of General Psychiatry 35:705-712, 1978.

Weissman, M.M.; Myers, J.K.; and Harding, P.S. Psychiatric disorders in a U.S. urban community: 1975-1976. American Journal of Psychiatry 135:459-462, 1978.

World Health Organization, Expert Committee on Mental Health (1960). Epidemiology of Mental Disorders. World Health Organization Technical Report Series, 185.

INTRODUCTION TO THE ECA PROJECT AS A SOURCE OF EPIDEMIOLOGICAL DATA ON ALCOHOL PROBLEMS*

Lee N. Robins

ABSTRACT

This paper briefly reviews the history of general population surveys relating age to heavy drinking behavior and alcohol problems. The elderly regularly show low rates of both lifetime and current excess drinking.

The ECA, a survey employing a standardized method of making psychiatric diagnoses, has provided reliable evaluations of the frequency of lifetime and current diagnoses of alcohol abuse and dependence according to DSM-III criteria in five samples of all ages from the general population. However, implementation of the DSM-III criteria was not without problems. This paper describes the difficulties encountered and solutions found.

In addition to getting information needed for making diagnoses, the survey asked about onset of drinking problems, age at last drinking problem, tee-totaling, history of heavy drinking, number of drinking problems, health problems caused by drinking, symptoms explained by alcohol ingestion, and use of alcohol treatment facilities.

In all three ECA sites providing data for this series of papers, alcohol abuse and dependence was found to be the most common psychiatric disorder for men and among the five most common disorders for women. In every site the elderly (age 65 or older) had the lowest rate of alcohol disorder, both on a lifetime and current basis. Rates in men greatly exceeded rates in women, but social class and race showed virtually no relationship to the prevalence of alcohol disorder. Rates of experiencing individual

---

*This paper acknowledges support of the ECA program as well as Research Scientist Award MH 00334.

alcohol symptoms were remarkably similar across sites. Almost one-quarter of the population had had at least one alcohol problem at some time in their lives.

Previous Surveys

The history of surveys concerning alcohol is a history of attempts to quantify both the amounts usually consumed at a drinking session by beverage type and the frequency with which drinking sessions occur. This approach was initiated by the California Drinking Practices Group in 1960, under the direction first of Genevieve Knupfer, and later Don Cahalan and Robin Room (Knupfer 1960). It soon spread worldwide. After some years, inspired in part by our own success in assessing alcoholism in ex-child guidance clinic patients and control subjects (Robins et al. 1962), the California Drinking Practices Group began to assess problems associated with drinking, as well as measures of quantity and frequency (Clark 1966). However, there was no attempt to equate problems with a diagnosis of alcoholism. Similarly, Mulford (1960) added the study of preoccupation with alcohol and problems resulting from drinking to the study of quantity-frequency. He defined high scorers on the "preoccupation" scale as alcoholics, justifying the cutoff point by the fact that they were also high on measures of heavy drinking, problems, and a "definitions" scale. In a review of existing surveys concerning alcoholism per se at about the same time, Lipscomb (1966) found only surveys of physicians' practices and social agency clients, not any direct estimations of the population, except for the study by Bacon (1960), which defined alcoholism in terms of problems in living.

One of the earliest attempts to ascertain prevalence rates of alcoholism in the general population through personal interviews was the study in southern Sweden initiated by Essen-Moller and carried on by Hagnell (1972). During the 1957 followup, a definition of alcohol abuse and addiction, with brief but reasonably specific criteria for diagnosis, was used. A point prevalence of 10.3 percent was found among men, with almost total absence of the disorder among women. Prevalence was low in the youngest men (6.5 percent in those under 30) and in the oldest men (6.0 percent in those over 69). However, the "younger elderly," those 60 to 69, had the highest rate, 16.2 percent. When followed again in 1972 (Ojesjo 1980), the overall prevalence rate was slightly lower (9.5 percent). Rates were again lowest in the youngest age group (6.3 percent). The oldest group had an average rate (9.8 percent), and the group with the highest rate had become the 50 to 59 age group (12.3 percent). Age differences had tended to disappear over time, and the elderly were no longer distinctive.

In London, a survey of men living in housing estates (Edwards et al. 1972) used a semistructured interview that inquired about 25 problems associated with drinking. Six percent of the population were positive for at least five of these problems, asked about on a lifetime basis. Using this as a rough definition of alcoholism, Edwards found the frequency of alcoholism highest (13 percent) in the youngest age group (18 to 24); there were no cases at all among those over 60. There was a sharp dropoff in prevalence with age, beginning at age 40.

A third-wave assessment of a sample in New Haven (Weissman et al. 1980) was probably the first to use fully explicit criteria for diagnosis in a random sample of the general population. RDC criteria for probable and definite alcoholism were ascertained by means of a semistructured interview schedule, the SADS-L. A lifetime prevalence rate of 6.7 percent and a point prevalence rate of 2.6 percent were found. When these interviews were rediagnosed using DSM-III criteria, the lifetime prevalence fell to 5.3 percent, and the point prevalence rate to 2.2 percent (Boyd et al., unpublished). The lifetime prevalence rate was lowest in the youngest (26 to 35) and oldest (76 or older) groups, and the highest rate was in the group aged 56 to 65. Point prevalence showed the same age pattern.

These surveys generally suggest that alcohol problems are infrequent among the elderly, whether one considers lifetime histories or current status. The findings are consistent with results of surveys that do not attempt diagnosis but cover only quantity of alcohol consumed. For instance, in a survey of persons 60 and over in Washington, D.C., more than half used little or no alcohol (Guttman 1978). Only 1 percent reported any problems with alcohol at all.

In addition to these few general population surveys on the extent of alcoholism in the community, there are assessments of alcoholism in special populations. One of the earliest was our own followup of child guidance clinic patients and matched control subjects. In this study, structured questions were asked, but two psychiatrists independently made judgments based on interview and extensive record information. The psychiatrists made a single diagnosis, and they agreed to make a diagnosis of alcoholism only in the absence of antisocial personality and schizophrenia. Thus, the finding that 7 percent of the patients and 2 percent of the control sample were alcoholic must be adjusted to add the respondents with antisocial personality and schizophrenia who met criteria for alcoholism. This produces an estimated rate of 29 percent in the ex-patient group vs. 5 percent in the control sample. We also surveyed young black men (Robins et al. 1968), Vietnam veterans (Wish et al. 1979), and men 45 to 64 (the latter in a search for the causes of excess suicides in older white men) (Robins et al. 1977). In these surveys we asked fully structured questions about the presence or absence of a specified list of problems due to alcohol in order to make a diagnosis according to Feighner criteria. Taking all these studies together, we found alcoholism less common in older than in younger samples, and we found the rates for blacks exceeded the rates for whites among younger persons, while the rates for whites exceeded the rates for blacks among older persons. These findings are questionable because they are based on studies from different samples; however, they are confirmed by studies of patient populations (Schuckit et al. 1978).

It would be little exaggeration to say that almost all that we now know about alcoholism in the elderly population on the basis of previous general population surveys is that it is rare, particularly among blacks and women. We do not know to what extent elderly alcoholics are survivors from among those whose alcoholism began young or whether they are predominantly late onset cases. Neither do we know whether their symptom patterns are identical to those of younger alcoholics nor whether the predictors of alcoholism are the same for younger and older cases.

A Brief History of the ECA

The ECA project now in progress has markedly changed that picture. It provides information about alcohol dependence and abuse as well as other diagnoses in very large samples of the general population aged 18 and over. In addition, it provides information on a number of risk factors including demographics, preexisting psychiatric disorders, physical health, and occupational activities. At three of five sites, an oversample of the elderly has provided samples that are particularly generous with respect to those 65 or older. At all sites, there is an oversample of institutionalized persons, making it possible to compare elderly living in nursing homes with those living in the community. One site has a large Hispanic population; two have large black populations; and in a third, blacks were oversampled, allowing ethnic contrasts.

The five sites are New Haven, Baltimore, St. Louis, Los Angeles, and in North Carolina, Durham and the surrounding counties. Because of the inclusion of rural counties in North Carolina and near St. Louis, it is possible to contrast rural and urban elderly with respect to their alcohol dependence and abuse.

Respondents are being surveyed three times at 6-month intervals. The first and third interviews (and in New Haven, the second as well) obtain diagnostic information. This allows assessing not only the prevalence of alcoholism, but also rates of incidence, remission, and relapse over a 1-year period.

The instrument used to collect diagnostic information, the Diagnostic Interview Schedule (DIS), was specially designed for this study. The instrument covers diagnostic criteria in three diagnostic systems: DSM-III, RDC, and Feighner. Respondents are asked whether they have ever had each of the symptoms, and then asked a standard set of probes to learn whether criteria are met for possible psychiatric significance, i.e., whether the symptom was severe enough to be of clinical significance and whether it could be explained entirely by physical causes. If a sufficient number of symptoms in each of the required clusters of symptoms for a diagnosis are reported, the respondent is considered to have met the symptom criteria for that psychiatric disorder at some time in his life. In addition to symptoms, some diagnoses require a clustering of symptoms into episodes; some have maximum ages of onset; and some have exclusion criteria, i.e., meeting criteria for one disorder may make it impossible to meet criteria for another. Multiple diagnoses are allowed.

If a respondent meets lifetime criteria, his disorder is determined to be either active or in remission on the basis of the most recent date at which he suffered from any of its symptoms. Its date of onset is the date at which the first criterion symptom appeared.

Because symptom questions and probes are predetermined, the interview can be administered by lay interviewers after a training period of about 2 weeks. Interviewers are required to make relatively few judgments; they largely ask a series of fixed questions and record the respondents' answers. However, they must be certain that the questions asked were understood and appropriately answered. If they are, a computer program can provide a reasonable facsimile of the diagnoses a psychiatrist using the same diagnostic criteria would arrive at. This was demonstrated in a test of the interview's validity with a predominantly patient population (Robins et al. 1981).

As compared with other diagnoses, the diagnosis of alcohol abuse and alcohol dependency requires the least interviewer skill. (It is, in fact, the diagnosis we teach the interviewers first because of its simplicity.) Lacking the somatic symptoms characteristic of many psychiatric disorders, the criterion symptoms of the alcohol diagnoses cannot be confused with the symptoms of physical disorders. Nor, since the symptom questions mention the etiological factor alcohol, are the symptoms likely to be confounded with the effects of other drugs. Further, each symptom carries its own criteria for severity (e.g., binges must occur more than once and last at least two days accompanied by a failure to meet responsibilities). Therefore, no special probing is required.

Not surprisingly then, the alcohol diagnoses are among the most reliable of all diagnoses. In our test-retest design of psychiatrists vs. lay interviewers giving the interviews independently, the kappa for the DSM-III diagnosis of alcohol abuse or dependence was .86 with a sensitivity of 86 percent and a specificity of 98 percent, compared with an average kappa of .69 for all diagnoses, an average sensitivity of 75 percent, and an average specificity of 94 percent. This relative reliability of the alcohol diagnoses is being substantiated in the household portions of the ECA in Baltimore and St. Louis in studies of subsets of the respondents who are being reinterviewed and clinically evaluated by psychiatrists.

Interviewers had little difficulty in obtaining cooperation from respondents in answering these questions. Like most symptom questions in the DIS, no alcohol question was refused by as many as 1 percent of those agreeing to be interviewed. The high reliability plus low refusal rate gives confidence that the questions were answered seriously and that responses probably give a reasonably accurate picture of the prevalence of alcohol symptoms in the general population.

The Diagnosis of Alcohol Dependence and Abuse in the DSM-III

Diagnoses related to the use or abuse of alcohol appear in two sections of the DSM-III, one titled Organic Mental Disorders and the other on Substance Abuse Disorders. As table 1 shows, there are seven diagnoses attributed to the use of alcohol under the general heading of Organic Mental Disorders. The first two, Alcohol Intoxication and Alcohol Amnestic Disorder, do not necessarily require either chronic or prolonged use of alcohol. (In laymen's terms, the first simply means being drunk, and the second means having a blackout, either of which can occur in association with a single bout of heavy drinking). The remaining diagnoses can occur only after heavy alcohol use for a considerable period of time. In RDC and Feighner diagnostic systems, these five diagnoses are considered criterion symptoms of alcoholism.

In the papers to be presented here, we will be discussing only the DSM-III diagnoses that appear under the Substance Abuse category; i.e., alcohol abuse and alcohol dependence. Table 2 shows the five major criteria used in these diagnoses: (1) pattern of pathological use, (2) impairment in social or occupational

Table 1.—Diagnoses Related to Alcohol in DSM-III

Alcohol Organic Mental Disorders

    303.00 Alcohol intoxication
    291.40 Alcohol idiosyncratic intoxication
    291.10 Alcohol amnesic disorder
    291.2x Dementia associated with alcoholism
    291.80 Alcohol withdrawal
    291.00 Alcohol withdrawal delirium
    291.30 Alcohol hallucinosis

Substance Abuse

    303.9x Alcohol dependence
           Alcohol abuse
           Alcohol dependence

Table 2.—Outline of Diagnostic Criteria

Alcohol Abuse

    1. Pattern of pathological alcohol use

    2. Impairment in social or occupational functioning due to alcohol use

    3. Duration of disturbance at least 1 month

Alcohol Dependence

    4. Either 1 or 2 above

    5. Either tolerance or withdrawal

functioning, (3) duration of disorder for at least a month, (4) tolerance, and (5) withdrawal. Items 1 through 3 are required for a diagnosis of alcohol abuse; item 4 or 5 plus item 1 or 2 are required for a diagnosis of alcohol dependence. It is possible to qualify for dependence without qualifying for abuse. Thus, abuse is not necessarily a milder disorder than dependence by DSM-III criteria.

For item 1, pattern of pathological use, the DSM-III requires the meeting of at least one of eight specific criteria. These specific criteria are as follows: need for daily alcohol use in order to function normally, inability to cut down or stop drinking, repeated use of abstinence or rules about when to drink in order to control drinking, binges, occasional drinking of a fifth of whiskey or its equivalent in other beverages in one day, blackouts, drinking in the face of a serious medical illness known to contraindicate alcohol, and drinking nonbeverage alcohol. The DIS provides questions to identify each of these behaviors except the last, drinking nonbeverage alcohol. That question was tested but dropped when it was found that not only were positive answers rare, but they occurred only in persons who already met criteria on the basis of several other of these symptoms.

For item 2, impairment in social or occupational functioning, the DSM-III does not provide an exhaustive list of criteria, but mentions examples of problems that would qualify. These include violence while drunk, missing work because of drinking, being fired because of drinking, arrests for drinking or traffic accidents while drinking, and difficulties with family or friends. The DIS covers each of these, without adding other examples, except that a doctor's statement that the respondent is drinking too much is included along with difficulties with family or friends.

DSM-III provides no definition for item 3, duration of disturbance of at least one month. We found this statement difficult to interpret since the specific criteria in items 1 and 2 can each occur on a single day or on two or three single days. We were not sure whether item 3 meant that at least a month must elapse between the first and last event, or that there must be a problem on every day for a month, or that there must be at least 30 consecutive days of heavy drinking that on some occasions led to these events, or that there must be at least 30 days over one's lifetime on which some drinking problem occurred. Because of this confusion, we did not attempt to write a question to cover this criterion. However, it seems improbable that criteria 1 and 2 would be met in the absence of at least the minimum interpretation—heavy drinking for 30 days.

Item 4, tolerance, is defined as a need for markedly increased amounts of alcohol to achieve the desired effect or a markedly diminished effect from the same amount. This definition is troublesome, because it is a well-known fact that tolerance increases with regular drinking, even in people who only drink modestly by conventional standards. And in alcoholics, the increase in tolerance may be so gradual that they would not report much change, having forgotten how little alcohol was required to get drunk in their teens. We compromised by using a positive answer to a question asking whether they had ever consumed seven or more drinks every day for 2 weeks. We reasoned that drinking this heavily would be either an indicator of preexisting tolerance or would itself produce tolerance.

Item 5, withdrawal symptoms, like social or occupational impairment, is not defined in the DSM-III, but examples of signs that would meet criteria are given. These are limited to "shakes" and morning malaise relieved by drinking, but the reader is then referred to a page in the section on organic mental disorders on which the full diagnosis of alcohol withdrawal occurs and the diagnosis of alcohol withdrawal delirium begins. Under alcohol withdrawal, in addition to the "shakes," one finds nausea and vomiting, malaise and weakness, autonomic hyperactivity, anxiety, depressed mood, and orthostatic hypotension. Here again there were serious problems in the design of an interview. While the "shakes" indicate a fairly advanced stage of dependence on alcohol, the other symptoms listed under Alcohol Withdrawal are common in anyone who has a hangover, even if the person is a very inexperienced drinker. Indeed, the common view of the hangover is that it is a form of withdrawal, as proven by its response to taking a drink. Since the principal description of alcohol withdrawal delirium was on a page not mentioned, it was unclear whether or not that was to be included. Our solution was to ignore the referral to the diagnoses of alcohol withdrawal and alcohol withdrawal delirium and to limit ourselves to the symptoms mentioned in the description of alcohol dependence: the "shakes" and morning drinking.

This description of the problems inherent in translating DSM-III diagnostic criteria into a form concrete enough to enable us to write algorithms for a computer program should make it clear that the statement in each of two studies that DSM-III criteria were used should not be taken to mean that the two studies have used identical criteria. Although the DSM-III is light years beyond the DSM-II in terms of the clarity of its criteria, there are still sufficient ambiguities to allow persons to apply the criteria in differing ways.

Information about Drinking and Its Consequences Produced by the DIS and Its Programs

The computer programs designed for the DIS combine symptoms as directed by the DSM-III. This means that a diagnosis of alcohol abuse is made if at least one question referring to the criteria for pathological alcohol use and at least one question referring to the criteria for impairment in social or occupational functioning due to alcohol use are answered positively. A diagnosis of dependence is made if at least one question referring either to criteria for pathological alcohol use or to criteria for impairment in social or occupational functioning is answered positively, and the respondent reports either daily drinking of seven or more drinks for 2 weeks or more or having the "shakes" or drinking on awakening. A respondent may meet criteria for both abuse and dependence. For those who meet criteria for one of these diagnoses, the program ascertains the age at the time of the first positive symptom and the recency of the last positive symptom. Recency is assessed as occurrence within the last 2 weeks, between 2 weeks and a month previous to interview, between a month and 6 months previous to interview, between 6 months and a year previous to interview, between a year and 3 years previous to interview, and more than 3 years previous to interview. (The Hopkins interview does not distinguish between those symptom-free for 2 to 3 years and those symptom-free longer, but this distinction can be made by use of age at last symptom.) When the interval has been more than 3 years, the age at last symptom is recorded, allowing one to calculate years since last symptom or the total duration of the symptomatic period.

The program also counts the total number of positive symptoms regardless of whether the respondent does or does not meet diagnostic criteria. This makes it possible to separate clear cases from borderline cases among those with a positive diagnosis, and to identify problem drinkers among those who do not meet full diagnostic criteria. However, this count of symptoms is not truly comparable across sites, since the sites used somewhat different rules for allowing an interviewer to terminate the alcohol symptom questions once it was established that the respondent was not going to meet criteria for a positive diagnosis. Among the first three sites, New Haven allowed the earliest skipouts, Baltimore allowed none at all, and St. Louis allowed an intermediate number.

In addition to the information used by the computer for DSM-III diagnosis or for the other special assessments described above, the DIS provides information about the age at which the respondent first drank enough to get drunk and distinguishes those who claim never even to have had a single drink. It also identifies those who have been reasonably heavy drinkers--i.e., have for some period of time drunk seven or more drinks at least once a week (on a single day or evening). It also covers the personal belief that drinking has been excessive, whether at least one of a variety of health problems resulted from drinking (liver disease, gastritis, peripheral neuropathy, pancreatitis, and Korsakoff's syndrome), and whether withdrawal symptoms other than the "shakes" occurred (fits, delirium tremens, and alcoholic hallucinosis). These additional symptom questions are used in making RDC and Feighner diagnoses.

In addition to the required questions, the sites had the option of adding questions of special interest to them. With respect to drinking behavior, Hopkins added a series of questions that covered the traditional quantity-frequency topics that had been the content of the early drinking practices surveys. Hopkins, Duke, and UCLA added questions about the recency of each positive alcohol symptom, in addition to asking about the date of the most recent of all symptoms. This addition was also made by Washington University in its followup (wave 2) diagnostic interview. Also in the followup interview, Washington University asked each respondent with a total of three or more positive symptoms about the age of onset of each positive symptom, and also asked each respondent whether he or she had ever met the provided definition of a moderate drinker and, if so, the duration of the moderate drinking and whether or not any alcohol problems had occurred during the period of moderate drinking. Washington University also asked about stigmatization as a result of drinking--i.e., whether anyone had considered the respondent an alcoholic or excessive drinker, whether such stigmatization caused them any practical difficulties, whether they themselves accepted the label, and whether it was caused by seeking help for a drinking problem.

At all three waves of interviewing, respondents were asked whether they had ever had residential treatment in an alcohol treatment unit and, if so, the number of admissions and whether they had ever been to an alcohol clinic as an outpatient.

Ingestion of alcohol was recorded if it was offered as the only explanation for various somatic symptoms that can be attributable to alcohol intake. Although it cannot be directly entered into the computer, this information can be readily extracted if the interest exists, since a "3" code for each relevant symptom shows that the symptom has been attributed either to alcohol, drugs, or medication. Reference to the interview document for those so identified would then permit distinguishing attribution to alcohol from attribution to other substances.

Some Intersite Data on Drinking for the Total Sample

As background for the discussion of alcohol abuse or dependence in the elderly, it may be useful to look at the role alcohol abuse or dependence plays relative to other diagnoses in the sample as a whole. Whether we look at lifetime or recent diagnoses, alcohol abuse or dependence is the most common diagnosis for men in every site, varying from 19.2 percent of men in New Haven to 28.9 percent of men in St. Louis who have met the criteria at some time in their lives (see table 3). For women, alcohol abuse or dependence was the fifth most common diagnosis in every site, exceeded only by phobias, depressive episodes, dysthymia, and drug abuse or dependence. In each site, between 4 and 5 percent of women reported sufficient alcohol symptoms to meet criteria at some time in their lives.

As reported in other studies, the elderly in the ECA (defined as 65 years of age or older) had the lowest rates of alcohol abuse and dependence, ranging from 4 to 8 percent at some time in their lives. The elderly also had the lowest rate of recently affected persons, with about 3 percent of elderly males and less than 1 percent of elderly females meeting criteria. Rates for blacks and whites were similar, varying by not more than 3 percent in any site. Social class, as measured by possession of a college degree, did not have a large effect.

When the frequency of individual symptoms was compared across sites, a remarkable similarity was found. The rank order in St. Louis and Baltimore, for instance, correlated .98 (see table 4). The common symptoms were drinking a fifth in a single day, the family's objecting to the amount of drinking, believing oneself that the amount was excessive, fighting when drinking, and suffering blackouts. Overall, between one-fifth and one-quarter of the general population has experienced at least one alcohol problem. This is about 31 percent of those who have ever had a significant exposure to alcohol (approximately one-fourth of the general population claims never in their lifetimes to have drunk enough alcohol to get drunk).

With this picture of a very high frequency disorder, and with particular symptoms of even higher frequency, we can begin to look at the alcohol use and abuse of the elderly. We are prepared to find lower rates of alcohol problems than in the general population, but will the patterns of symptoms and the correlates of positive symptoms be similar or different for the elderly?

Table 3.--Five Most Common Diagnoses in Three Sites: Lifetime Prevalence

	Men			Women		
Diagnoses	NH (Percent)	St. L (Percent)	Balt (Percent)	NH (Percent)	St. L (Percent)	Balt (Percent)
Alcohol abuse/ dependence	19.2	28.9	24.9	4.8	4.3	4.2
Drug abuse/ dependence	6.5	7.4	7.1	5.1	--	4.4
Major depressive episode	4.4	2.5	--	8.7	8.1	6.4
Antisocial personality	3.9	5.6	4.9	--	--	--
Simple phobia	3.8	4.0	14.5	8.5	9.4	25.9
Agoraphobia	--	--	5.2	5.3	6.4	12.5
Dysthymia	--	--	--	--	5.4	--

Table 4.—Specific Alcohol Problems
(unweighted data)

	Percent positive	
	St. Louis	Baltimore
Any problem	22	24
Never drank enough to get drunk	29	24
Specific problems among the remainder		
Drank fifth in 1 day	21	16
Family objected	17	16
Himself thought excessive	15	13
Fighting when drinking	13	11
Blackout	11	9
Others object	8	8
Binge	7	7
Driving	7	6
Arrest	6	8
Shakes	5	6
Morning drink	5	5
Made rules to control	5	4
Couldn't quit	4	4
Drank despite medical contraindication	3	3
Job trouble	3	2
Stomach problems	3	3
Needed alcohol to feel normal	2	2
Lost job	1	1
	$r = .98$	

REFERENCES

Bacon, S.D. EM Jellinek 1890-1963. Quarterly Journal of Studies on Alcohol 24:587-590, 1963.

Boyd, J.H.; Weissman, M.M.; Thompson, W.D.; and Myers, J.K. "Different Definitions of Alcoholism. I: Impact of Seven Definitions on Prevalence Rates in a Community Survey." draft (c. 1982).

Clark, W. Operational definitions of drinking problems and associated prevalence rates. Quarterly Journal of Studies on Alcohol 27:316-327, 1966.

Edwards, G.; Chandler, J.; Hensman, C.; and Peto, J. Drinking in a London suburb. II. Correlates of trouble with drinking among men. Quarterly Journal of Studies on Alcohol Supplement 6:94-119, 1972.

Guttmann, D. Patterns of legal drug use by older Americans. Addictive Diseases 3:337-356, 1978.

Hagnell, O., and Tunving, K. Prevalence and nature of alcoholism in a total population. Social Psychiatry 7:190-201, 1972.

Knupfer, G. Berkeley Drinking Practices Questionnaire, 1960. Research Reference Files Doc. 907A.

Lipscomb, W.R. Survey measurements of the prevalence of alcoholism. Archives of General Psychiatry 15:455-461, 1966.

Mulford, H.A. Drinking in Iowa. V. Drinking and alcoholic drinking. Quarterly Journal of Studies on Alcohol 21:483-499, 1960.

Myers, J.K.; Weissman, M.M.; Tischler, G.L.; Holzer, C.E.; Leaf, P.J.; Orvaschel, H.; Anthony, J.C.; Boyd, J.H.; Burke, J.D.; Kramer, M.; and Stoltzman, R. Six-month prevalence of psychiatric disorders in three communities: 1980-1982. Archives of General Psychiatry, in press.

Ojesjo, L. Prevalence of known and hidden alcoholism in the revisited Lundby population. Social Psychiatry 15:81-90, 1980.

Robins, L.; Bates, W.M.; and O'Neal, P. Adult drinking patterns of former problem children. In: Pittman, D.J., and Snyder, C.R., eds. Society, Culture and Drinking Patterns. New York: John Wiley & Sons, Inc., 1962. pp. 395-412.

Robins, L.N.; Helzer, J.E.; Croughan, J.; and Ratcliff, K.S. The NIMH Diagnostic Interview Schedule: Its history, characteristics, and validity. Archives of General Psychiatry 38:381-389, 1981.

Robins, L.N.; Helzer, J.E.; Weissman, M.; Orvaschel, H.; Regier, D.A.; Gruenberg, E.; and Burke, J. The lifetime prevalence of specific mental disorders--Results from the ECA sites. Archives of General Psychiatry, in press.

Robins, L.N.; Murphy, G.E.; and Breckenridge, M.B. Drinking behavior of young urban Negro men. Quarterly Journal of Studies on Alcohol 29:657-684, 1968.

Robins, L.N.; West, P.A.; and Murphy, G.E. The high rate of suicide in older white men: A study testing ten hypotheses. Social Psychiatry 12:1-20, 1977.

Schuckit, M.A.; Morrissey, E.R.; and O'Leary, M.R. Alcohol problems in elderly men and women. Addictive Diseases 3:405-416, 1978.

Weissman, M.M.; Myers, J.; and Harding, P.S. Prevalence and psychiatric heterogeneity of alcoholism in a United States urban community. Journal of Studies on Alcohol 41:672-681, 1980.

Wish, E.D.; Robins, L.N.; Hesselbrock, M.; and Helzer, J.E. The course of alcohol problems in Vietnam veterans. In: Galanter, M., ed. Currents in Alcoholism. Vol. VI. New York: Grune & Stratton, 1979.

ANTECEDENTS AND CORRELATES OF ALCOHOL ABUSE AND DEPENDENCE IN THE ELDERLY

Charles E. Holzer III, Lee N. Robins, Jerome K. Myers,
Myrna M. Weissman, Gary L. Tischler, Philip J. Leaf,
James Anthony, and Philip B. Bednarski

ABSTRACT

The Epidemiologic Catchment Area (ECA) Study is a large, multi-site community survey providing diagnostic assessment of a number of major psychiatric disorders. It was conceived and funded by NIMH, with supplemental funding provided by NIA. The ECA project provides a unique opportunity to look at the prevalence of alcohol abuse and dependence among the elderly because it includes a diagnostic assessment of alcohol abuse and dependence provided by the Diagnostic Interview Schedule. Further, the combined samples of the first three of the five ECA sites--New Haven, Baltimore, and St. Louis--provide a total of over 11,000 adult respondents, of whom approximately 4,600 are 60 years of age or older.

Findings from the first three ECA sites show alcohol abuse and dependence to be much less prevalent among the elderly than among younger respondents. For males under age 40 years the 6-month prevalence exceeds 10 percent, but it decreases to between 1.9 and 4.6 percent for males 60 or older. Rates for females, which are much lower, decrease from between 1.4 and 3.3 percent for those under 40 to between 0.1 and 0.7 percent over age 60.

Among the correlates of alcohol abuse or dependence were marital status, education, and income, with similar though not identical relationships found among older and younger respondents. Race and employment appeared unrelated to alcohol problems. Having experienced a major depressive episode appeared related to alcoholism, although small cell sizes make those results less certain for the elderly.

INTRODUCTION

The purpose of the present paper is to examine antecedents and correlates of alcohol abuse and dependence among the elderly. It presents results from the Epidemiologic Catchment Area (ECA) Study, which is a large, multisite community survey providing diagnostic assessments of a number of major psychiatric disorders. The ECA project provides a unique opportunity to look at the prevalence of alcohol abuse and dependence among the elderly, because it provides a large sample of the elderly and because it includes a diagnostic assessment of alcohol abuse and dependence.

Most community studies have measured alcoholism in terms of the frequency and volume of consumption rather than in terms of alcohol abuse and dependence as used by most clinicians. This has made it difficult to relate the findings of community and clinical studies. In contrast, the ECA project uses the NIMH Diagnostic Interview Schedule (DIS), which provides an assessment of alcohol abuse and dependence based on the American Psychiatric Association's (APA) Diagnostic and Statistical Manual, DSM-III (American Psychiatric Association 1980).

The DSM-III definitions of alcohol abuse and alcohol dependence are presented in table 1. The first, criterion A, "pattern of pathological alcohol use," begins with excessive consumption but goes further by judging consumption pathological if it produces amnesia or blackouts or if drinking is continued despite a serious physical disorder.

Criterion B, "impairment of social or occupational functioning due to alcohol use," focuses on consequences. These consequences depend in part on how well a person can "hold his or her liquor" and in part on how tolerant the social milieu is to alcohol use and consequences. Both criterion A and B are required for a diagnosis of alcohol abuse, with the added requirement that the disturbance last at least 1 month.

A DSM-III diagnosis of alcohol dependence requires that either criterion A or B be met; in addition, the person must experience E, "tolerance or withdrawal," such as reduced effect or morning "shakes." Abuse and dependence are presented as separate "diagnoses," although the underlying disorder(s) may be closely related.

Although the DSM-III is the APA standard for diagnosis in this country, other sets of diagnostic criteria have been developed and used in various studies. These have been examined theoretically and compared empirically in papers by Boyd et al. (1983) using data from a community survey and an alcohol clinic. In general, the

Table 1.—Diagnostic Criteria for Alcohol Abuse and Dependence

---

Alcohol Abuse

A. Pattern of pathological alcohol use

   Need for daily use of alcohol for adequate functioning
   Inability to cut down or stop drinking
   Repeated efforts to control or reduce excess drinking by "going on the wagon" or restricting drinking to certain times of the day
   Binges, i.e., remaining intoxicated throughout the day for at least 2 days
   Occasional consumption of a fifth of spirits
   Amnesic periods for events occurring while intoxicated
   Continuation of drinking despite a serious physical disorder
   Drinking of nonbeverage alcohol

B. Impairment in social or occupational functioning due to alcohol use

   Violence while intoxicated
   Absence from work or loss of job
   Legal difficulties
   Arguments or difficulties with family or friends because of excessive alcohol use

C. Duration of disturbance of at least 1 month

Alcohol Dependence

D. Either A or B above

E. Either tolerance or withdrawal

   1. Tolerance: Need for markedly increased amounts of alcohol to achieve the desired effect, or markedly diminished effect with regular use of the same amount.

   2. Withdrawal: Development of alcohol withdrawal (e.g., morning "shakes" and malaise relieved by drinking) after cessation of or reduction in drinking.

---

different definitions of alcoholism identified the same individuals as cases. This suggests that the effects of alcoholism are sufficiently encompassing that case identification is not overly dependent on any one criterion.

While the DSM-III diagnostic criteria apply regardless of age, we are particularly interested in the correlates of alcoholism among the elderly. These criteria may be less intercorrelated in the aged. Mishara and Kastenbaum (1980) have reported that the physiological ability of the body to tolerate alcohol decreases in the elderly. Whether due simply to changes in physiological processes or to a decreased willingness by the elderly to tolerate the physical consequences, the result is that the elderly may suffer social consequences of drinking without intake sufficient to meet some of the heavy use requirements in criterion A. Additionally, one must take into account the reduced set of social demands placed on most elderly persons, which may mask changes in social functioning used in meeting criterion B. Consequently, we must consider the possibility that standard definitions of alcohol abuse and dependence have different meanings when used with the elderly.

Based on a number of community surveys of measures of frequency and/or volume of consumption as related to age, we expect rates of current alcohol symptoms to be low in the elderly. These include the survey by Cahalan, Cisin, and Crossley (1969) and a series of surveys funded by NIAAA between 1971 and 1979 (see Clark and Midanik 1982, p. 11ff). Although the age of peak consumption reported in these studies varies from young adulthood through middle age, the elderly uniformly report the least consumption.

Cahalan et al. (1969) have produced a detailed report of sociodemographic correlates of alcohol consumption. Males were reported as the heaviest drinkers in every age group, although the difference between men and women appeared to be decreasing (p. 21). Race appeared to make little difference in consumption (p. 21). Being single, separated, or divorced was associated with heavy drinking (p. 31). The report shows low rates of alcohol use by the widowed. Education presents a more complicated picture, with the college educated being more likely to drink than other groups but less likely to drink heavily than those who have completed only high school. Highest rates of total abstinence were found among those who had not gone beyond grammar school (p. 31). Perhaps as a corollary, low income was associated with low consumption (p. 28). These findings for widowhood, education, and income were not controlled for age.

We turn to the ECA results with a note of caution. Because these results come from a cross-sectional survey, we are often unable to infer the direction of causality operating in the relationships examined. Sex and age relationships may be confounded by factors such as differential mortality. Also, since drinking patterns are usually formed in early adulthood, there may be cohort effects. Changes in social attitudes toward alcohol over time will have differentially affected those of a different current age because they reached the ages at which drinking patterns are set in different eras. The social and legal acceptance of alcohol use has changed greatly during the lives of the current elderly. Those now in their seventies and eighties grew up in a time when there was widespread proscription of alcohol use, particularly for women. The degree of proscription varied widely, however, among various ethnic and religious groups. Consequently, a respondent's exposure to alcohol and its social significance will vary widely by year of birth and social background.

METHODS

The ECA Program of the National Institute of Mental Health (NIMH), in collaboration with Yale, Johns Hopkins, Washington, and Duke universities and the University of California, Los Angeles, has conducted longitudinal psychiatric surveys of community and institutional populations. This report presents data from the first wave of community interviews at the three initial ECA sites: New Haven (Yale University), Baltimore (Johns Hopkins University), and St. Louis (Washington University).

Sample Selection

The New Haven community sample was drawn in two stages as a systematic sample of households compiled from utility listings and supplemented from city directories. Clusters of eight households were drawn, with the first and fifth households designated for the random selection of one adult (Kish 1965, pgs. 396-401). The remaining households were designated for random selection of one person aged 65 or older based on Kish's procedure. These procedures are described in detail in Holzer et al. (in press).

The Baltimore sample was selected from households listed in segments, which were sampled from census tracts with probability proportionate to size. The oversample of elderly was accomplished by selecting, from each designated household, one person between the ages of 18 and 64 (using the Kish procedure) and all persons aged 65 or older.

In St. Louis, the sampling of households was accomplished by a multistage procedure using census tracts and block groups, with heavily black tracts being given a higher probability of selection. Respondents were selected from households by Kish's procedure.

Instrumentation

The interview instruments used in the ECA Program include three major elements that nearly uniform across sites: sociodemographic characteristics, utilization of health and mental health services, and the Diagnostic Interview Schedule (Robins et al. 1981). In addition, each site has designed unique sections dealing with possible risk factors of disorder and disability.

Through the Diagnostic Interview Schedule, DSM-III diagnoses can be generated by computer for various current periods or over the respondent's lifetime. The version of the DIS used in the present research covers the following major mental disorders: alcohol abuse/dependence, anorexia, antisocial personality, bipolar, drug abuse/dependence, dysthymia, major depression, obsessive-compulsive, panic, phobias, schizophrenia/schizophreniform, and somatization.

The section on alcohol abuse or dependence follows DSM-III criteria and provides diagnoses for alcohol abuse, alcohol dependence, or the two combined. The DIS elicits information about the age of onset (first symptom) and recency (last symptom). With the exception of table 4, which considers alternative periods, alcohol abuse or dependence is considered present for a respondent if diagnostic criteria have been met at any time in the respondent's life _and_ symptom (major problem) has occurred within the last 6 months. The complete syndrome may or may not have been present within the last 6 months.

Interviewing

All interviewing was conducted in the field by trained lay interviewers. Interviewers received at least 6 days of classroom training followed by field practice and were accepted for field work only after demonstrating competence with the instrument. Typically, interviews took about 60 to 90 minutes to complete. The completion rates at each site ranged from 77 to 80 percent, with refusals accounting for a high proportion of nonresponse.

Weighting of Data

The data are weighted to compensate for differing probabilities of selection and for refusal rates among respondents. Initial sample weights were constructed for each respondent based on selection probabilities. An additional poststratification adjustment was added to improve the fit of the sample to the 1980 U.S.

census. These procedures are described in Holzer et al. (in press) and Kessler et al. (in press). Percentages in this paper have been weighted as already described. However, sample sizes (N's) are presented in unweighted form.

Significance Testing

Conventional statistical procedures assume random sampling and so are not appropriate for the analysis of complex weighted samples (Cohen 1983).

To provide appropriate significance tests for weighted data, we first used the FUNCAT procedure (SAS Institute 1982) to estimate logistic regression parameters for the weighted data. The resulting chi-square statistic was then adjusted on the basis of estimated variances (design effects) from SURREGR (Holt 1977), which provides standard errors for regression coefficients. The estimated design effects range from 1.0 to 2.9. This adjustment provides more conservative estimates of significance than those obtained from FUNCAT directly and appears to provide a good approximation of the significance of weighted samples.

Tables 3 and 5 through 9 present results of applying logistic regression models. To simplify the tables, we have presented the significance level only for the main effect of the major control variable. Age and sex are significant control variables in each of these tables. Interactions are presented where significant. When the adjustment for design effects changed the significance level, we have presented both the adjusted and unadjusted results.

RESULTS

Description of Sample

Table 2 presents the demographic characteristics of the sample. For each site, the left column presents the actual number of respondents in the sample, while the right column presents the weighted percentage.

Of particular interest are the large numbers of respondents aged 60 or older within the New Haven (N = 2,809) and Baltimore samples (N = 1,185), produced by the oversampling of respondents aged 65 or older. Note that the elderly oversamples also increase the unweighted ratio of females to males, because of the greater life expectancy for females.

Table 2.—Demographic Characteristics of Sample by Site

Demographic characteristic	New Haven N	New Haven Percent*	St. Louis N	St. Louis Percent*	Baltimore N	Baltimore Percent*
Sex						
Male	2,063	46.3	1,202	46.7	1,322	45.4
Female	2,972	53.7	1,802	53.3	2,159	54.6
Age						
18-39	1,463	47.7	1,536	51.3	1,534	47.1
40-59	763	28.6	702	27.9	762	27.1
60+	2,809	23.7	766	20.8	1,185	25.8
Race						
White	4,437	86.6	1,743	77.6	2,193	65.0
Black	421	10.1	1,158	19.0	1,182	31.9
Other	131	3.4	103	3.3	106	3.1
Marital status						
Married	2,492	59.9	1,364	61.7	1,474	48.4
Widowed	1,232	8.1	398	8.2	570	11.9
Sep./div.	517	9.5	552	10.0	643	14.5
Single	792	22.5	672	20.1	793	25.2
Household income						
0,000-9,999	1,619	19.6		**	1,213	31.7
10,000-19,999	1,237	28.1		**	918	30.7
20,000+	1,476	52.4		**	862	37.6
Education						
0-11	1,918	25.1	1,158	33.3	1,886	52.0
12	1,340	30.9	869	33.1	948	28.8
13+	1,762	44.0	977	33.7	647	19.2

*Percentages are based on weighted data.
**Household income is not available for St. Louis.

Both St. Louis and Baltimore have more black respondents than does New Haven; in St. Louis, blacks were oversampled, and in Baltimore, the areas selected had relatively large black populations. The marital status distributions are similar between New Haven and St. Louis, with fewer currently married respondents in Baltimore. New Haven has more college-educated respondents than the other sites, while Baltimore has higher percentages of those who did not complete high school.

Age and Sex

Table 3 presents the 6-month prevalence of alcohol abuse and dependence combined--tabulated by age, sex, and study site. The prevalence rates are provided as percentages, weighted as already described. The major findings are higher prevalence rates for males than for females and a relatively consistent pattern of a decrease with age. The age and sex differences are significant ($p < .001$), but the differences among sites are marginal, initially yielding $p < .05$ but dropping to nonsignificance after adjustment for the design effects from the complex samples. As shown in the more detailed age breakout, the decrease with age continues among the elderly, particularly for females, who report no alcohol abuse or dependence past age 75.

The columns marked N provide the unweighted number of respondents in the specified age groups. For the groups aged 18 to 39 and 40 to 59 years, cell sizes are roughly comparable at all sites, with somewhat more females than males. Among the elderly, one can see the effects of oversampling those 65 and older in New Haven and Baltimore.

Although table 3 combines alcohol abuse and alcohol dependence, we have also looked at the two diagnoses separately. In general, alcohol abuse is more prevalent among the younger respondents, while elderly respondents report relatively less abuse than dependence.

Prevalence Period

Throughout this paper we consider alcohol abuse or dependence to be present among those meeting lifetime criteria if a major symptom has been reported as occurring within the last 6 months. Table 4 shows the impact of using alternative time periods to define prevalence rates. Overall, the 2-week rates are the lowest, being about half the 6-month rates. One-year prevalence rates are only slightly higher than the 6-month rates, while lifetime rates are as much as two or three times greater. The 6-month rates provide the same associations with sex and age obtained from using longer or shorter periods.

Table 3.—Six-Month Prevalence of Alcohol Abuse or
Dependence by Age, Sex, and Site

Sex Age	New Haven		St. Louis		Baltimore	
	N	Percent	N	Percent	N	Percent
Male						
18-39	636	11.7	625	10.8	581	11.9
40-59	312	6.3	280	6.9	277	12.4
60+	1,104	1.9	271	3.6	410	4.6
60-64	109	2.3	64	5.6	86	6.4
65-69	417	2.8	60	2.8	138	5.1
70-74	264	0.4	62	4.0	83	4.8
75-79	154	2.1	42	4.1	66	0.0
80-84	97	1.3	29	0.0	26	3.9
85+	62	0.0	14	0.0	11	0.0
Female						
18-39	821	3.3	900	1.4	935	2.2
40-59	449	1.4	409	0.4	454	2.1
60+	1,685	0.1	473	0.7	651	0.4
60-64	120	0.0	123	0.6	165	1.2
65-69	496	0.3	84	0.2	165	0.0
70-74	413	0.0	106	1.9	147	0.0
75-79	296	0.0	79	0.0	99	0.0
80-84	213	0.0	51	0.0	43	0.0
85+	146	0.0	30	0.0	32	0.0

Significance: Sex ($p < .001$), age ($p < .001$), site (.05, n.s. after design adjustment).

Table 4.—Effect of Prevalence Period on Rates
of Alcohol Abuse or Dependence

Prevalence period	Male			Female		
	18-39	40-59	60+	18-39	40-59	60+
New Haven						
2 week	6.0	4.1	1.7	1.2	0.6	0.0
1 month	7.4	4.4	1.7	1.9	0.6	0.0
6 month	11.7	6.3	1.9	3.3	1.4	0.1
1 year	14.1	6.6	2.7	4.6	1.9	0.4
Lifetime	23.4	20.2	7.4	7.3	4.1	1.1
St. Louis						
2 week	3.2	2.5	1.1	0.5	0.3	0.6
1 month	4.6	3.5	1.1	0.7	0.3	0.7
6 month	10.8	6.9	3.6	1.4	0.4	0.7
1 year	15.0	9.1	3.9	2.1	0.6	0.8
Lifetime	35.0	24.6	17.3	5.7	3.5	2.2
Baltimore						
2 week	7.2	6.3	3.8	0.7	1.2	0.4
1 month	9.8	7.5	4.0	1.4	1.2	0.4
6 month	11.9	12.4	4.6	2.2	2.1	0.4
1 year	13.9	15.1	6.6	2.3	2.1	0.4
Lifetime	22.9	32.8	19.7	4.3	6.1	2.1

The lifetime rate provides the percentage of respondents who report ever having met the criteria for alcohol abuse or dependence. People with lifetime but not current alcoholism may be considered recovered alcoholics. The proportion of lifetime alcoholics who have recovered is greater among older than younger persons, as might be expected. (The one exception is found in St. Louis women, probably accounted for by the small number of women over 60 who ever had an alcohol disorder.)

Race

Table 5 presents the 6-month prevalence of alcohol abuse or dependence for whites and blacks. The category "other" has been omitted because of small cell size. In most age and sex categories, racial differences are small, and there is no trend toward higher rates in either race. Further, in a logistic regression the main effect for race was minimal, with only one interaction approaching significance.

Table 5.—Six-Month Prevalence of Alcohol Abuse or Dependence by Race*

Site Race	Male			Female		
	18-39	40-59	60+	18-39	40-59	60+
New Haven						
White	11.1	6.5	1.8	3.3	1.1	0.1
Black	10.7	6.7	3.7	3.1	4.4	0.0
St. Louis						
White	11.7	6.8	3.7	1.6	0.1	0.6
Black	8.8	7.4	2.3	1.1	1.7	1.4
Baltimore						
White	14.1	9.2	4.8	2.1	1.2	0.4
Black	8.4	21.6	4.5	2.5	4.2	0.6

*Other race groups are not presented due to small N's.
Significance: Race (NS)

Marital Status

The distributions of alcohol abuse and dependence by marital status are shown in table 6. The major finding is that married respondents have significantly low rates of alcohol abuse or dependence, while the separated/divorced groups have the highest rates (p .001). In Baltimore, separation or divorce among the elderly is associated with an even higher rate of alcoholism than among the young. The never married appear to be intermediate in the risk of alcoholism. Only the elderly include enough widowed persons to allow the assessment of their alcoholism, and we were therefore unable to include widowhood as a separate category in the logistic regressions. Among the elderly in St. Louis and Baltimore, rates of alcoholism among the widowed were below those of the separated or divorced but higher than those of others. Among the New Haven elderly, the widowed had more alcoholism than the separated or divorced but less than the singles.

We have also looked at the effects of living arrangements in the New Haven data alone (data not shown). Results are consistent with those obtained for marital status, showing persons married and living with a spouse to have less alcohol abuse or dependence, regardless of age or sex. Highest rates were found for those living with nonrelatives. Rates for those living alone were almost as high.

Education

Table 7 presents alcohol abuse or dependence by highest grade completed. There is more alcoholism ($p < .05$) among those who have not finished high school than among those with more education. Differences between high school and college graduates are not significant.

Income

Table 8 presents alcohol abuse or dependence by total household income. We have used total household income because it is less affected by the nonemployment of the elderly than is personal income. The general trend ($p < .01$) shows increased alcoholism among those from the poorest households, regardless of age or sex.

Employment Status

The prevalence of alcohol abuse or dependence by employment status is presented in table 9. For younger men and women in Baltimore, nonemployment appears to be associated with higher alcohol abuse or dependence, but overall, no pattern is apparent.

Table 6.—Six-Month Prevalence of Alcohol Abuse
or Dependence by Marital Status

Site	Male			Female		
Marital status	18-39	40-59	60+	18-39	40-59	60+
New Haven						
Married	7.6	5.2	1.2	1.5	1.0	0.0
Single	12.4	0.0[a]	5.5	4.9	0.0	0.0
Widowed	[c]	[c]	4.8	0.0[c]	2.6	0.1
Sep./div.	31.0	13.5	4.2	5.2	3.5	0.5
St. Louis						
Married	8.7	5.1	2.4	0.6	0.1	1.4
Single	10.2	16.1[a]	1.6[b]	2.8	1.7	0.6
Widowed	[c]	31.4[b]	6.3	0.0[b]	0.0	0.1
Sep./div.	31.0	17.1	14.5	1.7	1.6	0.0
Baltimore						
Married	10.5	6.8	1.8	0.8	1.1	0.4
Single	12.0	20.3	3.7[a]	1.2	0.0	0.0
Widowed	[c]	15.9[b]	8.4	0.0[b]	4.9	0.5
Sep./div.	16.2	22.9	20.2	7.8	4.0	0.0

[a] = Cell with $N < 30$
[b] = Cell with $N < 20$
[c] = Cell with $N < 10$ (suppressed)
Significance: Marital status ($p < .001$).

Table 7.—Six-Month Prevalence of Alcohol Abuse
or Dependence by Highest Grade Completed

Site Grade	Male			Female		
	18-39	40-59	60+	18-39	40-59	60+
New Haven						
0-11	18.5	7.6	2.8	6.8	1.0	0.1
12	15.0	4.9	0.4	4.0	2.5	0.1
13+	8.3	6.5	1.9	1.9	0.6	0.0
St. Louis						
0-11	20.7	8.1	4.5	1.5	0.3	0.3
12	9.4	9.3	0.0<u>a</u>	1.9	0.7	2.3
13+	8.2	3.5	3.3	0.8	0.0	0.4
Baltimore						
0-11	17.1	16.0	4.3	4.0	2.8	0.5
12	9.5	7.6	5.3	1.8	1.0	0.0
13+	9.2	5.2	5.9	0.4	0.9	0.0

<u>a</u> = Cell with $\underline{N} < 30$.
Significance: Education ($\underline{p} < .01$, $\underline{p} < .05$ after design adjustment).

Table 8.—Six-month Prevalence of Alcohol Abuse or
Dependence by Household Income

Site	Male			Female		
Income	18-39	40-59	60+	18-39	40-59	60+
New Haven						
$ 0,000-9,999	12.4	11.4[b]	2.4	5.8	2.8	0.2
10,000-19,999	12.3	3.5	0.7	3.3	2.2	0.0
20,000+	10.4	7.4	2.3	2.2	0.5	0.0
Baltimore						
$ 0,000-9,999	15.8	23.8	6.6	5.9	5.7	0.3
10,000-19,999	10.0	17.1	4.9	1.2	0.4	1.2
20,000+	12.1	5.1	2.6	0.4	0.7	0.0

b = Cell with N < 20.
Significance: Income (p < .001, p < .01 after design adjustment).

Table 9.—Six-Month Prevalence of Alcohol Abuse
or Dependence by Employment Status

Site	Male			Female		
Employment status	18-39	40-59	60+	18-39	40-59	60+
New Haven						
Working	11.7	6.1	1.3	1.7	0.6	0.0
Not working	11.3	7.9	2.2	4.6	1.7	0.1
St. Louis						
Working	9.6	7.0	7.1	2.2	0.3	0.5
Not working	16.6	6.7	3.2	0.7	0.7	0.6
Baltimore						
Working	11.5	9.6	4.7	0.7	1.1	0.0
Not working	16.3	22.4	4.7	4.3	3.1	0.5

"Never worked" have been deleted from table.
Significance: Employment (n.s.).

Both the employment main effect and employment interaction terms in a logistic regression are nonsignificant.

Logistic Regression

To test the joint relationship of the foregoing variables to alcohol abuse or dependence, we used the FUNCAT procedure (SAS Institute 1982) to run a logistic regression. We dropped family income because of its unavailability for St. Louis and employment, because of its weakness in the initial tables. The data from the three sites were included in a single model. Respondent weights in each site were proportionately reduced so that they would sum to the actual sample sizes, rather than to the 1980 census of residents aged 18 and over. Interaction terms were tested, but all were dropped as nonsignificant or nonessential to the fit of the model.

The resulting model presented in table 10 includes six variables, four of which are strongly significant ($p < .001$) regardless of adjustment for the sample design. These are age, sex, marital status, and education. Also included are site and race. Race is initially significant ($p < .02$) but drops to nonsignificance after adjustment for the complex sample design. The lack of significant interactions with age indicates that the relationships between alcoholism and these sociodemographic factors are relatively independent of age.

Tabel 10.—Logistic Regression for 6-Month Prevalence of Alcohol Abuse or Dependence (N = 11,201)

Source	DF	Unadjusted Chi-Square	Prob.	Design effect	Adjusted prob.
Intercept	1	1,759.44	.0001	2.4	.001
Site	2	1.84	.3977	2.6	n.s.
Age	2	113.53	.0001	1.2	.001
Sex	1	275.45	.0001	1.8	.001
Race	1	6.11	.0135	2.8	n.s.
Marital status	2	127.38	.0001	1.9	.001
Education	2	47.74	.0001	2.4	.001
Likelihood ratio	305	334.41	.1187		

From the foregoing analysis it appears that alcoholism has correlates among the elderly that are similar to those among younger respondents. To test further the equivalence of these effects in younger and older respondents, we reran the preceding model separately in each of the three age groups. The models for younger respondents remained roughly as described, but for those 60 years old or older, many of the parameters dropped to nonsignificance. This may be due to differences in the effects among the elderly, but it may also result from the smaller number of respondents in the elderly model and the reduced range of variation for the risk variables among the elderly subpopulation.

Major Depressive Episode

Alcoholism may be related to psychiatric characteristics as well as to demographic variables. Attempts to look at its relationship to several diagnoses have been hampered by small cell sizes. Table 11 presents recent alcohol abuse or dependence for those who have ever experienced a major depressive episode. Although the cell sizes are small, particularly for the elderly, and there are some inconsistencies, depression is generally associated with increased alcoholism (p .001).

Table 11.—Six-Month Prevalence of Alcohol Abuse or Dependence by Major Depressive Episode

Site Prevalence	Male			Female		
	18-39	40-59	60+	18-39	40-59	60+
New Haven						
Lifetime	10.1	0.0[a]	6.8[a]	4.2	5.8	0.0
Never	11.8	6.4	1.8	3.1	1.0	0.1
St. Louis						
Lifetime	38.5[a]	52.8[b]	0.0[c]	2.6	0.8	10.4[a]
Never	9.7	6.2	3.7	1.3	0.4	0.5
Baltimore						
Lifetime	24.3[a]	35.0[b]	18.2[c]	2.0	8.4	6.6[a]
Never	11.5	11.8	4.3	2.2	1.6	0.2

[a] = Cell with $N < 30$.
[b] = Cell with $N < 20$.
[c] = Cell with $N < 10$.
Significance: Depression ($p < .001$).

Age of Onset

In examining alcoholism in the elderly, it is important to distinguish between those who have had difficulty with alcohol all their lives and those who began to have problems at a later age. We have used self-report of first problem before or after the age of 40 years to differentiate between early- and late-onset alcoholism. That cutoff is slightly lower than the ages of 45 to 50 that others have used to distinguish late onset (Mishara and Kastenbaum 1980). Further, we limited the analysis to respondents who were 60 or older at the time of interview and therefore had passed through most of the period of risk for late-onset alcoholism. Only seven respondents reported onset after age 65.

Table 12 presents the percentage of late versus early onset among elderly respondents with current (6-month) and lifetime alcohol abuse or dependence. Among elderly alcoholics reporting problems within the last 6 months, less than a third of the males reported an onset at age 40 or later. In contrast, more than half the females reported late onset. Because of the small cell sizes, this relationship reaches significance only for Baltimore ($p < .05$) or if the data from all three sites are pooled ($p < .05$).

The higher proportion of late onset for females is also found when the larger number of elderly with a lifetime diagnosis of alcohol abuse or dependence are included. The differences become significant for New Haven ($p < .01$) and remain significant for Baltimore ($p < .05$). The pooled result is also significant ($p < .001$).

We had hoped to examine specific risk factors for those with late onset, but as one can see, the cell sizes are too small to provide stable results.

Cohort Effects

The last issue addressed in the present analysis is cohort effects. It is clear from history, and from reviews such as that by Malin et al. (1982), that there have been changes in the pattern of alcohol consumption during the lives of our elderly respondents. This means that the lower rates of alcoholism among the present elderly may be due to their experience of Prohibition or other historical phenomena.

It is also true that the present study includes only survivors. Each earlier born age cohort had to survive longer to be included in the present survey. Because alcoholism is a risk factor for poor health and mortality, it is possible that the present elderly respondents are the healthy portion of their birth

Table 12.--Late versus Early Onset Among Elderly Respondents with Current or Lifetime Alcohol Abuse or Dependence

Site Sex	Current (6 mo.) Dx			Lifetime Dx		
	Number of cases	Percent with late onset*		Number of cases	Percent with late onset*	
New Haven						
Males	19	31.6		91	34.1	
Females	2	50.0	n.s.	14	71.4	$p < .01$
St. Louis						
Males	13	7.7		55	20.0	
Females	4	50.0	n.s.	21	33.3	n.s.
Baltimore						
Males	21	28.6		91	23.1	
Females	3	100.0	$p < .05$	15	53.3	$p < .05$

*This is the unweighted percentage of cases with their first problem occurring at age 40 or later. Significance levels for males versus females are Fishers exact test, without adjustment for sample design effects.

cohort, while others who were alcoholics have not survived. Although the present cross-sectional data do not provide direct evidence about the complete birth cohort, the retrospective information about age of onset and recency of last episode tell us about the lifetime experience of the survivors and thus provide a partial picture of the cohort's experience.

In figure 1 we have presented idealized profiles of alcohol prevalence for each cohort, reconstructed from the ages of onset and remission reported by the respondents. The profile is idealized in that it assumes that after the reported age of onset, a person has alcohol abuse or dependence continuously until the age a problem is last reported.

We have constructed a set of variables estimating whether a given respondent was actively alcoholic at any time in each decade of life. If, for example, a person started having alcohol problems at age 21 but stopped at age 28, he would be considered alcoholic in the age period from 18 to 24 years and from 25 to 34, but not during subsequent decades. If the problem lasted only a year, say during age 27, then only the age period from 25 to 34 would be considered positive. This provides a decade prevalence period. Age periods past the respondent's age at interview are considered missing.

Cohorts are defined by year of birth, with the oldest cohorts being born before 1905 (now age 75 or older) and the youngest born between 1956 and 1962 (now 18 to 24 years old). The prevalence of alcohol abuse and dependence by age and cohort is pressented in figure 1 for the data from New Haven. The results for other sites are similar.

As can be seen, the age-specific drinking profile rises sharply for the younger cohorts. Of those people born between 1956 and 1962, about 7 percent report drinking problems before age 18, and 17 percent report drinking problems during ages 18 to 24. For the second cohort, born between 1946 and 1955, about 5 percent had drinking problems before age 18 and 13 percent had problems between 18 and 24, but the proportion having problems decreased to 12 percent between ages 25 to 34. The next cohort, born between 1936 and 1945, reports fewer alcohol problems before age 18 (3 percent), increasing to 6 percent by ages 18 to 24 and 12 percent by ages 25 to 34, and decreasing to 9.5 percent by ages 35 to 44.

This pattern is repeated, with each successive age cohort reporting a smaller proportion having problems before age 18, with lower and later peak prevalence. In each cohort but the first, the reported prevalence of alcohol abuse and dependence decreases between the last two decades. The oldest cohorts, those born before

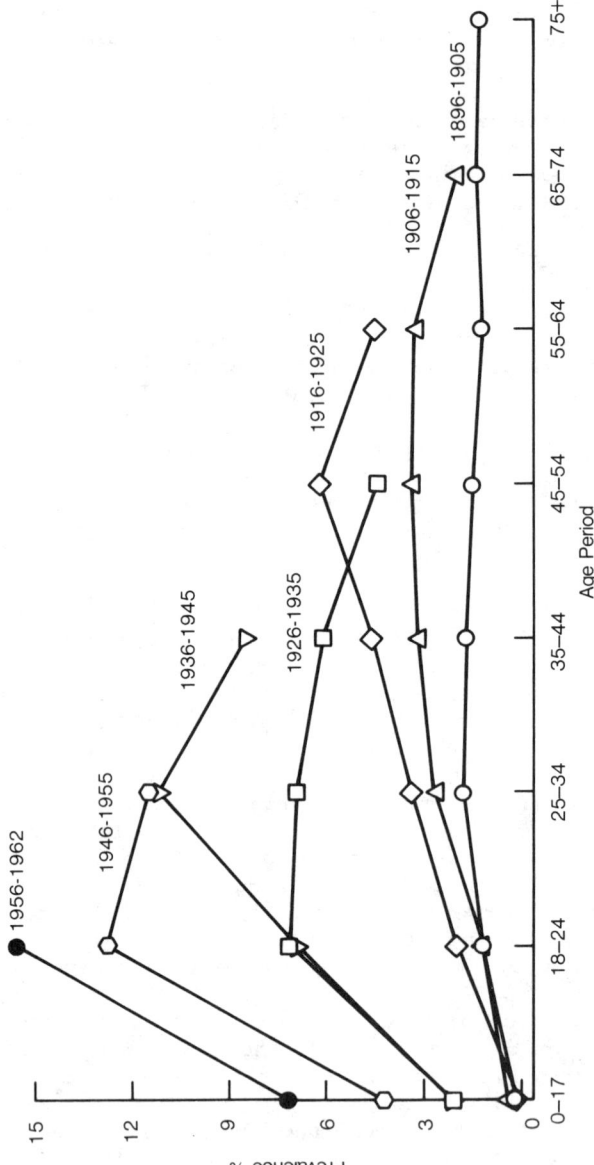

Figure 1.—Prevalence of Alcohol Abuse or Dependence by Age Period and Birth Cohort

1905 (now age 75 or older), report low prevalences throughout, although we have relatively few respondents in that category (see table 3).

DISCUSSION

The present data are some of the first to be based on large-scale application of DSM-III criteria in the community. Because these results are based on DSM-III diagnoses, they might have been quite different from the results of surveys based solely on frequency-volume measures of alcoholism. However, they appear to be quite similar to results of previous studies (Cahalan et al. 1969; Mishara and Kastenbaum 1980), particularly in regard to age and sex distributions. Most studies have found generally lower rates of alcohol use among the elderly and among females of all ages. Prevalence rates for a DIS/DSM-III diagnosis of alcohol abuse or dependence appear similar to Cahalan, Cisin, and Crossley's (1969) category "heavy" drinking, although there is no means of determining whether the same respondents would be identified by the two measures.

The major thrust of the present paper has been to examine sociodemographic variables that are correlates of alcohol abuse and dependence, and to determine whether these operate differently as risk factors for alcoholism in the elderly than they do in younger age groups.

In particular, we have examined age, sex, race, marital status, education, employment, and study site as correlates of current alcohol abuse or dependence. A higher prevalence of alcoholism is associated with being young, with being male, with being separated or divorced, with being poor, and with having less than a high school education. These factors were associated with alcohol abuse or dependence regardless of age. On the other hand, three of the variables examined--site, race, and employment status--had no apparent relationship to the prevalence of alcoholism.

These relationships are consistent with previous studies based on frequency and volume of alcohol consumption, although Cahalan found the widowed drinking less heavily than others, while we found an intermediate level of alcoholism among widowers. This difference can probably be explained by Cahalan's failure to control for age.

We wanted to know whether these variables are related to alcoholism differently among the elderly than among younger groups. To test for that possibility, we have presented the tables showing age comparisons and have included variable by age interaction terms in the logistic regression models used to test significance. In both the individual models and the combined logistic regression, the age interactions were not significant, indicating that the relationships between these variables and alcohol abuse or dependence are much the same for the elderly as for younger populations. On the other hand, when we reran the model for the elderly alone, a number of the previously significant parameters became nonsignificant. Therefore, our view that sociodemographic factors relate to alcoholism in a similar way in the elderly and younger respondents must remain tentative.

Of the correlates found, only sex can be seen distinctly as a cause of alcoholism. While drinking may be a response to poverty and marital breakup, excessive drinking may also lead to school dropout and to job loss, causing low earnings and marital instability. Depression also may either prompt early drinking or be its consequence.

Of great interest is the role of age in alcoholism. Our finding that alcohol abuse and dependence are less prevalent among the elderly is consistent with previous studies (Cahalan et al. 1969; Clark and Midanik 1982). These authors and others (Mishara and Kastenbaum 1980, p. 51) have attempted to explain the apparent low rate of alcoholism in the elderly. Specifically, four alternative explanations have been proposed: (1) the earlier (older) birth cohorts never reached the levels of alcohol abuse and dependence of the younger cohorts; (2) people drink less as they get older; (3) alcoholics die early, leaving fewer alcoholics among the surviving elderly; (4) the elderly forget or underreport their problems with alcohol.

Any of the foregoing arguments may contribute to the observed pattern, although decline in drinking among the elderly, explanation 2, cannot be the whole story, as shown in figure 1, which presents prevalence of alcoholism by age for seven birth cohorts. The elderly report very few problems with alcohol even between the ages of 18 and 30, the time of greatest risk for all cohorts.

However, this second explanation is partially supported by the data. In table 4 we found that lifetime prevalence rates were substantially higher than prevalences for 1 year or less. That indicates that a large proportion, about two-thirds, of the respondents who had ever met criteria for alcohol abuse or dependence reported that they had not had problems with alcohol during the last 6 months. This rate of remission appears high in comparison to the results of clinical studies following treated alcoholics. Both the Rand report (Armor et al. 1978) and Vaillant and Milofsky

(1982) report recovery and abstinence in less than a quarter of the alcoholics followed, regardless of treatment status.

The first explanation, that the decline is explained by changes in the drinking patterns of successive cohorts, would be a parsimonious explanation of figure 1. But some degree of caution is necessary before adopting a cohort explanation. Malin, Coakley, and Kaelber (1982, p. 104) report historical figures on the per capita consumption of alcohol in the United States. They show consumption rising from 0.97 gallons per capita in 1934 to 1.5 by 1936, 2.06 in 1944, and 2.51 in 1969. This increase does not appear great enough to explain the great changes in figure 1. Further, the per capita consumption before Prohibition (1919-1933) reached 2.60, similar to per capita rates for 1969. Based on these results, our oldest cohort, those born before 1905, might be expected to have pre-Prohibition rates in their youths similar to those of our youngest cohort, with those reaching maturity during Prohibition falling below; but we do not find this pattern. Still, our sample of the very elderly may simply be too small and too pruned by alcohol-associated deaths to show such an effect.

The third and fourth explanations for the age decline in the prevalence of alcoholism, mortality and underreporting, must also be considered viable, but the present data set provides little opportunity to test them.

In conclusion, the ECA project has permitted us to look at alcohol abuse and dependence as defined by DSM-III in large samples of community resident elderly. We have found that the elderly report less alcohol abuse and dependence, but at present we cannot be certain why. Historical change in alcohol use is undoubtedly important in this picture, but many respondents appear to have given up earlier alcohol problems, despite increasing consumption overall. Beyond their lower rates of alcohol abuse and dependence, the elderly appear to have sociodemographic correlates of alcohol abuse or dependence that are similar to those of younger respondents. Women of all ages drink less; the single, separated, and divorced drink more, as do those with less education or income.

ACKNOWLEDGEMENTS

The Epidemiologic Catchment Area (ECA) Program is a series of five epidemiologic research studies performed by independent research teams in collaboration with staff of the Division of Biometry and Epidemiology of the National Institute of Mental Health and the staff of the Epidemiology, Demography, and Biometry Program of the National Institute on Aging. The NIMH Principal

Collaborators are Darrel A. Regier, Ben Z. Locke, and Jack D. Burke; the NIMH Project Officer is Carl A. Taube. The NIA Principal Collaborator is Jacob A. Brody. The Principal Investigators and Co-Investigators from the five sites are: Yale University, U01 MH 34224--Jerome K. Myers, Myrna M. Weissman, and Gary L. Tischler; Johns Hopkins University, U01 MH 33870--Morton Kramer, Ernest Gruenberg, and Sam Shapiro; Washington University, St. Louis, U01 MH 33883--Lee N. Robins and John Helzer; Duke University, U01 MH 35386--Dan Blazer and Linda George; University of California, Los Angeles, U01 MH 35865--Richard Hough, Marvin Karno, Javier Escobar, Audrey Burnam, and Dianne Timbers.

REFERENCES

American Psychiatric Association, Diagnostic and Statistical Manual of Mental Disorders. 3d ed. Washington, D.C.: The Association, 1980.

Armor, D.J.; Polich, J.M.; and Stambul, H.B. Alcoholism and Treatment. New York: Wiley, 1978.

Boyd, J.H.; Weissman, M.M.; and Thompson, W.D. Different definitions of alcoholism. I: Impact of seven definitions on prevalence rates in a community survey. American Journal of Psychiatry 140:1309-1313, 1983.

Cahalan, D.; Cisin, I.H.; and Crossley, H.M. American Drinking Practices: A National Study of Drinking Behavior and Attitudes. New Brunswick, N.J.: Rutgers Center of Alcohol Studies, 1969.

Clark, W.B., and Midanik, L. Alcohol use and alcohol problems among U.S. adults: Results of the 1979 national survey. In: NIAAA Alcohol and Health Monograph No. 1: Alcohol Consumption and Related Problems. DHHS Pub. No. (ADM)82-1190. Washington, D.C.: Supt. of Docs., U.S. Govt. Print. Off., 1982.

Cohen, S.B. Present limitations in the availability of statistical software for the analysis of complex survey data. Review of Public Data Use 11:338-344, 1983.

Holt, M.M. SURREGR: Standard Errors of Regression Coefficients From Sample Survey Data. Research Triangle Park, N.C.: Research Triangle Institute, 1977.

Holzer, C.E.; Spitznagel, E.; Jordan, K.; Timbers, D.; Kessler, L.; and Anthony, J. Sampling the household population. In: Eaton, W.W., and Kessler, L.L., eds. Epidemiologic Methods in Psychiatry: The NIMH Epidemiologic Catchment Area Program, Academic Press, in press.

Kessler, L.; Folsom, R.; Royall, R.; Forsythe, A.; McEvoy, L.; Holzer, C.; Rae, D.; and Woodbury, M. Parameter and variance estimation. In: Eaton, W.W., and Kessler, L.L., eds. Epidemiologic Methods in Psychiatry: The NIMH Epidemiologic Catchment Area Program, Academic Press, in press.

Kish, L. Survey Sampling. New York: Wiley, 1965.

Malin, H.; Coakley, J.; and Kaelber, C. An epidemiologic perspective on alcohol use and abuse in the United States. In: NIAAA. <u>Alcohol and Health Monograph No. 1: Alcohol Consumptions and Related Problems</u>. DHHS Pub. No.(ADM)82-1190. Washington, D.C.: Supt. of Docs., U.S. Govt. Print. Off., 1982.

Mishara, B.L., and Kastenbaum, R. <u>Alcohol and Old Age</u>. New York: Grune and Stratton, 1980.

Robins, L.N.; Helzer, J.E.; Croughan, J.; and Ratcliff, K.S. The NIMH Diagnostic Interview Schedule: Its history, characteristics and validity. <u>Archives of General Psychiatry</u> 38:381-389, 1981.

SAS Institute, <u>SAS Users Guide: Statistics</u>. Cary, N.C.: SAS Institute Inc., 1982.

Vaillant, G.E., and Milofsky, E.S. Natural history of male alcoholism. <u>Archives of General Psychiatry</u> 39:127-133, 1982.

ALCOHOL ABUSE AND DEPENDENCE AS A RISK FACTOR ACROSS THE ADULT MALE AGE SPAN*

James C. Anthony

ABSTRACT

This paper presents results from an initial exploration of prospective data from the Baltimore Epidemiologic Catchment Area (ECA) Program. To investigate whether the consequences of alcohol abuse/dependence vary across the adult male age span, it examines what happened to 982 male Baltimore household survey respondents during a 1-year followup period, presenting cumulative incidence rates specific for age and alcohol abuse/dependence. As in the accompanying papers on the ECA Program, cases of alcohol abuse and/or dependence have been identified by the NIMH Diagnostic Interview Schedule (DIS) administered during the baseline survey. Interviews 1 year later provided data on followup characteristics, which include pathological drinking behavior, psychopathology, use of mental and other health services, and health-related behavior or experiences involving family, peers, and work.

This exploratory study suggests that DIS-measured alcohol abuse/dependence functions as a risk factor or predictor for many health-related experiences and behaviors measured at followup. The causal implications cannot be resolved at present. Though limited by small numbers of elderly cases, the analyses usually suggested very little age-related variation in the associations with baseline alcohol abuse/dependence. The discussion of these results includes an examination of methodologic limitations and strengths of this exploratory effort and points toward some specific directions for future investigations of the consequences of alcohol abuse and dependence in relation to age.

---

*William W. Eaton, Michael R. Von Korff, Elizabeth Ann Skinner, and Survey Research Associates of Baltimore played critically important roles in the Baltimore survey work.

PREFACE

The ECA Program data set is not yet fully prepared for prospective data analyses, so this report is somewhat premature. At the time of writing, all five ECA field sites continue to collect data or prepare followup data for file construction. It has been possible to extract a small number of variables from the Baltimore followup data set in order to begin exploration of questions indicated by this report's title. However, the work is intended to be essentially exploratory and descriptive, with some interval estimation and testing for the significance of observed associations when this might increase an understanding of the findings. Given the preliminary and incomplete nature of the data, there has been no attempt to evaluate, control, or clarify the status of confounding variables or effect modifiers other than gender. This is an important limitation of the findings presented here.

INTRODUCTION

Locke (this volume) and Robins (this volume) have explained how trained lay interviewers administered the Diagnostic Interview Schedule (DIS) as part of a more comprehensive health-oriented interview in field surveys for the NIMH Epidemiologic Catchment Area (ECA) Program. Information from the DIS has been processed for the computer, and computerized decision rules have been used to sort the survey respondents into diagnostic categories of the American Psychiatric Association's current Diagnostic and Statistical Manual (DSM-III). Alcohol abuse and alcohol dependence are two of the diagnostic categories covered by the DIS.

In line with DSM-III criteria, every respondent given a DIS diagnosis of alcohol abuse has reported evidence that suggests both a pattern of pathological alcohol use and impairment in social or occupational functioning because of alcohol use. Every respondent given a DIS diagnosis of alcohol dependence has reported evidence that suggests either tolerance to alcohol or symptoms of the alcohol withdrawal syndrome, as well as either a pattern of pathological alcohol use or impairment in social or occupational functioning due to alcohol use. However, the DIS classification of respondents vis a vis DSM-III alcohol abuse/dependence should do more than merely indicate their verbal behaviors during the DIS interview. To the degree that it is comprehensively useful and valid, this DIS diagnosis should also help in predicting and understanding what happens to respondents over time (see, for example, Guze 1967; Nunnally 1978; Klerman 1980).

The present report gives results from an initial exploration of Baltimore ECA Program data on what has happened to the survey respondents over time. It presents a comparison of DIS alcohol abuse/dependence cases' followup experience with that of noncases. The issue of alcohol abuse/dependence as a risk factor across the adult age span is considered through evidence on whether the associations between DIS-ascertained alcohol abuse/dependence and followup status are uniform across three groups defined by age. Thus, this work drives toward a better understanding of the consequences of alcohol abuse/dependence in relation to the age span. The separate contributions of chronological age, birth cohort, and secular periods are not taken up in this report.

MATERIALS AND METHODS

Population Sample and Response Rates

The study population was the adult household population living within the boundaries of three contiguous mental health catchment areas in eastern Baltimore City (Johns Hopkins Hospital, Baltimore City Hospitals, and Harbel). There were approximately 175,000 adult household residents 18 years of age and older in this urban area in 1981. About 35 percent were black. Additional details about the survey population in Baltimore are presented in Holzer et al. (this volume).

The survey team drew a probability sample of adults in this population, using methods described in detail elsewhere (Kramer et al. in press). Trained lay interviewers administered the DIS at baseline in 19818 and again during a followup personal interview about 1 year after baseline. Other sections of the interview covered sociodemographic factors, physical health and functional status, employment, interpersonal relationships, and use of health services. (The analysis on use of ambulatory services for mental health care makes use of additional data from a brief followup interview conducted by telephone 6 months after baseline.)

At baseline, there were 3,481 participating respondents, 78 percent of the sample. Of 3,360 respondents eligible for this analysis, 2,678 (80 percent) completed the initial interview, the telephone interview after 6 months, and the followup interview after 1 year. Whenever possible, subjects who moved to a new household or institutional residence within the greater metropolitan area of Baltimore were traced and interviewed at followup. Subjects who moved away from Baltimore or could not be located, subjects who died, and subjects who refused to be interviewed are counted among the nonparticipants at followup. The data to discriminate causes of nonparticipation were not available at the time of data analysis for this study. (The 121 subjects who participated at either baseline or followup by means of proxy interview with a key informant were excluded from this analysis because of uncertainty regarding completeness and validity of data gathered by proxy.)

Baseline Assessment of Alcohol Abuse/Dependence

The baseline DIS lifetime diagnosis has been used in this study. This lifetime diagnosis sorts the respondents into two groups: those with current alcohol abuse and/or dependence or with a past history (the cases) versus those without (the noncases).

The ECA Program has included investigations of DIS diagnoses made by the lay interview method in relation to criterion diagnoses made by psychiatrists. The currently available results suggest that the DIS "lifetime diagnosis" of alcohol abuse/dependence has sensitivity in a range from 75 to 90 percent and specificity in a range from 90 to 97 percent, as compared with the criterion diagnoses (Anthony et al. submitted; Robins et al. 1981).

The utility of DIS lifetime diagnosis at baseline was given additional support by preliminary work for this report. This work indicated that (1) for many analyses the strength of relationships between DIS/DSM-III alcohol abuse/dependence and later experiences did not vary substantially when DIS current diagnoses and DIS lifetime diagnoses were used to designate separate strata; and (2) very few Baltimore subjects developed alcohol abuse/dependence as a new condition between baseline and followup. Analytic refinements suggested by this preliminary work will be pursued in later multisite analyses of the ECA data.

The baseline DIS indicated that 297 of the male respondents and 87 of the female respondents had either current DSM-III alcohol abuse/dependence or a past history of these conditions. The DIS/DSM-III cases included 74 men aged 60 years and older. Fifty-four of these elderly men were interviewed at followup. Of 12 DIS/DSM-III female cases at baseline, 7 were interviewed at followup. With so few older female cases, the present report concerns only the males.

Measurement of Subject Status at Followup

In this report, data are presented on the relationships of baseline DIS alcohol abuse/dependence to subsequent occurrence of 14 health-related experiences and behaviors reported at followup. Listed in table 1, the 14 variables were selected to represent several categories and social fields: (1) pathological drinking

Table 1.--Health-Related Experiences and Behaviors Examined as Followup Characteristics in This Analysis

1. Pathological drinking behaviors

    a. Sustained high-dose drinking
    b. Failed attempt to reduce drinking

2. Disturbances in the mental life ("psychopathology")

    a. Sustained depressed/dysphoric mood
    b. Sustained mod-related death wish

3. Behavior and experiences involving the family

    a. Family objections to drinking
    b. Physical fighting with spouse**

4. Behavior and experiences involving persons outside family

    a. Objections to drinking by persons outside the family
    b. Broken relationship with a lover or close friend**

5. Behavior and experiences involving work and the workplace

    a. Job trouble or job loss due to drinking
    b. At least one disability day during last half of followup**
    c. Job loss or layoff during followup**

6. Use of mental health and other health services during followup

    a. At least one ambulatory visit for mental health care**
    b. Admission for inpatient medical care**
    c. Admission for inpatient mental health care**

**is used to indicate a variable that has been constructed without regard to subjects' experiences prior to the initial interview. Hence, the associated incidence rate estimates reflect both "new" and "repeat" occurrences of the associated experiences.

behavior, (2) disturbances in the mental life ("psychopathology"), (3) behavior and experiences involving the family, (4) behavior and experiences involving peers and other interpersonal relationships outside the family, (5) behavior and experiences involving the workplace, and (6) use of mental health and other health services. A variable to represent ambulatory visits for physical health care was initially included in the analysis plan but was dropped because of technical difficulties.

These variables were selected after examination of basic cross-tabulations by age and sex but before cross-tabulation by the alcohol abuse/dependence variables. That is, the analysis began with selection of the 14 variables shown in table 1 and the ambulatory physical health care variable. At the time of writing, no other followup variables have been studied in relation to the alcohol abuse/dependence variables.

When appropriate and possible, the variables were selected in pairs or triplets, the first member based on an interview question or questions that had an explicit linkage to drinking (e.g., "Did you ever lose a job or get kicked out of school on account of drinking?") and the other member(s) based on questions that had no explicit linkage (e.g., "[Since the initial interview], were you laid off from work or did you lose a job?").

A list of the questions from the DIS and from other parts of the baseline and followup interviews that were used to determine occurrence of the 14 health-related experiences and behaviors is available upon request to the author. Panel analysis of responses to these questions suggests that the degree of these variables' reliability is generally moderate, sometimes lower. Hence, relationships between alcohol abuse/dependence and these variables are subject to attenuation because of unreliability and other effects of survey error, as discussed later.

Statistical Analysis

This initial exploration of data has been based on the concept of cumulative incidence (Miettinen 1976; Kleinbaum et al. 1982). For this analysis, cumulative incidence has been specified as the proportion of individuals who develop the experience or behavior in question during the followup period. In this report, "cumulative incidence" and "cumulative incidence rate" are used equivalently to refer to this proportion.

For some variables (marked in the tables with a double asterisk), all subjects were counted in the denominator of the cumulative incidence rate as being at risk of the experience or behavior during the followup period. Further, subjects were added to the numerator of the rate if they reported occurrence of the experience or behavior upon followup, whether this was a repeat occurrence or a first occurrence. For the other variables, cumulative incidence has been estimated only on the basis of first occurrence of the experience or behavior during followup, and the candidate population in the denominator of the proportion consisted only of subjects whose baseline interview indicated no history of prior occurrences. (For the cumulative incidence estimates of this study, an individual subject has been counted no more than one time for the numerator and no more than one time for the denominator. This was true no matter how many times the individual subject engaged in the behavior or had the target experience during followup.)

The ratio of cumulative incidence for cases to the cumulative incidence for noncases has been used as a measure of the degree of association between alcohol abuse/dependence and followup status in this analysis, following Kleinbaum et al. (1982). Under the null hypothesis of no association, the value of this ratio (RR) is 1. With positive association, the rate ratio exceeds 1; with negative association, the rate ratio is less than 1 but greater than or equal to 0.

The degree of consistency of the association across age groups was tested by a chi-square statistic proposed by Miettinen (1975) except when there were contrary indications judged to be important (e.g., opposite direction rate ratios in the age strata; poorly distributed empty cells). When this test statistic indicated no departure from uniformity of effect, a Mantel-Haenszel test for significance of the common degree of association was conducted and a 90 percent confidence interval for the cumulative incidence ratio was estimated by the test-based interval estimation procedure proposed by Miettinen (1976). The Rothman-Boice statistical package was used for these exploratory analyses (Rothman and Boice 1979).

Proper consideration of the study findings requires attention to several issues of the exploratory and illustrative methods used here. First, these analyses are based upon ECA Program data tapes and the DIS computer program in use in October 1983. Second, these data have not been weighted to adjust for sample selection probabilities, and there has been no poststratification adjustment. Third, the statistical testing and interval estimation have not addressed possible survey design effects. Fourth, the work assumes its statistical models, and there is no evaluation of confounding or effect modification beyond the consideration of age. Fifth, the small number of subjects, particularly the small number of older cases, limits this single-site ECA study of age-related differences in the degree of association between alcohol abuse/dependence and followup status. It is unlikely that future refinements in analysis concerning the first three methodologic points will produce major changes in the overall pattern of findings. The problem of limited statistical power will affect any single-site analysis of the questions raised here. Future multi-site analyses will have some capacity to overcome this limitation.

It may be of some interest that the cumulative incidence estimates from this analysis have some applicability as annual incidence rates. This is not simply a consequence of the 1-year followup research design, because there was some inter-subject variation in the actual number of days between baseline and followup. However, review of this variation across groups defined by age, sex, and DIS diagnosis indicates average followup periods of between 360 and 378 days (i.e., close to the target of 1 year). In addition, a preliminary comparison suggested small differences between the cumulative incidence values and annual incidence rate estimates based on a person-time estimation procedure.

RESULTS

Cumulative Incidence by Age

Table 2 shows age-specific cumulative incidence rates for each of the target behaviors and experiences selected for this analysis, as well as rates of nonparticipation at followup.

Of 1,265 male participants at baseline, 22.4 percent did not complete followup interviews. Nonparticipation at followup was greatest for the oldest males, in part because of mortality.

Cross-sectional surveys of drinking practices and problems generally find age-related differences in prevalence (see, for example, Clark and Midanik 1982). Based on DIS questions that concern taking seven or more drinks every day for 2 weeks or more, this study's cumulative incidence estimate for first-time occurrence of sustained high-dose drinking was 5.4 percent among adult males 18 years of age and older. The estimated rate was lowest for males 18 to 24 years of age. It was substantially higher for males 35 to 44 years old and for those 60 and older, the age groups 25 to 34 and 45 to 59 having rates with intermediate values.

The overall cumulative incidence of a failed attempt to cut down or stop drinking was lower than the overall incidence of sustained high-dose drinking--3.1 percent compared with 5.4 percent. The youngest males had the lowest rate, but variation of the estimates with age was not pronounced.

Table 2.—Estimated Cumulative Incidence of Selected Followup Experiences of Males, By Age Unweighted Data from the 1981-82 Baltimore ECA Household Survey, Waves I and II

Age:	18-24	25-34	35-44	45-59	60+	All ages
Nonparticipation at followup						
Rate of nonparticipation (percent)	14.6	20.3	22.0	23.2	27.4	22.4
N at risk*	198	300	159	207	401	1,265
Sustained high-dose drinking						
Cumulative incidence rate (percent)	1.4	4.5	8.2	3.6	8.3	5.4
N at risk*	142	198	97	112	216	765
Failed attempt to reduce drinking						
Cumulative incidence rate (percent)	2.0	2.8	4.5	3.9	2.9	3.1
N at risk*	149	217	111	127	243	847
Sustained depressed/dysphoric mood						
Cumulative incidence rate (percent)	8.7	15.5	7.2	8.8	9.1	10.3
N at risk*	127	181	83	125	242	758
Sustained mood-related death wish						
Cumulative incidence rate (percent)	2.5	2.7	2.6	2.7	2.6	2.6
N at risk*	163	226	114	147	268	918
Family objections to drinking						
Cumulative incidence rate (percent)	14.0	13.6	18.3	15.5	13.4	14.5
N at risk*	121	162	82	97	201	663
Physical fights with spouse**						
Cumulative incidence rate (percent)	10.3	5.3	7.1	1.2	0.0	3.1
N at risk*	29	114	70	84	193	519

Table 2.—Estimated Cumulative Incidence of Selected Followup Experiences of Males, By Age Unweighted Data from the 1981-82 Baltimore ECA Household Survey, Waves I and II (cont'd.)

Age:	18-24	25-34	35-44	45-59	60+	All ages
Objections to drinking by persons outside the family						
Cumulative incidence rate (percent)	0.7	4.4	9.8	5.1	7.0	5.3
$\underline{N}$ at risk*	143	204	102	117	228	794
Broken relationship with lover or close friend**						
Cumulative incidence rate (percent)	16.0	14.2	11.4	2.5	2.1	8.7
$\underline{N}$ at risk*	169	239	123	159	289	979
Job trouble/loss due to drinking						
Cumulative incidence rate (percent)	0.7	0.9	1.9	3.6	1.6	1.6
$\underline{N}$ at risk*	149	219	108	137	247	860
At least 1 day of disability experienced during the 6th through final month of followup**						
Cumulative incidence rate (percent)	33.7	37.7	37.9	36.5	22.8	32.4
$\underline{N}$ at risk*	169	239	124	159	290	981
Job loss or layoff among persons who worked for pay during followup**						
Cumulative incidence rate (percent)	22.5	17.9	18.8	12.3	6.5	16.9
$\underline{N}$ at risk*	151	224	112	130	62	679
Sought ambulatory mental health care**						
Cumulative incidence rate (percent)	7.1	7.1	9.7	6.3	2.1	5.8
$\underline{N}$ at risk*	169	239	124	159	289	980

Table 2.--Estimated Cumulative Incidence of Selected Followup Experiences of Males, By Age Unweighted Data from the 1981-82 Baltimore ECA Household Survey, Waves I and II (cont'd.)

Age:	18-24	25-34	35-44	45-59	60+	All ages
Admitted for inpatient medical care**						
Cumulative incidence rate (percent)	1.2	4.2	12.9	15.1	19.4	11.0
N at risk*	169	239	124	159	289	980
Admitted for inpatient mental health care**						
Cumulative incidence rate (percent)	0.0	0.8	0.8	1.3	0.0	0.5
N at risk*	169	239	124	159	289	980

*These numbers indicate the baseline sample size. The number of subjects who completed the followup examinations can be obtained by multiplying the baseline sample size by the complement of the nonparticipation rate. The denominators for the cumulative incidence rates are somewhat less than the number of subjects who participated at followup when the analysis pertains to first-time occurrences of the experience or behavior.

**is used to indicate a variable that has been constructed without regard to subjects' experiences prior to the initial interview. Hence, the associated incidence rate estimates reflect both "new" and "repeat" occurrences of the associated experiences.

Epidemiologic studies have frequently found age-related variation in the prevalence of depressive symptoms and disturbances (e.g., Myers et al. in press). Based on DIS questions about 2 weeks or more of feeling depressed or being dysphoric, this study's cumulative incidence estimate for sustained depressed and/or dysphotic mood among males was 10.3 percent, with a peak value among males 25 to 34 years old.

Based on a DIS depression section question about 2 weeks of feeling "like you wanted to die," the cumulative incidence of mood-related death wish was found to be 2.6 percent for the males. There was very little age-related variation in the estimates for this mood-related disturbance among males.

Family objections to drinking and physical fighting with a spouse were studied as examples of health-related experiences and behaviors involving the family. The family objections are explicitly linked with drinking (i.e., they require drinking behavior on the part of the respondent). In contrast, physical fighting with a spouse may or may not be related to drinking, and the DIS questions used for this variable do not refer to drinking.

Among the men whose baseline record indicated no prior family objections to drinking, more than 14 percent reported family objections to drinking at followup. The age group 35 to 44 years had the highest rate, but there was comparatively little age-related variation in the study estimates for cumulative incidence of this drinking-related problem.

The cumulative incidence of physical fights with a spouse was 3.1 percent among the married males followed up in this study. Age-related incidence variation was observed, with males age 18 to 44 having substantially higher rates than those 45 years old and older. Two special features of this preliminary analysis should be noted. First, for this variable, the estimates are not based on a restriction to the first-time occurrence of the behavior (indicated by the double asterisk in the table). Second, the analysis concerns married males only. It was not possible to take into account whether each married subject had an opportunity for contact with his spouse, but this refinement would not be likely to produce major changes in the tabled estimates.

During the followup period, slightly more than 5 percent of the men at risk were told that they were drinking too much by persons outside the family (such as friends, coworkers, and doctors). The age-specific rates suggest that the youngest males were at lowest risk of this outcome, and the highest rates were observed for men 35 to 44 years old. Men aged 60 years and older were found to have the second highest rate.

A different pattern of age relationships was found with respect to the occurrence of broken friendships and love relationships. Males in the age range 18 to 34 were most likely to report that relationships with lovers or close friends had broken off during the followup period. The estimates indicate declining cumulative incidence with increasing age.. Different results might be obtained if the analysis were restricted to men with one or more close friendships or love relationships at baseline, but this analytic refinement could not be implemented.

The followup data indicate that slightly more than 1.5 percent of men in the sample reported alcohol-related trouble on the job or at school for the first time during the followup period, with the highest rates in the middle-aged and older age groups. (This preliminary analysis has not taken the employment status of the subjects into account.)

Based on a standard question about being kept from work, school, or usual activities because of injury or not feeling well, more than 32 percent of men in the sample reported experiencing disability days during the last half of the followup period (i.e., during the 6 months prior to followup interview). The men age 25 to 59 had the highest disability day rates; the oldest men were least likely to report disability days; and the youngest men had intermediate values.

Among the 670 men in the sample who worked for pay between baseline in 1981 and followup in 1982, almost 17 percent experienced job loss or layoff during that period. Cumulative incidence of this experience was higher for males in the younger age groups and lowest for working males 60 years of age and older.

The numerators of the estimated rates for mental health and medical care are based upon the numbers of men in the followup sample who reported at least one ambulatory visit or at least one admission for either mental health care or physical health care during followup. Mental health care was specified to include chemical dependency treatment and attendance at self-help groups in connection with problems involving use of alcohol and other drugs.

Five men reported being admitted for inpatient mental health care during the followup period, yielding an overall cumulative incidence rate of 0.5 percent. None of these men were 18 to 24 or 60 years old or older, so the point estimates for cumulative incidence in these age groups equaled 0.0 percent.

Ambulatory mental health care was more common than hospitalization, with cumulative incidence estimates from 6 to 10 percent of the men in the age groups 18 to 24, 25 to 34, 34 to 44, and 45 to

59. Only 2 percent of the men 60 years of age and older reported this type of health care. In contrast, the cumulative incidence of admission for inpatient medical care increased with age from 1.2 percent among men 18 to 24 to almost 20 percent in the group 60 years of age and older.

Alcohol Abuse/Dependence as a Prognostic and Risk Factor

Table 3 provides evidence on two important sets of relationships. First, the table shows cumulative incidence rates for males with a lifetime history of DIS-ascertained alcohol abuse and/or dependence by age, and also shows the number of cases at risk of each specific health-related experience and behavior. Variation in these rates for cases suggests the prognostic significance of cases' membership in the age-specified groups without taking into account the followup experience of noncases. Second, for each of the experiences and behaviors, the table also shows the ratio of the cumulative incidence rate for cases to the cumulative incidence rate for noncases (indicated by the row labeled "Estimated R.E."). Except where indicated by a footnote, the chi-square test to examine whether the association varies with age group has been found to be nonsignificant. (There were very few test statistics with p values below 0.10.) When the data indicate consistency of association across the age groups, the tables include results from a test of the significance of overall association. The approximately 90 percent confidence intervals for each rate ratio indicate the size of the estimated degree of association and its statistical precision. In reviewing these results, it is important to remember that neither prognostic significance nor degree of association bears an implication of causal significance.

Nonparticipation at Followup. The data in table 3 show that the rate of nonparticipation at followup was 19.2 percent among the 104 baseline alcohol abuse/dependence cases aged 18 to 34 years, 25.2 percent among 119 baseline cases aged 35 to 59 years, and 27.0 percent among 74 baseline cases aged 60 years and older. This suggests that classification by age at baseline was a prognostic factor that helped to discriminate followup participants among the cases from nonparticipants. However, the association between the cases' nonparticipation and age was not statistically significant. This result illustrates that here and throughout this report the statistical power of tests for association with age is limited because of small numbers of cases at risk within male subgroups defined by age. Unless the age relationships are fairly strong, the test statistics do not achieve statistical significance. Similarly, the age-specific cumulative incidence estimates for the cases of alcohol abuse/dependence have relatively large standard errors (i.e., low precision).

Table 3.—The Degree of Association Between a History of DIS/DSM-III Alcohol Abuse/Dependence and Later Experiences, Among Males, By Age: Unweighted Data from the 1981-82 Baltimore ECA Household Survey, Waves I and II

	Males			M-H Chi*	Approximate
Age:	18-34	35-59	60+	(p value)	90% CI for RR*
Nonparticipation at followup					
Number of cases at risk	104	119	74	1.2	(0.9, 1.4)
Rate of nonparticipation among cases (percent)	19.2	25.2	27.0	(0.11)	
Estimated RR*	1.1	1.3	1.1		
Sustained high-dose drinking					
Number of cases at risk	52	42	22	5.1	(2.7, 6.9)
Cumulative incidence rate for the cases (percent)	9.6	14.3	27.3	(<0.01)	
Estimated RR*	4.6	4.0	4.4		
Failed attempt to reduce drinking					
Number of cases at risk	74	69	38	5.4	(3.8, 12.4)
Cumulative incidence rate for the cases (percent)	8.1	8.7	13.2	(<0.01)	
Estimated RR*	7.9	3.7	13.5		
Sustained depressed/ dysphoric mood					
Number of cases at risk	58	64	39	4.4	(1.8, 3.7)
Cumulative incidence rate for the cases (percent)	27.6	15.6	12.8	(<0.01)	
Estimated RR*	3.0	3.2	1.5		
Sustained mood-related death wish					
Number of cases at risk	80	83	49	N/A	RR not uniform form across age strata (1). Chi for males 18-34 18-34 = 3.9, p < 0.001.
Cumulative incidence rate for the cases (percent)	8.1	3.6	2.0		
Estimated RR*	7.9	1.6	0.7		

Table 3.--The Degree of Association Between a History of DIS/DSM-III
Alcohol Abuse/Dependence and Later Experiences, Among Males, By Age:
Unweighted Data from the 1981-82 Baltimore ECA Household Survey,
Waves I and II (cont'd.)

	Males			M-H Chi*	Approximate
Age:	18-34	35-59	60+	(p value)	90% CI for RR*
Family objections to drinking					
Number of cases at risk	30	29	13	5.4	(2.1, 4.2)
Cumulative incidence rate				(<0.01)	
for the cases (percent)	40.0	37.9	23.1		
Estimated RR*	3.7	3.0	1.8		
Physical fights with spouse**					
Number of cases at risk	35	43	28	2.4	For males
Cumulative incidence rate				(<0.01)	18-59:
for the cases (percent)	11.4	9.3	0.0		(1.4, 6.9)
Estimated RR*	2.4	5.0	0/0		
Objections to drinking by persons outside family					
Number of cases at risk	58	49	25	3.0	(4.1, 9.9)
Cumulative incidence rate				(<0.01)	
for the cases (percent)	10.3	20.4	28.0		
Estimated RR*	7.5	5.8	6.3		
Broken relationship with lover or close friend**					
Number of cases at risk	84	88	53	2.5	(1.2, 2.5)
Cumulative incidence rate				(<0.01)	
for the cases (percent)	22.6	9.1	1.9		
Estimated RR*	1.7	1.9	1.1		
Job trouble/loss due to drinking					
Number of cases at risk	74	74	42	5.2	(7.3, 46.1)
Cumulative incidence rate				(<0.01)	
for the cases (percent)	2.7	8.1	9.5		
Estimated RR*	5.2	13.9	r/0		
At least 1 day of disability experienced during the 6th through final month of followup**					
Number of cases at risk	84	89	54	3.4	(1.2, 1.6)
Cumulative incidence rate				(<0.01)	
for the cases (percent)	42.9	46.1	35.2		
Estimated RR*	1.3	1.4	1.8		

Table 3.—The Degree of Association Between a History of DIS/DSM-III Alcohol Abuse/Dependence and Later Experiences, Among Males, By Age: Unweighted Data from the 1981-82 Baltimore ECA Household Survey, Waves I and II (cont'd.)

	Males			M-H Chi*	Approximate
Age:	18-34	35-59	60+	(p value)	90% CI for RR*
Job loss or layoff among persons who worked for pay during followup**					
Number of cases at risk	78	72	12	N/A	RR is not uniform across age strata (2). Age-specific chi have probabilities between 0.05 and 0.07.
Cumulative incidence rate for the cases (percent)	25.6	9.7	16.7		
Estimated RR*	1.4	0.6	4.1		
Sought ambulatory mental health care**					
Number of cases at risk	84	89	54	3.7	(1.7, 4.0)
Cumulative incidence rate for the cases (percent)	16.7	10.1	3.7	(<0.01)	
Estimated RR*	3.6	1.7	2.1		
Admitted for inpatient medical care**					
Number of cases at risk	84	89	54	1.6	(0.99, 1.8)
Cumulative incidence rate for the cases (percent)	6.0	15.7	24.1	(<0.06)	
Estimated RR*	2.7	1.2	1.3		
Admitted for inpatient mental health care**					
Number of cases at risk	84	89	54	3.6	Not calculated due to zeros in 4 of 10 cells.
Cumulative incidence rate for the cases (percent)	2.4	3.4	0.0	(0.01)	
Estimated RR*	r/0	r/0	0/0		

*The ratio of the rate for cases (r) to the rate for noncases is designated "RR." The Mantel-Haenszel chi statistic is designated "M-H chi."

Table 3.—The Degree of Association Between a History of DIS/DSM-III Alcohol Abuse/Dependence and Later Experiences, Among Males, By Age: Unweighted Data from the 1981-82 Baltimore ECA Household Survey, Waves I and II (cont'd.)

**Is used to indicate a variable that has been constructed without regard to subjects' experiences prior to the initial interview. Hence, the associated incidence rate estimates reflect both "new" and "repeat" occurrences of the associated experiences.

Note: The test for departure from a uniform RR across age strata was via Miettinen's asymptotic likelihood ratio method. It is distributed as chi-square with two degrees of freedom. Except where noted below and in the text, these tests have indicated uniformity of effect across the age strata.
1. In this analysis, the likelihood ratio test equaled 5.995, with p = 0.050.
2. In this analysis, the likelihood ratio test equaled 6.058, with p = 0.048.
All other analyses gave test statistics with p values greater than 0.15; most p's exceeded 0.40.

Though the data on cases suggested a tendency for age-related variation in nonparticipation, there was uniformity in the cumulative incidence ratios concerning the association between alcohol abuse/dependence and nonparticipation within each age-defined subgroup. The ratios were 1.1 for the youngest males, 1.3 for males age 35 to 59, and 1.1 for males 60 years of age and older. All of these estimated cumulative incidence rate ratios (RR) exceed unity, but this level of association between a baseline history of alcohol abuse/dependence and the probability of nonparticipation at follow-up might be a function of sampling variability alone and, in any case, was not strong. The Mantel-Haenszel (M-H) chi statistic was not large (p = 0.11), and the approximate 90 percent confidence interval for the overall rate ratio (RR) included 1.0 within its span (congruent with a null hypothesis of no association). Moreover, the upper bound for the approximate confidence interval was only 1.4.

Pathological Drinking Behavior. Among the male cases of alcohol abuse/dependence studied in this eastern Baltimore community survey, age appears to have had some prognostic significance in relation to sustained high-dose drinking. However, there was less variation with age among cases for the variable concerning failed efforts to reduce alcohol consumption.

Consistent with concepts of alcohol abuse and dependence, the test statistic and confidence interval suggest that alcohol abuse/ dependence at baseline was a risk factor for both types of pathological drinking behavior. The associations between baseline alcohol abuse/dependence and first-time occurrence of these behaviors were consistent across the age groups.

Symptoms of Depression. In the data on male cases, there is an apparent inverse relationship between age and the cumulative incidence rate for first-time occurrence of sustained depressed mood, but the relationship was not statistically significant. The association between alcohol abuse/dependence and sustained depression was uniform across the three age groups; it was moderately strong and achieved statistical significance (as indicated by the confidence intervals for the RR and the p values associated with the test statistic).

The association of baseline alcohol abuse/dependence and incidence of mood-related death wishes was found to vary across the male age strata (see footnote in table 3). Among men aged 18 to 34, there was a strong and statistically significant relationship between alcohol abuse/dependence and the cumulative incidence of this symptom (chi = 3.9, $p <$ 0.001). The data on the other two age groups indicate no similar associations.

Problems Involving Family. Many subjects with a history of alcohol abuse/dependence had reported problems involving family at baseline. As a result, the number of cases at risk of first-time occurrence of the problems during followup was exceptionally small. Thus, there are special limits on statistical power and other aspects of the analysis on this set of target behaviors and experiences.

Among the cases, there was a nonsignificant tendency for an age-related decline in the cumulative incidence of problems involving family. However, the statistics indicate a significant and strong association between baseline alcohol abuse/dependence and family objections to drinking. The degree of association with family objections to drinking was found to be consistent across the age groups.

For married males 18 to 34 and 35 to 59 years of age, the data show an association between the baseline diagnosis and physical fighting with a spouse. However, this behavior was not reported by subjects age 60 and older, and this suggests discontinuity in the association across the adult male age span.

Problems Outside of Family. The data on interpersonal relationships outside the family indicate the prognostic importance of age. In addition, the data sustain an impression that alcohol abuse/dependence is a risk factor for the target experiences that concern interpersonal relationships. The association between diagnosis and the cumulative incidence of objections to drinking by persons outside the family was very strong, as one might expect. In addition, there was a significant association with cumulative incidence of broken love and friendship relationships. These associations were consistent across the male age span.

Troubles in the Workplace. Among the male cases, there was age-related variation in the occurrence of drinking-related troubles at work (job or school), disability days, and job loss or layoff not explicitly linked to drinking. There were statistically significant associations between alcohol abuse/dependence and cumulative incidence of alcohol-related work troubles, as well as occurrence of disability days. However, the strength of association between alcohol abuse/dependence and disability days was not strong (as indicated by the confidence interval). In addition, it was noteworthy to find that baseline alcohol abuse/dependence was not, in the overall data, a strong risk factor for job loss and layoff among those who worked for pay during followup. The data on job loss and layoff indicate variability in the degree of association across the age span, and the test statistics for significance of association in each of the male age strata had p values at the margin of conventional statistical significance (0.06, 0.07, 0.06).

Use of Health Services. The data indicate that age was a prognostic factor and that baseline alcohol abuse/dependence was a risk factor for use of mental health services, both inpatient and ambulatory. The cumulative incidence of admission for inpatient mental health care was significantly associated with baseline alcohol abuse/dependence. However, there were no recorded admissions for the oldest age groups, which suggests age-related variation in the potency of alcohol abuse/dependence as a risk factor for this health-related experience.

Among male cases, age was a prognostic factor for seeking mental health care as an ambulatory patient or client, but the degree of association between diagnosis and subsequent use of mental health services did not vary with age.

There was, in addition, a relationship between age and inpatient medical care among male cases. The association of baseline alcohol abuse/dependence and subsequent inpatient medical care seems to have been consistent across age groups for men and was at the margin of conventional statistical significance ($p = 0.057$).

DISCUSSION

Followup Experience in Relation to Age

The data indicate that there were frequent but not always strong relationships between age and cumulative incidence of the 14 health-related experiences and behaviors examined for this report on the Baltimore ECA household survey. Some of the relationships were predictable. For example, the youngest males under study were more likely to report physical fighting with spouses. In contrast, the oldest males were more likely to report having been admitted for inpatient medical care.

There were also some unanticipated findings that concern age and cumulative incidence. For example, the estimated cumulative incidence rates for drinking-related problems among the oldest men were not dramatically lower than the estimated rates for middle-aged men. In addition, the cumulative incidence of these problems among the youngest subjects was frequently low in relation to that among the older subjects.

Myers et al. (in press) have reported that the current (6-month) prevalence of DIS/DSM-III major depression is low among persons age 65 and older as compared with younger age groups. This analysis indicates that the elderly men (age 60+) have a cumulative incidence of two types of depressive symptoms that is generally comparable to rates in the younger persons. Multisite analyses of the ECA Program data will help to clarify whether the depressive symptom experience of the elderly in the other ECA household samples has been similar. If there is consistency across sites, the multisite analyses will be able to clarify the meaning of this difference in findings about depressive symptoms as compared with major depressive disorder.

Alcohol Abuse/Dependence as a Risk Factor

As summarized in table 4, the ratios of cumulative incidence among cases to cumulative incidence among noncases generally indicated that the baseline DIS diagnosis of alcohol abuse/dependence was a risk factor or predictor for the occurrence of the target experiences and behaviors during the 1-year followup period in Baltimore. There were some observed instances of age-related variation in the potency of the risk factor.

Among the males under study, there was age-related variation in the association between alcohol abuse/dependence and occurrence of mood-related death wishes, and occurrence of job loss or layoff during followup. The data also indicated age-related variation in the association between baseline diagnosis and occurrence of physical fighting with a spouse. For each of the other variables, there was apparent consistency in the associations across age strata, with some possible age-related variation not detectable in this analysis. Generally, the risk factor status of baseline DIS/DSM-III alcohol abuse/dependence could be tested, and the associations were found to be significant or nearly so.

This exploratory analysis has not controlled for various confounding and effect-modifying factors that might account for the observed associations between alcohol abuse/dependence and subjects' status at followup. For example, a history of antisocial personality (ASP) disorder has been found to be associated with DIS alcohol abuse/dependence (Blazer et al. this volume). ASP is also quite likely to be associated with followup characteristics studied here (e.g., physical fighting with spouse, loss of job). As progress is made in the continuing analyses of these data, the influence of such factors will be taken into account so that the potency and mechanism of associations between subjects' alcohol abuse/dependence and their characteristics at followup can be better understood.

Variation with Age

Some prior research and commentaries have suggested that the consequences of alcoholism for the elderly are different from those experienced by younger cases (e.g., Schuckit and Miller 1976;

Table 4.—Summary of Findings on Male Respondents

	Do the data suggest that alcohol abuse/ dependence functioned as a risk factor?	Do the data indicate age-related variation? in the association?
Pathological drinking behaviors		
Sustained high-dose drinking	Yes	No
Failed attempt to reduce drinking	Yes	No (1)
Disturbances in the mental life ("psychopathology")		
Sustained depressed/dysphoric mood	Yes	No
Sustained mood-related death wish	In part	Yes
Behavior and experiences involving the family		
Family objections to drinking	Yes	No
Physical fighting with spouse**	Yes	Yes (3)
Behavior and experiences involving persons outside family		
Objections to drinking by persons outside the family	Yes	No
Broken relationship with a lover or close friend**	Yes	No
Behavior and experiences involving work and the workplace		
Job trouble or job loss due to drinking	Yes	No (1)
At least 1 disability day during last half of followup**	Yes	No
Job loss or layoff during followup**	No (2)	Yes

Table 4.—Summary of Findings on Male Respondents (cont'd.)

	Do the data suggest that alcohol abuse/ dependence functioned as a risk factor?	Do the data indicate age-related variation? in the association?
Use of mental health and other health services during followup		
At least one ambulatory visit for mental health care**	Yes	No
Admission for inpatient medical care**	No (2)	No
Admission for inpatient mental health care**	Yes	No (1)

**is used to indicate a variable that has been constructed without regard to subjects' experiences prior to the initial interview. Hence, the associated incidence rate estimates reflect both "new" and "repeat" occurrences of the associated experiences.

1. "No (1)" indicates that some attribute(s) of this study's data (usually small numbers of cases within a subgroup and occurrence of a null cumulative incidence value) might have restricted its capacity to detect variation with age.

2. "No (2)" indicates that the test for significance of the association had a p value that was marginal (i.e., not much greater than the conventional standard of 0.05).

3. "Yes (3)" indicates that the data suggest possible age-related variation in the potency of the risk factor, though this could not be tested due to presence of empty cells.

"In part" indicates that within at least one age-defined subgroup there was a statistically significant association with alcohol abuse/dependence.

Atkinson 1981). On the surface, this study's findings were contrary: (1) age was not generally a prognostic factor that helped to predict the followup status of cases; and (2) the associations between baseline history of alcohol abuse/dependence were generally uniform across age groups. However, there are a number of methodological issues and questions to be considered.

As already noted, the relatively small subgroup sizes limited this study's statistical power to detect age-related differences unless they are fairly large. Moreover, the number of female cases was too small for study of age-related differences. The remedy for these limitations is to study larger numbers of subjects. This can be achieved through future multisite analyses of the ECA data.

Available evidence suggests that many of the questions used to measure subject status at followup had moderate to low levels of reliability in the field survey context. These reliabilities can produce attenuated relationships in the analyses, including attenuated associations with age. Moreover, it is conceivable that the item reliabilities and their validity are different for the elderly as compared with the younger subjects and for the cases as compared with the noncases. These are possibilities worth further inquiry, since they could introduce bias in the observed associations. The elaboration of ECA Program analyses on consequences of alcohol abuse/dependence should include development, psychometric evaluation, and use of multi-item scales that will provide more precise and valid measurement of subject characteristics at followup.

There are separate issues that concern the assessment of alcohol abuse/dependence at baseline. First, in this study, the baseline history of alcohol abuse/dependence has been designated by DIS lifetime diagnosis according to DSM-III diagnostic criteria. Evidence from earlier studies indicates that the DIS lifetime diagnosis of alcohol abuse/dependence has been generally congruent with lifetime diagnoses made by psychiatrists. Evidence from this study indicates that the DIS lifetime diagnosis of alcohol abuse/ dependence was generally helpful in predicting what happened to the survey respondents over time. Notwithstanding these signs of diagnostic validity, it is possible that the DSM-III criteria and the DIS diagnosis have more utility in studies of younger alcoholics or problem drinkers, with less utility in studies of the elderly and a resulting bias in this study's findings. Resolution of this issue will require future studies with larger numbers of elderly cases and with greater attention to the validity of the DIS/DSM-III method and other diagnostic methods used to evaluate alcohol abuse and dependence in the elderly.

A second issue related to diagnostic assessment concerns use of the DIS lifetime diagnosis, which makes no distinction between cases that were active at baseline and past cases with no recently active drinking practices or problems. Preliminary work indicated that for many analyses the strength of relationships between DIS alcohol abuse/dependence and later experiences did not vary substantially when DIS current diagnoses and DIS lifetime diagnoses were used to designate separate strata. However, future ECA multisite analyses with larger numbers of cases will provide a better opportunity to test for age-related differences that might be found when the recency of drinking practices and problems is examined or controlled.

A third assessment issue involves the stages or phases of drinking practices and problems as discussed by Mandell (1983). This study has not addressed possible differences in stages of alcohol abuse/dependence, though it is likely that stage and age are interrelated predictors of certain consequences of alcohol abuse and dependence. At present, there is no generally accepted method for specifying which DIS cases are at earlier, middle, or later stages in their course, but this could be a useful development for future analyses on age-related variation in consequences of alcohol abuse or dependence.

Methodologic Strengths

The methodologic limitations of the present effort have been emphasized because the study was intended as a preliminary exploration of newly available data. Nevertheless, the ECA Program and the present study have some noteworthy methodologic strengths that enhance their capacity to clarify the potential consequences of alcohol abuse/dependence and age-related variation in these consequences.

The prospective research design represents an important methodologic strength not frequently encountered in the published scientific literature on drinking practices and problems. The prospective design brings many advantages, including a limited susceptibility to biases associated with selective recall or retrospective construction of events. Further, with several notable exceptions (e.g., Kozarevic et al. 1982), most of the previously reported prospective studies in this field have emphasized tangible consequences of drinking measured through survey questions with an explicit linkage to drinking. In contrast, this study's coverage extended to survey questions without this explicit linkage. Further, reports on prior survey-based prospective studies have not generally included estimates for cumulative incidence rates or other forms of incidence (e.g., Cahalan and Room 1974; Clark 1976; Clark and Cahalan 1976; Roizen et al. 1978). There are inherent weaknesses in survey-based estimates of incidence, but they convey information about the dynamics of alcohol-related consequences that are not readily communicated by other statistical indices.

The value of ECA Program incidence estimates is enhanced by the procedural independence of its baseline assessments of DSM-III alcohol abuse and dependence and the measurement of subjects' status at followup. The followup interviewers had no knowledge of DIS diagnosis at baseline; the standardized format and independence of the measurements reduced the likelihood of biases due to systematic variation in the amount of probing during assessment of followup characteristics.

Though the DIS is a relatively new diagnostic method subject to continuing study and refinement, it provides a substantially standardized diagnostic assessment with relatively little opportunity for the interviewer to manipulate the method based on preconceptions about age, alcohol use, or other characteristics of the subject. Moreover, the DIS diagnostic method consists of a comprehensible process in the sense that it is possible to inspect the interview record concerning what each subject was asked and how he or she responded to the interview questions, and it is possible to know precisely how the computer algorithm put the responses together for the diagnosis.

One general limitation of prospective studies, including this one, concerns sample attrition during the followup period. Followup participation in the Baltimore ECA study was not perfect but was generally good. In most subgroups there was no association between alcohol abuse/dependence and nonparticipation at followup.

CONCLUSION

The evidence from this exploratory study indicates that alcohol abuse/dependence is a risk factor or predictor of selected health-related experiences and behaviors over a 1-year followup period. This evidence helps substantiate the utility of the DIS lifetime diagnosis of DSM-III alcohol abuse/dependence in predicting and understanding what happens to subjects over time. Issues concerning confounding factors, effect modifiers, and other aspects of the mechanisms that account for the observed associations will be taken up as progress is made in the multisite analyses of ECA data.

This study's findings did not generally indicate that there was great variability in the potency of alcohol abuse/dependence as a risk factor across the adult age span. More often than not, the associations between alcohol abuse/dependence and followup characteristics were consistent across the three age groups studied. However, the subgroup analyses were based upon rather small numbers of subjects, and there are some other unresolved methodologic issues that require further attention before firm conclusions about age-related variation can be made. The discussion of these results includes an examination of methodologic limitations and strengths of this exploratory effort and points toward some specific directions for future investigations of the consequences of alcohol abuse and dependence in relation to age.

REFERENCES

Anthony, J.C.; Folstein, M.F.; Romanoski, A.J.; Von Korff, M.R.; Nestadt, G.N.; Chahal, R.; Merchant, A.; Brown, C.H.; Shapiro, S.; Kramer, M.; and Gruenberg, E. M. Comparison of Lay D.I.S. and a Standardized Psychiatric Diagnosis: Experience in Eastern Baltimore. Submitted.

Atkinson, J.H. Alcoholism and geriatric problems. Part II. Advances in Alcoholism 2(9):1-3, 1981.

Cahalan, D., and Room, R. Problem Drinking Among American Men. New Brunswick, N.J.: Rutgers Center of Alcohol Studies, 1974.

Clark, W.B. Loss of control, heavy drinking and drinking problems in a longitudinal study. Journal of Studies on Alcohol 37(9):1256-1290, 1976.

Clark, W.B., and Cahalan, D. Changes in problem drinking over a four-year span. Addictive Behavior 1(3):251-259, 1976.

Clark, W.B., and Midanik, L. Alcohol use and alcohol problems among U.S. adults: Results of the 1979 national survey. In: NIAAA. Alcohol and Health Monograph No. 1: Alcohol Consumption and Related Problems. DHHS Pub. No. (ADM)82-1190. Washington, D.C.: Supt. of Docs., U.S. Govt. Print. Off., 1982.

Guze, S.B. The diagnosis of hysteria: What are we trying to do? American Journal of Psychiatry 124:491-498, 1967.

Kleinbaum, D.G.; Kupper, L.L.; Morganstern, H. Epidemiologic Research, Belmont, CA: Lifetime Learning Pubs., 1982.

Klerman, G.L. Long-term outcomes of neurotic depressions. In: Sells, S.B.; Crandall, R.; Strauss, J.S.; and Pollin, W., eds. Human Functioning in the Longitudinal Perspective. Baltimore: Williams and Wilkins, 1980. pp. 58-70.

Kozarevic, D.; Demirovic, J.; Gordon, T.; Kaelber, C.T.; McGee, D.; and Zukel, W.J. Drinking habits and coronary heart disease: The Yugoslavia Cardiovascular Disease Study. American Journal of Epidemiology 116(5):748-758, 1982.

Kramer, M.; Anthony, J.C.; and Von Korff, M.R. Patterns of mental disorders among the elderly residents of eastern Baltimore. Journal of the American Geriatrics Society in press.

Mandell, W. Types and phases of alcohol dependence illness. In: Galanter, M., ed. <u>Recent Developments in Alcoholism</u>. Vol. 1. New York: Plenum Press, 1983. pp.. 415-447.

Mantel, N., and Haenszel, W. Statistical aspects of the analysis of data from retrospective studies of disease. <u>Journal of the National Cancer Institute</u> 22(4):719-748, 1959.

Miettinen, O.S. "Principles of Epidemiologic Research." Department of Epidemiology and Biostatistics, School of Public Health, Harvard University. Unpublished course text, 1975.

Miettinen, O.S. Estimability and estimation in case-referent studies. <u>American Journal of Epidemiology</u> 103(2):226-235, 1976.

Myers, J.K.; Weissman, M.M.; Tischler, G.L.; Holzer, C.E.; Leaf, P.J.; Orvaschel, H.; Anthony, J.C.; Boyd, J.H.; Burke, J.D.; Kramer, M.; and Stoltzman, R. The prevalence of psychiatric disorders in three communities: 1980-82. <u>Archives of General Psychiatry</u> in press.

Nunnally, J. <u>Psychometric theory</u>. 2d ed. New York: McGraw-Hill, 1978.

Robins, L.N.; Helzer, J.E.; Croughan, J.; and Ratcliff, K. National Institute of Mental Health Diagnostic Interview Schedule. <u>Archives of General Psychiatry</u> 38:381-389, 1981.

Roizen, R.; Cahalan, D.; and Shanks, P. "Spontaneous remission" among untreated problem drinkers. In: Kandel, D.B., ed. <u>Longitudinal Research on Drug Use--Empirical Findings and Methodological Issues</u>. Washington, D.C.: Hemisphere, 1978. pp. 197-221.

Rothman, K.J., and Boice, J.D. <u>Epidemiologic Analysis With a Programmable Calculator</u>. DHEW Publ. No. (NIH)79-1649. Washington, D.C.: Supt. of Docs., U.S. Govt. Print. Off., 1979.

Schuckit, M.A., and Miller, P.L. Alcoholism in elderly men: A survey of a general medical ward. <u>Annals of the New York Academy of Sciences</u> 273:558-571, 1976.

THE ELDERLY ALCOHOLIC: A PROFILE*

Dan Blazer, Linda George, Max Woodbury, Ken Manton, and
Kathleen Jordan

ABSTRACT

Nearly 4,000 persons 18 years of age and older, including over 1,500 persons 60 years of age and older, were sampled and interviewed within a 5-county area of North Carolina as part of the Epidemiologic Catchment Area Project. Data from this study were used to contrast elderly and young subjects currently suffering from a DIS/DSM-III diagnosis of alcohol abuse/dependence as well as a larger group of subjects with at least one symptom of alcohol abuse/dependence. By means of simple comparisons as well as a new method for deriving symptom profiles, the Grade of Membership analysis, a profile of the elderly alcoholic emerges. This profile suggests that the elderly alcoholic is more likely to be black, less educated, and from a rural residence than his or her younger counterpart. In addition, the elderly alcoholic is relatively free of other psychiatric symptoms and/or disorders, with the exception of cognitive impairment.

INTRODUCTION

Clinicians have become increasingly aware of the significance of alcohol problems in later life. Epidemiologic studies can provide even further information to clinicians. Results have suggested that alcohol problems in late life are qualitatively different than those in earlier stages of the life cycle (Dunham 1981). One reason for this observation may be the cohort effect, a phenomenon recognized in most longitudinal studies. Rates of alcohol consumption and patterns of drinking may have been different

---

*The data are derived from the NIMH Epidemiologic Catchment Area Program.

for the present cohort of older adults throughout their lifespan, and thus cannot be attributed to a generalized process of aging.

On the other hand, despite the implications of cohort differences, there are a number of aspects of social and biological aging processes that may affect the nature and impact of alcohol consumption. For example, physiological aging may lead to decreased tolerance, which in turn may require the older adult to adapt to new relationships with family and society. These new relationships may, in turn, lead to changes in the rate of alcohol consumption and patterns of drinking. Older adults with mild to moderate physical or mental health impairments, such as cognitive decline, may be forced to live with relatives or companions, thus exposing their alcohol intake to close monitoring by others.

Social relations affecting alcohol consumption may change with the aging process as well. For example, older adults may seek companionship in social settings where alcohol consumption is not tolerated (such as senior centers or in churches) or, at least, the pattern of alcohol intake is modified. For example, the individual who frequented bars and sought companionship with drinking buddies may in later life find that these former relationships are no longer available or meaningful. In addition, lack of transportation and eco- nomic constraints may have an impact upon the drinking behavior of the elderly.

On the other hand, anecdotal evidence suggests that persons who rarely drank earlier in life sometimes relax certain prohibitions regarding alcohol consumption and even develop abuse and dependence syndromes for the first time in late life (Mishara and Kastenbaum 1980). For example, women who have difficulty in adjusting to the retirement of their husbands and the absence of children from the household have been thought to be at particular risk for late onset alcohol problems.

Unfortunately, it is difficult for clinicians to evaluate the frequency of the inhibitory or facilitating effects of aging on alcohol problems because they see a biased sample of elderly persons with alcohol problems. For example, physicians serving hospital emergency rooms are more likely to see elderly male alcoholics who demonstrate overt problems with abuse (i.e., public drunkenness or alcoholic stupor) and poor social networks (Schuckit and Miller 1976). The prototype for such individuals is the skid row alcoholic (Bahr and Caplow 1973). In addition, symptoms of abuse and/or dependence are often overlooked when the elderly alcoholic presents with symptoms of cognitive impairment or chronic illness as opposed to complaints of overt alcohol difficulties.

Thus, a comprehensive community profile of drinking problems among the elderly can be of great benefit to clinicians working with older adults. Broadening the horizons of the clinician should increase his or her sensitivity to potential and actual alcohol abuse and/or dependent syndromes in late life. Because older persons are especially likely to be vulnerable to multiple impairments if they suffer problems in any one area, elderly alcoholics are probably at greater increased risk for impairment in other areas of functioning than are younger alcoholics.

In this paper, a profile of the elderly community alcoholic will be described, based on a community sample of adults from the Piedmont Health Survey, part of the National Institute of Mental Health Epidemiologic Catchment Area Program. Nearly 4,000 persons 18 years of age and older, including over 1,500 persons 60 years of age and older, were sampled and interviewed within a five-county area of the North Carolina Piedmont. Data from this study will be used to contrast elderly alcoholics with younger alcoholics. In particular, a new statistical procedure for deriving clinical syndromes from epidemiologic data will be applied.

METHODS

In this paper, results are reported from the National Institute of Mental Health Epidemiologic Catchment Area Program. Five sites geographically distributed through the continental United States (New Haven, East Baltimore, Greater St. Louis, the Piedmont of North Carolina, and East Los Angeles), were each randomly sampled to yield approximately 3,000 interviews, one per household. In addition, samples to yield 500 institutional respondents were drawn in each area. In the Duke ECA study (i.e., the Piedmont Health Survey), a supplementary sample was drawn to yield an additional 900 interviews from elderly (60+) community residents. Though the survey included both community and institutional residents, only results from community respondents are reporting.

In the Piedmont Health Survey all housing units from segments throughout a five-county area in the north central Piedmont of North Carolina were enumerated. The segments were selected to be demographically representative of the population within the five counties on the dimensions of race, rural/urban residence, and socioeconomic status. Households were selected at random. Once a household was selected and rostered for all residents 18 and over, the Kish method was used to select one potential participant from each household (Kish 1965). For the elderly oversample, the same method was applied to select one potential participant 60 years of age and older. For the general community survey, 3,911 households were screened; 3,371 households were screened for the elderly oversample. They yielded 3,015 respondents in the community sample and 906 respondents in the elderly oversample.

There were 3,798 interviews usable for this study. Reasons that certain interviews could not be used included the availability of information only from a proxy respondent ($\underline{n}$ = 80), a partial interview ($\underline{n}$ = 37), and a determination by the research team that interview information was not reliable ($\underline{n}$ = 6). The overall response rate was 79 percent; the response rate in the elderly sample was 81 percent. Reasons for nonresponse included the inability to screen a household to determine a respondent (10 percent) and the refusal of a designated respondent to participate in the survey (11 percent).

Rural/urban residence was determined on the basis of the county in which the respondent resided. Durham County, which contains the city of Durham, is part of a Standard Metropolitan Statistical Area (SMSA). Four counties to the northeast of Durham in the North Carolina Piedmont--Granville County, Vance County, Warren County, and Franklin County--do not contain an SMSA. These four counties are contiguous and form a catchment area for one mental health center. Two of these counties are contiguous with Durham County.

The demographic profile of respondents by age is presented in table 1. As is readily apparent, selection of an elderly oversample results in a large proportion of widowed and few single persons, many who did not complete high school, and many who are living along. Otherwise, demographic characteristics of the sampled respondents do not differ significantly from those of the general adult population of these five counties.

Each participant in the survey underwent a 2-hour interview, including the Diagnostic Interview Schedule (DIS), a highly structured interview schedule developed for use by lay interviewers in epidemiologic studies from which computer-based diagnoses can be generated in terms of selected DSM-III dis- orders (Robins et all. 1981). The DIS is designed to elicit the elements of a diagnosis, including the presence or absence of symptoms; their severity, frequency, and distribution over time; and whether or not they can be explained by physical illness, drug and/or alcohol use, or another psychiatric diagnosis. It is structured both for the main questions and followup probes of the answers to those questions. It is precoded so that answers can be data entered directly after editing. Both current and lifetime diagnoses can be generated.

Table 1.—Demographic Profile of Respondents in the
Piedmont Health Survey
(Percentage)

Variable	Elderly (≥60) (n = 1,620)		Young (<60) (n = 2,176)		Total (n = 3,796)	
Age						
18-40	0	(0)	1,433	(66)	1,433	(38)
41-59	0	(0)	743	(34)	743	(20)
60-74	1,196	(74)	0	(0)	1,196	(31)
75+	424	(26)	0	(0)	424	(11)
Sex						
Male	561	(35)	927	(42)	1,488	(39)
Female	1,059	(65)	1,249	(57)	2,308	(61)
Race						
White	1,038	(64)	1,373	(63)	2,411	(64)
Nonwhite	582	(36)	802	(37)	1,384	(36)
Marital status						
Married	699	(43)	1,266	(58)	1,965	(52)
Widowed	721	(45)	95	(4)	816	(21)
Separated/ divorced	117	(7)	321	(15)	438	(12)
Never married	83	(5)	494	(23)	577	(15)
Residence						
Urban	897	(55)	1,199	(55)	2,096	(55)
Rural	723	(45)	977	(45)	1,700	(45)
Education						
< HS	1,014	(63)	551	(26)	1,565	(41)
≥ HS	588	(37)	1,599	(74)	2,187	(59)
Living arrangements						
Alone	645	(40)	294	(14)	939	(25)
With someone else	973	(60)	1,881	(86)	2,854	(75)

Five current (within the past year) diagnoses are considered in this study--alcohol abuse and/or dependence, major depressive episode, antisocial personality disorder, cognitive deficit, and sexual difficulties. The first two are from Axis I of DSM-III, the third is from Axis II, and the fourth, cognitive deficit, represents those individuals who score within the severe range on the Folstein Mini Mental State Exam (APA 1980; Folstein et al. 1975). A diagnosis of "sexual difficulties" is based on a cursory evaluation of general difficulties that an individual may suffer in sexual functioning. In addition to the DIS, data were recorded on a series of sociodemographic characteristics and behaviors, as well as the use of health services. The data presented in this paper derive from DIS computer-generated DSM-III diagnoses, individual items from the DIS, and additional questions regarding characteristics and behavior of the individual subjects sampled.

Several cautions should be observed in interpreting the results presented. First, though the survey included both households and institutions, the data presented are only from the unweighted household sample respondents. Therefore, the rates for alcohol abuse and/or dependence may be significantly lower than if cases from the institutional sample were included. Consequently, comparisons with other ECA sites could also be affected by differential rates of institutionalization. In addition, the data are exclusively dependent upon the accuracy of reporting of respondents. No medical records were reviewed. Therefore, memory loss of symptoms over time coupled with underreporting due to embarassment or other reasons may adversely bias these results. Memory loss may also differentially affect the report of symptoms across age groups. Nevertheless, no evidence exists to date suggesting that this particular survey suffers from defects greater than any other community-based epidemiologic survey of alcohol use among the elderly. As the analyses presented below rely upon current (within the last year) symptoms, bias secondary to memory problems should be minimized.

Analyses in this paper will not attempt to separate the subcategories of alcohol use but rather will combine all three categories (abuse, dependence, and abuse plus dependence) into one category. If symptoms leading to a DIS/DSM-III diagnosis of alcohol abuse and/or dependence are reported for the year preceding the interview, these subjects are classed as current alcoholics. Current diagnoses of alcohol abuse and/or dependence were found in only 1.4 percent of the elderly compared with 3.9 percent of those persons less than 60 years of age.

Two approaches to data analysis are taken in this paper. The first is simply a comparison of elderly vs. young current alcoholics according to demographic characteristics, other DIS/DSM-III diagnoses, characteristics of alcohol consumption, health care needs, and health care utilization. Results demonstrating clinically meaningful differences will be presented. Because of the relatively small numbers of subjects in individual cells, substantial percentage differences did not always reach significance. Chi-square tests of significance were performed for all comparisons.

The second analytic approach takes advantage of a new methodology to identify and describe profiles of disease symptomatology and abnormal behavior. This methodology, called Grade Of Membership (GOM) analysis (Woodbury and Manton 1982), overcomes simultaneously the problems of case clustering and estimation of discriminant coefficients that describe the empirically derived clusters.

Significant is the fact that the clusters found are based upon a concept of "fuzzy" as opposed to the more usual "crisp" clustering. That is, instead of assessing that each case belongs exclusively to a single group or cluster, a coefficient (g_{ik}) is calculated, which states the degree to which the symptoms of the i-th person is described by the k-th group or cluster. In this way, gradations in the individual expression of psychiatric symptoms may be represented. Strauss et al. (1979) found that failure to represent such individual gradations in symptomatic expression was a problem both in current psychiatric disease classification and in many of the multivariate procedures used to evaluate those classifications. The greater flexibility of the "fuzzy" clustering logic used in GOM analysis means that the procedure can be used in the assessment of the reliability of externally defined psychiatric diagnoses, multiple diagnoses for individuals, symptom presentation, and severity. It represents patient heterogeneity within the traditionally defined DIS/DSM-III diagnostic categories.

Briefly, the GOM analysis produces maximum likelihood estimates of two types of coefficients. The first type, the g_{ik} alluded to above, relates each case (i = 1,2,...I) to each of K pure types. The second set of coefficients, the λ_{kjl}, describes each of the K pure types in terms of the probability that each will have the l-th response to the j-th variable. Both coefficients are constrained to be between 0 and 1. The g_{ik} must sum to 1.0 for each person over all of the K groups. If the g_{ik} for a given pure type is exactly 1.0, then that individual has exactly the attributes described by the λ_{kjl}. If all of the cases had g_{ik}'s of exactly 1.0 or 0.0, then we would have an analogous situation to that in standard or "crisp" clustering. If, as is generally the case, the g_{ik}'s are neither 1.0 nor 0.0, we have heterogeneity residing within the classification system. If the g_{ik}'s do not cluster near 0.0 or 1.0, then, to adequately describe the data, a "crisp" clustering procedure would have to produce more groups (because there is no other way to represent the heterogeneity in a "crisp" clustering procedure).

It is important to understand that the g_{ik} are not probabilities. Rather, they are weights that relate the observed symptom pattern to the pattern of response for each of the K pure types described by the λ_{kjl}. Since the g_{ik} are forced to lie between 0.0 and 0.1, the λ_{kjl} must be viewed as external points within which the sample points are distributed.

This attribute of the GOM model has several important analytic implications when applied to diagnostic criteria. First, since all sample points must be distributed between the symptom profiles described by the λ_{kjl}, the model has a certain degree of sample invariance. That is, the individual sample points could be moved somewhat and not necessarily change the λ_{kjl} coefficients. Indeed, we have found this illustrated in a number of studies where a λ_{kjl} profile was identified, which because it implied a high rate of death or institutionalization, had few cases where the g_{ik} was near 1.0. Second, because we estimate coefficients that empirically describe the distribution of cases (i.e., the distribution of g_{ik}), the model does not make assumptions about the form of the distribution of cases.

Third, with these concepts, one can see how GOM can represent disease progression in individual heterogeneity. As extreme points, pure types may emerge that represent the furthest progression of disease. Differences in individual coefficients represent differences in the degree to which an individual has progressed to that end point. Furthermore, different individuals may, because of individual differences, progress toward end points via different paths.

These concepts are also important in understanding how error in the diagnostic categories can be evaluated. Given that the pure types represent extreme points in the space of clinical attributes, it is an inference that these extreme points correspond to end points of specific disease processes. To the degree that epidemiologic data represent the sum total of information about underlying disease states, this assumption is reasonable. It should also be clear that pure types are features of the total clinical picture. Thus, their interpretation depends on their relation to clinical variables, which may possibly indicate that two pure types represent (a) different disease processes, (b) the same disease process that is expressed differently because of different patient attributes, or possibly (c) different stages in disease progression.

Variables can actually be employed in the GOM analyses in two logically distinct ways, i.e., as internal and external variables. In general, symptoms will be used as internal variables. Internal variables are used to define the groups. External variables are not allowed (in the likelihood calculations) to affect the definition of the clusters. The λ_{kjl}'s for external variables thus are really measures of association between those variables and the groups defined by the internal variables. The external variables are typically the externally derived diagnostic variables (e.g., the DSM-III diagnostic classification) but may include other factors, depending upon the goals of the analysis. In the present analysis, both the DIS/DSM-III diagnoses and demographic variables are used as external variables.

In order to perform a GOM analysis on the present data set, all individuals 18 and above who positively responded to at least one item in the alcohol abuse and dependence section of the questionnaire and who stated that they suffered from this symptom of alcohol abuse and/or dependence within the year prior to the interview were included (n = 295). As can be seen, this is nearly three times the number of subjects who had a current alcohol diagnosis (n = 106). Of the subjects, 183 were 18 to 39 years of age, 63 were between 40 and 59 years of age, and 49 were 60+ years of age. Age was entered as an external variable to determine the age distribution for persons in each of the pure types.

The number of pure types in this analysis was a priori set at four. This allows for the emergence of pure types that can be related to the three alcohol abuse/dependence categories (i.e., alcohol abuse, alcohol dependence, and combined alcohol abuse/dependence) plus a group with no diagnosis.

RESULTS

The demographic profile of both the young and the elderly DIS-diagnosed DSM-III current alcoholics is presented in table 2. Compared with the overall elderly population, current elderly alcoholics are more likely to fall into the 60 to 74 age range (the young old), to be male, to be non-white, to be separated or divorced, to have less than a high school education and to live with someone else. In comparison to younger alcoholics, elderly alcoholics have a greater likelihood of being non-white. However, elderly alcoholics are similar to their younger alcoholic counterparts in more often living with someone else than does the general population.

Table 2.—Demographic Characteristics of Elderly and
Young DIS/DSM-III Current Alcoholics
(Percentage)

	Elderly (n = 21)	Young (n = 85)	Total (n = 106)
Age			
18-40	0	67	49
41-59	0	33	24
60-74	81	0	14
75+	19	0	3
Sex			
Male	86	86	86
Female	14	14	14
Race			
White	43	59	51
Nonwhite	57	41	49
Marital status			
Married	38	42	41
Widowed	33	5	10
Separated/divorced	19	19	19
Never married	10	34	30
Residence			
Urban	57	54	55
Rural	43	46	45
Education			
HS	76*	46	52
HS	24	54	48
Living arrangements			
Alone	29	18	20
With someone else	71	82	80

(Lifetime includes both current and inactive)

*$p < .05$

Both young and elderly alcoholics are compared by a series of DIS-generated DSM-III diagnoses in table 3. Except for moderate and severe cognitive deficit, current elderly alcoholics are less likely to demonstrate concurrent diagnoses, supporting previous contentions that late life drinking problems are more likely to exist independent of concurrent psychiatric disorder.

Elderly alcoholics are compared with young alcoholics in table 4 with respect to their alcohol consumption. The elderly have very heavy levels of alcohol intake less often but are more likely to demonstrate evidence of dependence, such as a need for a drink before breakfast.

Table 5 presents the health care needs and utilization of the same groups. The elderly are more likely to have talked to an M.D. about their drinking and to admit that they have wanted to stop drinking but could not, again emphasizing a general trend toward dependence rather than abuse. Older alcoholics tend to use drug or alcohol clinics more frequently than younger alcoholics but are less likely to have used self help groups. When current elderly and current young alcoholics are compared for the frequency of certain alcohol related symptoms, the elderly are less likely to report blackouts than the young, but are much more likely to report "the shakes," again evidence of a pattern of dependence. Despite the higher rate of cognitive deficit by test (table 3) there is virtually no difference between reports of memory problems by elderly alcoholics when compared with young alcoholics (10 percent and 7 percent respectively). Elderly alcoholics are much more likely to report fights while drinking (51 percent compared with 19 percent), but the rates of being arrested for drinking and drunken driving are similar for the two groups of alcoholics (38 percent compared with 36 percent and 33 percent compared with 46 percent, respectively). In a review of physical symptoms, elderly alcoholics generally complain of more symptoms such as chest pain, constipation, and fainting spells as well as present an overall increased rate of reporting physical symptoms, but for none of these symptoms does the rate exceed 20 percent. Surprisingly, only 5 percent of elderly alcoholics report significant sleep difficulties.

The GOM model was applied to all individuals suffering from at least one current symptom of alcohol abuse, alcohol dependence, and alcohol abuse/dependence (n = 295). Internal symptomatic variables used included indicants of drinking behavior, indicants of depressive symptomatology, and a series of miscellaneous symptoms (see table 6). External variables, as noted above, included the three DIS/DSM-III diagnostic categories for alcoholism and a no diagnosis category plus demographic variables. The number of pure types was a priori set at four for this analysis. The four pure types that

Table 3.—Rates for a Series of DIS/DSM-III Diagnoses
in Current Elderly and Current Young Alcoholics
Stratified by Age
(Percentage)

	Current elderly (n = 21)	Current young (n = 85)	Total (n = 106)
Major depressive disorder	5	11	9
Antisocial personality disorder	5	13	11
Cognitive deficit	57*	12	21
Sexual difficulties	5	7	7

*$p < .05$

Table 4.—Elderly vs. Young Current Alcoholics by the
Characteristics of Their Alcohol Consumption Within the Year
(Percentage)

	Elderly (n = 21)	Young (n = 85)	Total (n = 106)
Consumed a fifth of liquor in one day	43*	68	63
Two weeks of heavy drinking	33	41	39
Two months or more of heavy drinking	24*	60	53
Gone on binge	14	18	17
Needed a drink before breakfast	62*	25	32
Needed a drink to work	19	12	13
Drank even when ontraindicated by illness	33	19	22

*$p < .05$

Table 5.—Elderly vs. Young Current Alcoholics by Health Care Needs and Utilization (Percentage)

	Elderly (n = 21)	Young (n = 85)	Total (n = 106)
Told MD about drinking problem	38	20	24
Wanted to stop drinking but couldn't	52*	25	30
Health services use within last 6 months	67	48	52
Ever used alcohol or drug clinic	24	12	14
Ever used self-help groups	5	12	11

*$p < .05$

Table 6.—Internal Variables Included in Grade of Membership (GOM) Analysis (Percent Frequency in the Sample of Subjects with at Least One Current Symptom of Alcohol Abuse/Dependence, n = 295)

Characteristics of alcohol
    consumption

Family and friends object to drinking (32)

Heavy drinking in 1 day (33)

Thinks self excessive drinker (18)

Two weeks of constant drinking (13)

Wanted to stop but couldn't (9)

Two months of constant drinking (36)

Drunk driving (5)

Binges (6)

Physical fights (5)

Needs drink before breakfast (9)

Blackouts, the shakes, seizure, and/or DT's (11)

Work difficulties from clinic (5)
Drink even when ill (6)
Told MD about drinking (8)
Needs drink to work (3)
Sought help from alcohol clinic

Current symptoms of depression

Depressed for 2 weeks (12)
Lost appetite (7)
Lost weight (4)
Gained weight (14)

Miscellaneous current symptoms

Abdominal pain (13)
Back pain (23)
Headaches (15)
Weakness (11)
Anxiety (6)
Memory loss (2)
Phobias (21)
Drug problems (12)

Trouble sleeping (17)
Less interest in sex (11)
Agitation (8)
Feels worthless (8)
Trouble concentrating (10)
Thought of death (19)
Suicidal thoughts (6)

emerged in the GOM analysis are presented in table 7 and can roughly be described as follows: type I--asymptomatic; type II--mixed, episodic drug and alcohol abuse; type III--depressed; and type IV--classic alcohol abuse and dependence. Those symptoms that best describe each of the pure types are presented in the table along with the coefficients. Only symptoms with a coefficient greater than .60 were included. These pure types do demonstrate the emergence of a classic combined alcohol abuse/dependence type, but not separate abuse and dependence types. As expected, an asymptomatic pure type emerges, given that persons with only one symptom were included in the analysis. The other two types are interesting, but not unexpected. Type II is a combined drug and alcohol abuse pattern, but is otherwise relatively asymptomatic. One might expect this type to be more typical of the young rather than older persons. Type III is a typical pattern of major depression without a significant relationship to any one alcohol symptom. This type may represent individuals with a more random and minor collection of alcohol symptoms that are associated with the depressive symptomatology, but which do not progress to a classic picture of alcohol abuse and/or dependence.

Table 8 presents the distribution of the individual coefficients (g_{ik}'s) for 295 subjects with symptoms of alcoholism. As noted above, each subject is assigned a coefficient for each of the four pure types, which represents the proportionate contribution of the pure types to each subject's characteristics of alcohol consumption and psychiatric symptomatology. As would be expected, only a small number of individuals will possess all or nearly all of the characteristics of these extreme points. For example, a minimal number of persons have a coefficient above the .5 level for types II-IV. Even so, these may represent extreme points of clinical symptoms where few persons would be expected to demonstrate all or most of the symptoms. In contrast, the majority of subjects have coefficients above the .5 level for type I, the asymptomatic group. It is important to note that most (267 of 295) of the cases can be unambiguously assigned (i.e., a $g_{ik} > 0.5$) to one of the 4 groups.

Coefficients relating the four pure types to demographic variables are presented in table 9. The elderly (60+) load predominantly on the classic type (type IV) and not on the depressed or the mixed drug/alcohol abuse type. Therefore, persons in late life with at least one alcoholic symptom are likely either to demonstrate a classic picture of alcohol abuse/dependence or to be virtually asymptomatic. Alcoholic symptoms as a secondary characteristic of other problems, such as depression, are seen less in the elderly than at other stages of the life cycle. In addition, blacks are more likely to load on the classic alcohol symptom pattern (type IV), thus reiterating the increased likelihood of

Table 7.—Symptomatic Description of the Pure Types I to IV.
(Coefficients Relating Four Pure Types to Symptoms)

Type I	Type II	Type III	Type IV
(No symptoms)	Drug problems (1.00)	Depressed for 2 weeks (1.00)	Thinks self excessive drinker (1.00)
	Thinks self excessive drinker (.99)	Weight gain (1.00)	Family/others say too much drinking (1.00)
	Heavy drinking in 1 day (.65)	Trouble sleeping (1.00)	Two months of constant drinking (1.00)
		Tired out (1.00)	
		Feels worthless (1.00)	Needs drinks before breakfast (1.00)
		Thoughts of death (1.00)	Needs drink to work (1.00)
		Phobias (1.00)	Wanted to stop but couldn't (1.00)
		Headaches (1.00)	
		Trouble concentrating (.77)	Blackouts (.96)
			Binges (.90)
			Told MD about drinking (.81)
			Sought help from alcohol clinic (1.00)

Summary description of the four pure types

Type I - Asymptomatic

Type II - Mixed episodic drug and alcohol abuse

Type III - Depressed

Type IV - Classic Alcohol Abuse and Dependence

Table 8.--Number of Subjects by GOM Range for Four Pure Types (n = 295)

Range	Type I	Type II	Type III	Type IV
0.000 - .250	29	221	245	269
.251 - .500	39	55	38	17
.501 - .750	85	17	10	6
.751 - 1.000	142	2	2	3
Total	295	295	295	295

Table 9.—Coefficients Relating Pure Types from Isolates with $\underline{K}$ = 4 to a Series of External Demographic Variables

Demographic factors (percentage distribution)	Type I (Asymptomatic)	Type II (Mixed drug/ alcohol abuse)	Type III (Depressed)	Type IV (Classic alcohol abuse/ dependence
Age				
18-39 (62)	0.64	0.95	1.00	0.00
40-59 (21)	0.23	0.00	0.00	0.45
60+ (17)	0.13	0.05	0.00	0.55
Sex				
Male (75)	0.84	0.77	0.00	0.99
Female (25)	0.16	0.23	1.00	0.01
Race				
White (62)	0.67	0.71	0.51	0.22
Nonwhite (38)	0.33	0.29	0.48	0.78
Education				
HS grad (64)	0.75	0.82	0.35	0.09
HS (36)	0.25	0.17	0.65	0.91
Marital status				
Married (45)	0.52	0.51	0.23	0.15
Widowed (7)	0.04	0.00	0.00	0.40
Separated/ divorced (16)	0.16	0.33	0.06	0.45
Never married (32)	0.28	0.46	0.71	0.00
Living arrangements				
Alone (22)	0.21	0.18	0.13	0.45
With someone else (78)	0.79	0.82	0.87	0.55
Residence				
Rural (38)	0.43	0.10	0.24	0.55
Urban (62)	0.57	0.90	0.76	0.45

blacks to be prevalent among elderly alcoholics. The classic (type IV) alcoholic is also more likely to be male, less educated, widowed, separated or divorced, and a rural resident. Therefore, the classic (type IV) symptom profile confirms the previous demographic comparisons to some extent. Finally, in table 10, the classic (type IV) profile is most likely to show a combined abuse/dependence diagnosis.

In summary, these preliminary data present an interesting emerging picture. First, there are few individuals in late life who report alcohol-related symptoms to a degree that qualifies them for a current diagnosis of alcohol abuse and/or dependence. The current elderly alcoholics are more likely to demonstrate a pattern of dependence and to have more physical symptoms. Current alcoholics are more likely to be black in contrast with the predominantly white current young alcoholics.

The frequency data coupled with the GOM analysis do not identify readily a progression of alcohol problems from early life through old age. What happens to the middle-aged heavy drinker? If we ignore the potential for a cohort effect--that current middle-aged white alcoholics will appear in community surveys as elderly white alcoholics 20 years from now--at least three possibilities exist. First, the middle-aged white alcoholic does not survive to late life. (Edwards et al. 1983) Second, these individuals are institutionalized and, therefore, not identified in the community survey. (Bozzetti and MacMurray 1977; Gaitz and Baer 1971). Finally, these individuals may cease drinking and appear as the inactive alcoholics of late life (Drew 1968). Data suggests that only those with less severe alcoholic symptoms who do not have concomitant other psychiatric disorders will fall into this last category.

Finally, these analyses do not help to identify the origin of the older black male alcoholic. Perhaps by extending the GOM procedure to include more pure types, a precursor type may appear. Cross-site ECA data analysis with more subjects included may be of aid in these analyses, yet the regional differences that are controlled in the Piedmont Health Survey would complicate the analyses.

CONCLUSION

Many of the hypotheses stated in the introduction to this paper are substantiated in this preliminary analysis of data from the Piedmont Health Survey. Yet in retrospect, one must consider the possibility of a cohort effect as an explanatory factor for many of these findings. For example, males do represent a greater

Table 10.—Coefficients Relating Pure Types from Solutions with $\underline{K} = 4$ to External or Criteria Diagnostic Variables

Diagnostic category (percentage distribution)	Type I	Type II	Type III	Type IV
No alcohol diagnosis (54)	0.73	0.35	0.35	0.00
Alcohol abuse (15)	0.16	0.39	0.08	0.00
Alcohol dependence (4)	0.06	0.04	0.00	0.00
Alcohol abuse/dependence (27)	0.05	0.22	0.57	1.00

proportion of elderly than younger alcoholics, yet this elderly cohort of alcoholics may have always been very heavily male even when they were younger. Likewise, older alcoholics are less likely to be divorced or have never married than younger alcoholics, but again, this may be a cohort phenomenon. Even the findings concerning treatment may represent more of a cohort phenomenon than may at first be readily apparent. Data from this survey suggest that older alcoholics are more likely to have been hospitalized or to have sought medical treatment for their alcoholism and are less likely to seek self-help groups, such as Alcoholics Anonymous. The use of self-help groups requires, to some degree, a self-admission of problems. Older persons may be more reticent about admitting to themselves or others that they in fact have a problem with alcohol and are therefore less likely to seek such self-help groups. If a problem is recognized, older persons may be more likely to seek traditional forms of care, such as the primary care physician.

Certain demographic characteristics associated with alcoholism apply only to older alcoholics. For example, older alcoholics are less likely to live alone than are other older persons, while no marked difference is found for younger alcoholics. Because of increasing difficulties, elderly alcoholics may need to reestablish social relations to a degree that were not previously necessary.

Data on the cognitive impairments seen in elderly alcoholics, compared with young alcoholics, certainly needs more thorough evaluation. It is somewhat surprising that the high level of cognitive impairment is not accompanied by an equally high level of symptomatic complaints. In fact, the group of older alcoholics do not report appreciably higher rates of other symptomatology than would be expected in a general group of older adults.

The most consistent trend in this study to date is that current elderly alcoholics are characterized more by symptoms suggestive of dependency than are younger alcoholics. A number of explanations is possible. For example, a chronic pattern of dependence may be more likely to persist into late life, especially if alcohol use begins to interfere with social or physical functioning; i.e., episodic abusive drinking may be more easily stopped than chronic alcohol use. Another explanation might suggest that those persons who demonstrated more abusive symptoms earlier in life may have changed their drinking patterns over the life cycle and now have, because they are less physically tolerant of excess alcohol intake, changed their pattern of drinking to one that reflects dependence. The question remains unanswered as to why current alcohol use is more common among nonwhites (predominantly blacks in this population). A cursory review of the data does not suggest that education, rural/urban residence, or other obvious factors explain this particular racial difference. Further analyses are necessary so that this observation can be understood.

Finally, these data verify results found in other studies, namely, that older current alcoholics are less likely to have concurrent psychiatric disorders than are young alcoholics (Rosin and Glatt 1971). This group does not show an excessively high rate of the disorders surveyed--major depressive episodes, antisocial personality disorder, and sexual difficulties--but certainly does show a higher rate of cognitive impairment, as discussed earlier.

In conclusion, one must recognize that these data come from one geographic region--the southeastern United States--and represent a group of both urban and rural residents in these areas. Though there is definite value in analyzing data from geographic areas where factors like rural/urban residence can be compared without the usual regional differences that must be taken into account, there are nevertheless some problems with generalizing these data to the entire U.S. population. In determining the profile of the elderly alcoholic, however, the authors believe that an indepth analysis of ECA data from an individual site is the appropriate first step toward a better understanding of this not infrequent and potentially dangerous psychiatric disorder in late life.

REFERENCES

American Psychiatric Association. *Diagnostic and Statistical Manual of Mental Disorders*. 3d ed. Washington, D.C.: the Association, 1980.

Bahr, H.M., and Caplow, T. *Old Men Drunk and Sober*. New York: New York University Press, 1973.

Bozzetti, L., and MacMurray, J. Drug misuse among the elderly: A hidden menace. *Psychiatry Annals* 7:155, 1977.

Drew, L.R. Alcoholism as a self-limiting disease. *Quarterly Journal of Studies on Alcohol* 29:957-967, 1968.

Durham, R.G. Aging and changing patterns of alcohol use. *Journal of Psychoactive Drugs* 13:143-151, 1981.

Edwards, G.; Hoppenheimar, E.; Duckitt, A.; et al. What happens to alcoholics? *Lancet*, July 30, 1983, pp. 269-271.

Folstein, M.F.; Folstein, S.E.; and McHugh, P.R. Mini mental state: A practical method for grading the cognitive state of patients for the clinician. *Journal of Psychiatric Research* 12:189-198, 1975.

Gaitz, C., and Baer, P. Characteristics of elderly patients with alcoholism. *Archives of General Psychiatry* 24:372, 1971.

Kish, L. *Survey Sampling*. New York: John Wiley and Sons, 1965.

Mishara, B.L., and Kastenbaum, R. *Alcohol and Old Age*. New York: Grune and Stratton, 1980.

Robins, L.N.; Helzer, J.E.; and Croughan, J.; et al. National Institute of Mental Health Diagnostic Interview Schedule: Its history, characteristics and validity. *Archives of General Psychiatry* 38:381-389, 1981.

Rosin, A.J., and Glatt, M.M. Alcohol excess in the elderly. *Quarterly Journal of Studies on Alcohol* 32, 1971.

Schuckit, M.A., and Miller, E.L. Alcoholism in elderly men: A survey of a general medical ward. *Annals of the New York Academy of Sciences* 273:558, 1976.

Strauss, J.S.; Gabriel, K.R.; Kokes, R.F.; et al. Do psychiatric patients fit their diagnoses: Patterns of symptomatology as described with the biplot. Journal of Nervous and Mental Disease 167:105-113, 1979.

Woodbury, M.A., and Manton, K.G. A new procedure for analysis of medical classification. Methods of Information in Medicine 21:210-220, 1982.

GENERAL DISCUSSION PANEL

Jacob Brody

I would like to voice my excitement about participating in this NIAAA workshop on the Nature and Extent of Alcohol Problems among the Elderly. It is a subject that has received a great deal of lip service, but to be present when data are finally emerging is truly a privilege. The problems of alcohol are great and the problems of aging are great and the potential of an alcohol problem among the elderly is a very real one. Thus, developing the information presented at the meeting and the suggestion that more solid data are forthcoming is very exciting and gratifying. We have heard data from a longitudinal study and from the ECA cross sectional surveys. These two types of studies are, of course, only two among several that will be needed in the long run to determine "the nature and extent of alcohol problems among the elderly." Also necessary will be clinical studies of the natural history of alcoholism and alcohol abuse in older individuals. Case control studies would surely be rewarding if alcohol abusers and nonalcohol abusers were matched by age, sex, and other variables in order to determine the risk factors for developing an alcohol problem in later life. Another area that needs study is the mode of treatment for alcoholics at specific ages, and, of course, specifically at older ages.

Although these studies will be coming, the excitement we feel today arises from data before us that is accumulating from the five ECA sites and the one longitudinal study. It is certainly to be hoped that the five cross sectional studies will be converted into longitudinal studies, which will greatly enrich the information available in numerous areas, including information on alcohol-related problems. Such difficult problems as identification of a late onset alcoholic or even a person who starts to drink more heavily and abusively with age can be explored. Let me once again signal my great relief at not having to go over the same tedious reviews of alcohol problems and the elderly, and at being at the threshold of the collection of a real data base.

Again, I must say I am pleased with the conference and its success in terms of its stated mission.

Editors' Note: We believe that the paper prepared by Dr. Brody for the White House Conference on Aging, and published in the Journal of the American Geriatrics Society, provides some additional perspective, and we are including the paper as part of the Proceedings.

Papers Prepared by the National Institute on Aging for the
White House Conference on Aging (WHCoA)

AGING AND ALCOHOL ABUSE*

Jacob A. Brody, M.D.**

Demographic information suggests that the problems of alcohol abuse among the elderly will increase at least in proportion to the population growth of that sector. While fewer older people drink and average consumption declines, four factors that promote alcohol abuse are noted. These are: 1) retirement, with its attendant boredom, change of role status, and loss of income; 2) deaths occurring among relatives and friends and the awareness that more deaths are coming; 3) poor health and discomfort; and 4) loneliness, a particular problem among elderly women. Surveys in older age groups, in addition to being costly, are of questionable value. Anecdotal evidence and several early studies, however, suggest that a high proportion of elderly (10 to 15 percent) who seek medical attention for any reason have an alcohol-related problem, and that elderly alcoholics, whether alcoholism is of early or recent onset, are relatively easy to treat. If these findings can be confirmed, then detection during health-seeking encounters could have great potential value. Research in detection and treatment is critical. A prevention strategy involving the

---

*From Brody, J.A. (Aging and Alcohol Abuse) Journal of the American Geriatrics Society 30:123-126, 1982.

**Associate Director of Epidemiology, Demography, and Biometry Program, National Institute on Aging, National Institutes of Health, Bethesda, Maryland 20205.

Presented at the White House Conference on Aging, sponsored by the National Institute on Aging (NIA), Washington, D.C., November 1981.

Address correspondence and reprint requests to Dr. Brody.

cohort 55 to 64 years of age could have the dual effect of preventing subsequent alcohol problems among these people and offering a message that would be heard by those at older and less accessible ages.

A PONDERABLE

Alcohol abuse is not the biggest problem in gerontology, and aging is not the major concern of alcohol abuse workers. This manuscript is written in the hope of fostering thoughtful awareness that a problem does exist and should be of concern to the fields of alcoholism treatment and gerontology. An opportunity exists for tangible and timely progress in research, preventive strategies, and active interventions. The size of the aging population is growing, and alcohol remains abundant.

Defining aging and the aged is difficult, but I use the common, if arbitrary, convention, and refer to the population aged 65 years and older. Stereotypically, we conjure up a picture of the abandoned sick in decaying nursing homes throughout the land. This allows us to muster up a full measure of guilt about the sad and forsaken elderly sector of the country. In fact, however, only 5 percent of the people over age 65 are in nursing homes. The rest are out there, and for the most part, doing rather well. Riley and Foner[1] noted, "The typical older person seems to have a strong sense of his own worth, to minimize his self-doubts, and not even to regard himself as old. The older person seems at least as likely as the younger person to feel adequate and to have a sense of satisfaction in playing his various marital, parental, occupational, or housekeeping roles. To be sure, he does not perceive old age as the happiest period of his life. Nevertheless, he does not worry any more than the young person about his health, his finances, or any of the other difficulties to which he is subject."

Having thus with some smugness said that most of our notions about the aged are misconceptions and stereotypes, let me turn to another aspect of aging. The Elisabeth Kubler-Ross book "On Death and Dying"[2] observes ". . . we are impressed that death has always been distasteful to man and will probably always be."

Thus, we have a theme to ponder from the statements by these great women. The elderly are doing rather well but they are facing and surrounded by an ultimate.

ASSUMPTIONS

A priori notions plus experience and common sense inform us that the elderly are likely to be a highly susceptible group for alcohol problems. Common conditions in later life include: 1) retirement, with its attendant boredom, change of role status, and loss of income; 2) deaths occurring among relatives and friends and the awareness that more deaths are coming; 3) poor health and discomfort; and 4) loneliness, particularly among elderly women.

Thrown into this background is the imponderable effect created by the fact that all those who are more than 65 years old in 1981 were born no later than 1916. Thus, the entire population lived through the entire period of Prohibition, experiencing not only the moral outrage that produced this social experiment but the problems engendered by its failure. We lack knowledge of the impact of Prohibition on these people over 65, an obstacle in trying to understand and deal with the target population.

STATISTICS

I shall present generally accepted and available data that describe the elderly population, and emphasize the aspects that tend to make them susceptible to problems related to alcohol.[3] In 1977, one in nine, or approximately 23.5 million, Americans were 65 years old or older. Among whites, 11 percent of the population was over 65, while among blacks 8 percent were in this age group and among Spanish-surname populations the figure was approximately 4 percent. The net increase per day of the population 65 years old or older is approximately 1,500 people. This takes into account the number of people becoming 65 and subtracts the deaths in the age group 65 and over. Modestly projecting to the year 2000, there will be 32 million people over the age of 65 in the United States. Currently, 45 percent of those 65 or older live in seven states. There are more than 2 million in this age group in California and New York. More than 1 million people over age 65 live in Florida, Illinois, Ohio, Pennsylvania, and Texas. There is a slight tendency for more elderly to live in rural areas and in the central cores of large cities.

In 1975, about 11 percent of the elderly population lived below poverty level. Massachusetts had the lowest rate, with approximately 6 percent below the poverty line, while Mississippi and Georgia had the highest percentages, 37 and 32 percent, respectively.

Life expectancy in the United States in 1976 was 73 years, or approximately 69 years for males and 77 for females. An infant girl born today has a 50-50 chance of being 80 years old. At age 65 the subgroup with the most favorable life expectancy is the black female. Approximately 82 percent of females and only 65 percent of males survive to age 65. At age 65, the average male can expect to live another 14 years, while females can expect to live another 18 years. The differential survivorship between males and females causes a potentially devastating imbalance over age 65. For every 100 males there are approximately 150 females.

In terms of living arrangements, somewhere between 4 and 5 percent over age 65 are in institutions, the great majority, of course, being in nursing homes. The average age in nursing homes is approximately 82 years, with two thirds of the population being female. Almost 50 percent of people in nursing homes have no living relatives. Among those residing in the community, 1.6 million males, or 17 percent of the total male population over age 65, live alone or with non-relatives. An almost staggering 5.5 million females in this age group, 42 percent of the total female population over 65, live alone or with non-relatives. Because women live longer but tend to marry older men and older men who are widowed find it easier to remarry, at present, of those over the age of 65, 77 percent of men, and only 48 percent of women are married.

The present cohort aged 65 or more has an average of 9.5 years of education. About a third have finished high school, and 8 percent have finished college. Along with the increase in the absolute number of people aged 65 or older, the median level of education is rising, so that within the next few decades there will be little difference in educational levels at any adult age. This has considerable significance in terms of planning, since the people who will be joining the ranks of the elderly will be better educated and hence more vocal and demanding than the present constituency.

At present only 8 percent of women over age 65 are working. This is not a great departure from the past. Among men, however, only 20 percent of the population are working. In 1900, 67 percent of the male population over age 65 were employed. Leisure time, however, may be diminishing in recent years as financial needs cause more elderly people to remain employed.

A total of 40 percent of people 65 or older have a serious health problem that causes some limitation in conducting normal daily activities. This compares with approximately 7 percent of the population under age 65. Each year 17 percent of those over 65 are hospitalized at least once, and each hospitalization lasts for an average of 12 days. For those under 65, 10 percent are hospitalized annually and stay approximately seven days. The average annual cost for health, per capita, per year, for those over age 65 is estimated to be approximately $1,500, while for those under age 65 it is $550.

ALCOHOL ISSUES

There are few hard data about drinking patterns in the elderly population. Reviews are available,[4,5] and I shall attempt only to cull out data and concepts that relate to areas of potential development and progress. There are two major sources for information. The first is through surveys of the general population. Various surveys suggest that the absolute number of abstainers increases and the total amount of alcohol consumed decreases with age. Estimates of alcoholism range from about 1 to 5 percent of the population over age 65. Thus, in a survey to detect about 25 patients we would have to interview 1,000 people, assuming total cooperation and candor in responses. Not knowing the effects of Prohibition, etc., on this age group, and giving some credence to the belief that this population and their families are inclined to deny alcohol problems, this estimate of sample size may be much too low. It would appear that surveys are a costly and potentially unreliable measure of alcoholism in the elderly.

The second approach involves individuals being hospitalized or being seen by medical or paramedical personnel for any and all problems. Within this population it is estimated that 10 to 15 percent have a drinking problem that is in some way related to the presenting illness. Both Zimberg[6] and Schuckit[7] discuss this issue and the attendant difficulty in establishing the diagnosis of an alcohol-related problem in this population. There is some evidence that alcohol has unusual effects on elderly people. They appear to be less tolerant at lower doses of alcohol, and since many have heart conditions and alcohol is a cardiac muscle irritant, the role of alcohol in the patient's cardiovascular condition is difficult to evaluate; many patients are taking other drugs that may produce reactions with even small amounts of alcohol; and finally, alcohol seems to produce transient syndromes in the elderly which are industinguishable from senile dementia. The latter is potentially tragic, because a person could easily be labeled as having senile dementia when he has only a mild alcohol problem. Once the diagnosis of dementia is made, his chances of spending most of the rest of his life in an institution increase considerably.

CLINICAL OBSERVATIONS

Major clinical observations by Zimberg[6] and by Rosin and Glatt[8] were made in the early 1970s or before. None of their work has been expanded or repeated. Their initial reports described fewer than 200 patients, and their populations tended to be atypical, in that they contained an excess of females, from urban and impoverished areas such as Harlem or parts of London.

Key points have emerged from their studies. These authors tend to agree that there are two broad types of elderly alcohol abusers. One is the long-term abuser or survivor, who apparently has whatever mystic psychological problems cause early alcoholism, but this particular group is simply tougher and survives into old age. Estimates suggest that two thirds of the elderly alcoholics are in this group. The second group includes those in whom the onset of alcoholism occurs late in life. In contradistinction to the former, these are referred to alcohol specialists through geriatric practice rather than psychiatric practice. Their drinking is generally situational, exacerbated by failing physical and mental health and by emotional and environmental stresses.

A major claim is that elderly alcoholics, with either early or late onset, are easier to treat than other alcoholics. It is further suggested that their treatment need not be through classic mechanisms used for younger alcoholics such as Alcoholics Anonymous (AA) and routine alcohol counseling, but that their alcoholism is amenable to simple socialization. When in treatment programs, the elderly tend to be more responsive and more faithful in attendance. The surprising claim is that therapeutic methods that are of little use in earlier years are successful for both early-onset and late-onset elderly alcohol abusers. Surely it is time to stop writing reviews and quoting vintage Zimberg, Rosin and Glatt. These assertions need repetition and proof, a matter of critical importance since the need for treatment will grow at least in proportion to the rate of growth of the elderly population.

If these studies can be confirmed, they will offer a rational modus operandi to find and treat large numbers of elderly alcoholics. As mentioned above, it is claimed that 10 to 15 percent of elderly individuals seeking medical or paramedical attention have an alcohol problem. This should certainly be extensively investigated and confirmed, since the rate of 10 to 15 percent is sufficiently high that a fairly intensive effort would yield a large number of suffering individuals. If the yield is high, we must develop methods to make care-givers more sophisticated so that they can diagnose the alcohol problems in the patients they see. The reason I stress the foregoing is that if the treatment is as simple and successful as is suggested by the classic writers, then we have a relatively efficacious and available mechanism to deliver a great deal of medical and social help to a large group of people. Please note that throughout this I am emphasizing that the early studies and assumptions must be confirmed before massive programs can be embarked upon with optimism.

DISCUSSION

We have evidence and anecdotes suggesting that there are many elderly alcoholics of both the early-onset and late-onset categories who would be easy to cure. While the rates of alcohol abuse and drinking are low, and decline with advancing age, it is reported that 10 to 15 percent of all those seeking medical help have an alcohol-related problem.

A persistent source of anecdotes that do not appear in the literature is people who run housing authorities or large housing projects, or manage retirement communities. Since urban housing and retirement communities are becoming more numerous these observations demand attention and evaluation. Informants tell me that one of their most distressing and persistent problems is alcoholism and alcohol abuse, which causes an inordinately high proportion of serious and nagging difficulties. The rates of alcohol-associated fires, falls, starvation and neglect, and violence are simply unknown, but increasingly whispered about in these communities for the elderly.

Confounding the establishment of the veracity of these anecdotes is the barrier to collecting accurate data. There is no research in this age group concerning how to question about alcohol and get reliable answers. The nuances in working include the fact that there are more women, that their attitudes were formed and influenced before Prohibition, that surveys themselves are very expensive, and if the anecdotes are only partially true, it would take about a hundred interviews to find one patient given a predictably high denial rate. Some survey research should be done but my opinion is that firm data will not emanate from the age group currently under investigation.

It is likely that studies of the natural history and factors related to the decline in alcohol consumption with age would be rewarding, possibly in ways not immediately apparent. Another promising route of investigation is to learn more about late-onset problem drinkers. Case-control studies might identify the people at high risk as well as the precipitating circumstances. This should be accompanied by intense research to determine whether and why alcohol has an exceptionally deleterious effect on aging individuals and whether addiction is easily cured. Finally, I would give highest priority to straightforward case-finding studies in hospitalized series and to carefully documented treatment trials.

CONCLUSIONS

Concomitantly with survey research and clinical treatment research we should contemplate prevention efforts of the type that have done relatively poorly in the adolescent and young ages. It is likely that preventive efforts would find a much more responsive audience in the population that is now 55-64 years of age. A major prevention and education program would be of great interest to unions, management, the government, and anyone paying pensions or involved in health insurance. The staging would be to instruct this population that they are growing older and with age comes those risks that we know are associated with a greater likelihood for developing and perpetuating problems with alcohol. To repeat them once again, we would educate the target population that with retirement will come less money, a change in status and role, and free time to which they are unaccustomed. We must openly discuss the fact that death will be increasingly visible as they enter into the period when relatives and friends are passing away. We must present forcibly the information that health declines with age and that major and minor illnesses are an inevitable risk to the individual and his loved ones. Finally, we must emphasize the problem of loneliness and physically living alone, particularly for women but really for all elderly people. Throughout this, the message to be maintained is that alcohol, while tempting and abundant, is very likely to make things worse.

Encompassed in these suggestions are two goals. The first is to prevent alcohol problems from arising after age 65 by targeting the population aged 55 to 64. Secondly, it is likely that this is a fairly effective way to reach people already older than 65. This population is known to be sophisticated to the extent that they read newspapers and watch television more than most of their younger counterparts. Many of those who do have alcohol-related problems will identify with the messages being presented for the younger cohort and will seek help through medical sources, Alcoholics Anonymous, and other community resources. Thus, through practicing good prevention in one cohort we may be practicing good case detection in another. This is a time for research and a time for action. Our problems will be growing worse until our commitment becomes greater.

ACKNOWLEDGEMENTS

The author thanks Douglas A. Parker, Ph.D., Social Epidemiologist, Epidemiology, Demography, and Biometry Program, National Institute on Aging, NIH, for his assistance with the manuscript.

REFERENCES

1. Riley, M.W., Foner, A. *Aging and Society. Volume 1.* New York: Russell Sage Foundation, 1968, p. 1.

2. Kubler-Ross, E. *On Death and Dying.* New York: Macmillan, 1969, p. 2.

3. National Clearing House on Aging, AoA: Facts about Older Americans 1978. (DHEW) Publ. No. (OHDS)79-20006, 1979.

4. Keller M., Promisel D.M., Spiegler, D., et al. (eds.). Second Special Report to the U.S. Congress on Alcohol and Health June 1974. Chapter II. Alcohol and Older Persons. USDHEW, PHS, M.E. Chatetz, Chairman of the Task Force, p. 27.

5. Cahalan, D., Room, R. Problem Drinking among American Men. Monograph No. 7. New Brunswick, N.J.: Rutgers Center of Alcohol Studies, 1974.

6. Zimberg, S. The elderly alcoholic. *Gerontologist* June 1974, p. 221.

7. Schuckit, M.A., Pastor, P.A., Jr. The elderly as a unique population: Alcoholism. *Alcoholism Clin Exp Res* 2:31, 1978.

8. Rosin, A.J., Glatt, M.S. Alcohol excess in the elderly. *Quarterly Journal on the Studies of Alcohol* 32:53, 1971.

Tavia Gordon

I would like just to recall a few points that I mentioned yesterday. One is that if you are going to look at the relationship of alcohol to organic disease, it is particularly important to take into account concurrent cigarette smoking. Including cigarette smoking is important because it is clearly a major health factor; it is implicated in a variety of diseases and has a strong mortality effect. Any time there is a possibility that the data you are looking at are correlated with cigarette smoking, and data on alcohol consumption certainly are, you would certainly have to take that association into account if you could possibly do so. If you can't do so, I think you might have to ask whether it's safe to analyze the data.

The second comment concerns the notion of the elderly. We think of age as a continuous variable. Analytically, I would be inclined to treat it that way. There are certainly circumstances in which you would want to divide the data up into intervals, for instance if information at the upper end of the age scale is short. But arbitrary age cuts, whether at 50, 60, or 65, are sometimes treated as having some real meaning, and I really don't think they do. If you are going to hold a conference on the "elderly" you have to define elderly some way. Nor do I think that you can treat age as essentially a surrogate for other variables. While there are 40-year-old men who have difficulty in walking around the block and 90-year-old men who could walk a mile without great stress, the fact is that if you look at most characteristics across the age scale, on the average they do differ, both in their means and their standard deviations. I think it is well to keep in mind that all data in the papers presented here deal not with individuals but with populations, and that when you are dealing with populations, you need to be concerned about these average trajectories across the age scale. It is, of course, conceivable that in certain circumstances age is not an important variable, but in general, age usually is one of the most important variables that you have to take into account. Age may be a surrogate for things that you haven't looked at, which include things you never thought of looking at, and also things that you would like to look at but can't. I don't mean to lecture anyone about this particular analytical concern, but I think you always have to treat age with a great deal of respect and consideration because it is an important variable in what you are doing.

Rudolf Moos

I certainly would echo Jacob Brody's comments about the dearth of prior data. As I mentioned yesterday, John Kenny and I reviewed some work about a year and a half ago, both epidemiological studies and treatment studies, in which we particularly tried to look at work that has been done on older problem drinkers. I am certainly very aware of the dearth of prior data hidden in the literature.

I have just as many questions as I do comments on some of the things that intrigue me in the data presented today. While I am not as familiar with the DIS as I should be, one question I had as we were running through the criteria was whether the diagnostic criteria for alcoholism and alcohol abuse are a little bit too easy to meet. I worry about that.

Another issue that struck me as of particular interest in Anthony's paper, although I realize that the number of cases is small, was the incidence of new problems (symptoms and problems) within 1 year in a group of people already designated as lifetime alcohol abusers. How much of that is not remembering something at one time and remembering it later? But still I think it is very striking that in a 1-year period of time in a group of that sort there is as much new incidence, annual incidence as you call it, of problems as there was. You have already talked a little bit about what could explain that. There might be some further discussion.

I wish to raise again a question about "late onset." In the paper you presented it is not really, as you said, "late onset." You said onset after age 65 was not common. Looking at people who began to have problems after age 40, one would like information about experience at age 50 to 55 regarding new problems of alcohol abuse.

Robert Straus

One theme that I would like to reemphasize is the importance of looking at alcohol consumption within the same context in which we look at the consumption of medicines, foods, and other substances. The significance of smoking was mentioned, and I would add caffeine to the list. I have been struck, for example, by the fact that at AA meetings, both heavy smoking and caffeine use are in evidence among the people who have been problem drinkers. I think we need to reemphasize the importance of looking at the consumption of alcohol within the context of the use of other chemical substances.

In that context, I think that we also should think about getting information on exposure to environmental chemical substances that may have significant interactions with alcohol. Occupational histories should include data on exposure to the chemicals that have been identified as having potentially significant interactions with alcohol.

Some very important references have been made to cohort differences in drinking experience. There are similar differences in beliefs regarding alcohol. I am reminded that when my wife and I were married, my mother presented my wife with a case of medicines that included, among other things, a little bottle that was labeled "bourbon." It was really pre-Prohibition bourbon, because there had been a bottle of it in the medicine cabinet in my house for all those years. This episode illustrates the great significance that alcohol has had until recently as a medicine. This is particularly significant for many people who are now in the population we call elderly. I think both beliefs and practices are very important when we talk about cohort differences.

Another point I think we should consider is whether we are asking all the right questions. Are we asking all the questions that we might ask regarding why the liabilities of alcohol use may be different as we grow older? I am thinking of the special aging liabilities that are associated with falling down, the liabilities associated with changes in the capacity to metabolize alcohol, and the liabilities associated with interactions between alcohol and medications. In particular, with respect to the data that were presented on cognitive dysfunction, I wonder if there is a significant change with aging that is relevant to a different degree of liability with alcohol.

There are questions about alcohol in relation to food. With respect to appetite reduction, what role may alcohol play? Also, to what extent can alcohol actually interfere with the body's utilization of nutrients as we get older? If there are changes, this would be another liability factor for alcohol with respect to aging.

Still another question is whether we are including in our studies of alcohol and aging questions regarding the cumulative impact of nonproblem drinking. This is relevant to the alcohol-related diseases that may not be identified as alcohol problems, because they are not associated with the usual signs and symptoms of alcoholism or of alcohol disability.

This summarizes some of the questions that have come to my mind as I have sat through these very stimulating two days.

Lee Robins

Would anyone like to question the panel?

John Hermos

Not so much a question. In attending this workshop, the thing that I am most excited about, perhaps even more than results, is the development of a methodology for getting this information that will also be applicable to other populations. How can the validity of the testing measures be applied to different populations? I hope many papers come out on this topic as well as descriptions of results.

Tavia Gordon

One of the topics that has come up several times, and it is certainly an important topic, is the question of the differences by cohort. That is to say, people born in 1900 have a different life experience and arrive at old age with different kinds of problems or different characteristics than will people who were born in the 1930s. I haven't the slightest doubt there are differentials. But, unless you have some kind of evidence other than the internal appearance of your data, it becomes very difficult to determine whether what you are looking at are differentials of a cohort origin or differentials arising from some other source. If you look, for example, cross sectionally at a population, you will find height varies with age. Now height is a relatively invariant characteristic; once a person reaches full growth he begins to shrink a little bit with age, but not much. And so you can detect in a cross sectional cohort or population what are quite obviously (and we have other evidence to back it up) cohort differences. On the other hand, there are other differences that are not as easy to detect. I think when you analyze the data, if you are careful to think about what you are doing, you realize that in order to tease out what appears to be a cohort effect, you have to make certain assumptions about how things were going. So that your conclusions tend to be model dependent. I have done that, for example, with weight in the Framingham population. There does appear to be a clear cohort effect. Well, fortunately we have historical data that demonstrate that there is the cohort effect that you see in successive cross sections of the longitudinal data. Of course, if you have longitudinal data, you take the persons at a given age who achieve the next age group, whatever that may be, and then you compare them at this later age with persons who belonged to that age group earlier on.

Now the ECA, as I understand it, may serve as the basis for a longitudinal survey. Conceivably, by the time you get through with what you are doing, there will be extensions, additional contracts, and grants, so that there may be a longitudinal study that may give you a better hold on the differential between contemporaneous effects and longitudinal effects. But to determine cohort effects on a retrospective focus, especially when people are telling you what they remember about how things were when they were age 30, could be a fairly dangerous exercise. In most survey data, you will find that if you ask people when they were last hospitalized, you do quite well if you are within the last 60 days. If you go back a year or two you are beginning to have a very serious recall problem. I really am impressed with the amount of courage you have going back a whole lifetime for episodes of drinking. With hospitalization, people forget, so you get a dropping off of completeness of reporting. With drinking problems, you may not be getting biases in the other direction.

Lee Robins

Let me ask you a question, because this is something we have really thought about a great deal, and it has worried us a lot. I presented one table showing the frequency of individual drinking problems at two sites and showing the frequencies correlated at .98. Can that happen if you have a big recall error?

Tavia Gordon

Yes. Forgetting would follow the frequencies of the events themselves.

Lee Robins

If you can't remember them, wouldn't you get a very blurred picture rather than such a very consistent one?

Tavia Gordon

I have to think out loud. What about the frequency of the events themselves?

Lee Robins

The most frequent event was drinking at least a fifth a day.

Tavia Gordon

The event of being fired due to job difficulties?

Lee Robins

Very rare.

Speaker Unidentified

Rather than being related to the accuracy of recall, I thought of that table as being more related to the frequency of the events. It is very unlikely that somebody will be fired because of drinking. That is going to be as equally unlikely in Baltimore as it is in St. Louis. It just doesn't occur very much. In other words, you have events that range from zero to a hundred percent scale, and that is what gives you the high correlations.

Lee Robins

But wouldn't you have to say then that the chances of forgetting any particular event would have to be absolutely constant across events to reperoduce those frequency ranks in multiple settings? Why would you expect such regularity?

Speaker Unidentified

It would have to do with your preconception of what it should have been like in college. "Sure I drank a lot in college," you would say, although you don't really remember how much you drank in college. "Yeah, during Prohibition, anytime we could, we would all get drunk." You really might not have. So there are different reasons for giving a positive or negative answer that would be related not to reality, but to your preconceptions.

Let's say that the frequency of being fired through drinking is reported as 1 percent and let's say that a roughly constant 10 percent of people who have had this happen to them forget that it has happened to them and say that it hasn't happened. So in other words, rather than 1 percent, if recall were perfect, it would be 1.1 percent. That would not change the overall correlation.

J. Philip Miller, A.B., Associate Professor of Biostatistics in Preventive Medicine, Washington University School of Medicine, St. Louis, Missouri

I think it would be a better test for recall if you showed the symptoms to be the same in older people as in younger people. That is important, particularly if some of those activities are indeed associated with particular stages of alcohol dependence.

Lee Robins

The other thing we have done to try to test this hypothesis is to look at the power with which things remembered over different time spans predict recent events. We asked a number of questions about events in the last 6 months--for instance, have you moved? have you been fired? did someone in your household get sick? and so on. We argued that if events from childhood predicted these as well in older people as in younger people, then there can't be much forgetting, because the childhoods of the older people were much more distant in time than the childhoods of the younger people. Is that a reasonable conclusion? Neither young nor old have forgotten the recent events, but older persons would have had more chance to forget the childhood events.

Tavia Gordon

I feel more comfortable with the kind of data that has been done in validation of morbidity information, where in fact the investigators knew what had happened and then went to the population and asked them what had happened to them and compared known information, which was objective and was not a question of a person's impression, with what they were told. Those data are overwhelming in demonstrating the loss of information with increasing time between the event that is being recorded and the time that the information is being elicited by an interview. I think that there is a distinction between reliability, that is, if you ask a person the same question two times and you get the same answer, and validity, whether the answer you are getting really corresponds to the fact that you are trying to elicit. I don't think it is sufficient to be comfortable with a high reliability and infer from that that you have a high validity as well. I can't make a judgment as to the quality of recall over a long period of time with respect to alcohol-related episodes, but I really would be very surprised if it was as reliable as the reliability coefficients you recorded would suggest.

Dan Blazer

One thing that gives me more confidence in the alcohol section of this questionnaire is that in the elderly population we have many people reporting inactive as opposed to current problems. We feel that in our sample people are having difficulty in clustering events and symptoms. We found that our current rates of depression are only about .2 percent lower than our lifetime rates. Now that goes against all logic. You would imagine that lifetime instances of depression would be considerably higher than current rates, especially in an elderly population. Our first hypothesis is that we have considerable memory decay about lifetime episodes of depression. On the other hand, the fact that we have so few current alcoholics compared with lifetime alcoholics gives me a lot more confidence in that section of the questionnaire.

Lee Robins

There is evidence that certain things are more memorable than other things. You cited the poor recall of treatment. Interviews in those studies usually asked whether the respondent saw a doctor within a certain brief period of time. So there are two ways of making an error—making an error about whether the doctor was seen at all and making an error about whether it happened within the particular interval asked about. I think our recall for symptoms may be a lot better than those results about recall of treatment because we are asking only whether the symptom ever happened. People _do_ know if they have ever been arrested or not, even if they might not be able to tell you whether they were 16 or 17 the first time, or whether it was last month or 3 months ago.

Speaker Unidentified

But you also asked, "Did you ever --" with respect to depressive symptoms, and apparently recall was not that good.

Lee Robins

When you look at questions about a depressive episode, you find they are questions like, "Did you have a lot of trouble sleeping?" That is less concrete than "Did you ever drink a fifth of whiskey a day?" because you either did or didn't do that. Trouble sleeping is a continuum. Everyone has some. If I feel good today, I may not think having stayed awake for 40 minutes was a "lot of trouble." If I feel bad today, it might seem a terrible problem. That is, your current status may change your perception of history. I think the reason that alcohol questions are so reliable is that the questions are concrete. They ask about events that either happened or did not.

Speaker Unidentified

There is also a good deal of evidence that in the short run, i.e., last month, last 6 months, or even last year, contrary to what one might predict, the information that one gets from drinkers about drinking problems and drinking amounts, as compared with the criterion of records and collateral information, is just as likely to be overemphasized as to be minimized.

Speaker Unidentified

I would like to ask about the high sensitivity of the alcoholism or alcohol problem scale that you use, because you are reporting what seem to me to be very high lifetime prevalence rates. Does somebody on the ECA have a feeling as to whether perhaps the scale is too sensitive?

Lee Robins

You have to remember we are only applying rules in DSM-III. We are not making those rules.

Dan Blazer

Along these same lines, I don't think we have fully emphasized here the value of the DIS for eliciting the present symptomatology. We have, I think, for the first time in an epidemiologic survey of psychiatric disorders, questions that closely approximate the condition in which we are interested in terms of presence or absence of particular symptoms, and their severity. One of the advantages of that is that if we want to use more restrictive criteria in the future, we reanalyze the data using these new criteria, and come up with different rates. I don't think this is true of past surveys in psychiatry. As a result, 5, 10, or 15 years down the road, this set of interviews will still be of value and will allow us to do things we cannot do with data that were collected 15 years ago.

Jacob Brody

That is a point I was trying to make. There are data that have been available for many years that have considerable merit. We are, however, accumulating new data, not only from the studies presented, but from the many longitudinal and cross sectional studies underway. The statement by Dr. Riley in the opening section was that the elderly portion of society is growing very rapidly, and if there is no change whatsoever in the drinking patterns, the absolute number of problems must increase because of the demographic forces involved. There are clearly two constituencies involved, the aging and the alcoholic camps, and we must learn to work better with each other. There are researchers and treatment people involved primarily with alcohol. We hope that greater awareness of alcohol problems in the elderly is gradually achieved within the alcohol treatment network. Similarly, among those in gerontology, alcohol problems are now the first, or primary, issue that comes to mind. We must, however, acknowledge that the problem exists and perhaps at a much higher rate than we supposed, and therefore, those in gerontology must become more aware of the alcohol problem and those specialists who deal with alcohol.

The problem that Dr. Hermos mentioned is one that has also come to my attention. As our society evolves and has an increasing proportion of elderly citizens, there is an ever growing tendency for large communities of older people to exist. These are primarily retirement communities or public housing developments. In trying to set up studies for other purposes within such communities, I was surprised to hear how frequently the managers who run communities for elderly people are troubled and perplexed by the amount of drinking that they see and the problems that they encounter arising from drinking among the elderly. I must say I never got very far in establishing more than anecdotal evidence of this, since it is difficult to followup the impressions of these housing managers. I have the feeling, however, that as studies such as those being conducted and reported at this meeting extend into public housing and retirement communities, we will indeed find an alcohol problem that is larger than we currently think. Further, I have the optimism to believe that with a patient and thoughtful approach we will have the opportunity to address the problem of alcohol among the elderly, and that the rewards in terms of health and happiness and yes, even cost benefits, will be very great.

Matilda White Riley

I would like to comment on some ideas the panel of discussants has been discussing among itself at this exciting workshop. There is a clear interface here between interests of NIAAA and NIA, in that alcohol is associated both with mental health and with drug abuse, and the other concerns of ADAMHA on the one hand, and on the other hand with the kinds of concerns of NIA, as Bob Straus mentioned, such as changes with aging in nutrition, in pharmaceutical use, and the various other biological, social, and psychological aging changes that may interact with drinking phenomena. So alcohol use by the elderly is of interest in complex contexts. To bring all of this together, it is very clear that we need not only to design supplementary studies to answer some of these supplementary questions, but also that we need to put our efforts behind the ECA project to pursue this marvelous data base in the future. You have several cohorts here. You have the people who are starting off young now, and the people who are starting off old. If you are able to watch these people for 5 years or 10 years, some of the questions about what happens with aging will be uncovered. It is interesting to me to see the nice models of cohort and age differences that are being used. Such models have to form the background of the analysis. You have very provocative findings that show different drinking patterns and correlated drinking problems for young people and old people today. The older people are more dependent drinkers; the younger people are more abusive drinkers. You also do not find the high correlation between drinking and psychiatric symptoms among older people that you find among younger people. This raises critical questions that relate to socially significant issues, such as what is it that supports and reinforces these behaviors once they get started? We know that in adolescence and preadolescence, all the defiant behaviors like drinking and smoking and dropping out of school and teenage pregnancy, are very highly intercorrelated. We also know they are reinforced by the peer group. But it seems unlikely that the peer group sustains its importance into the later years. If this is indeed true, these defiant behaviors become less highly intercorrelated as people grow older and become more independent of peer influence. They must then be reinforced in a different way. As a representative of NIA, and because of my own interest in aging, I regard this research as highly important and very exciting. I agree with Jacob Brody that there should be future followups of these samples.

Phil Miller

I think one of the real exciting things for me is the data on the community as well on the institutionalized samples. I think the way you put those two data sets together will be important, and I see that as a real challenge for a statistician. I see it as important to the issue of cohort differences, because older people who abuse alcohol differentially may now be institutionalized. Perhaps they are being selected out of the community survey into institutions. So it seems you are going to have somehow to integrate the community data with the institutional data if you are going to make age inferences, in particular the kinds of cohort inferences you're taking on.

Charles E. Holzer

Oh yes, we're fully aware of that need.

Speaker Unidentified

I guess in that connection I have a question about categorizing the jail as you did in a category separate from prisons and mental hospitals, because there are people generally classified as alcoholics or alcohol abusers who are in and out of jails so constantly that from the point of view of an institutional impact, it wouldn't be very different from long-term institutionalization.

Charles E. Holzer

In terms of our sampling strategy, people who go in and out of jails are identified through their homes. The people sampled in prisons are in for over a year and may not maintain a community residence.

Lee Robins

Different sites have different definitions of institutional residents. We defined an institution as any place where the average stay is more than 2 weeks. This includes jails.

Robert Straus

I realize that these were done some time ago, but my own skid row studies suggested that there is a population who have, between jails and shelters and a whole variety of other institutional settings, a fairly continuous, if intermittent, institutional life, in which drinking often is significant between periods of institutionalization.

Lee Robins

It would be very useful to have another conference like this one in which we include the institutional sample.

REACTION PAPERS

George Maddox

When I was first confronted with the issue of aging and alcohol abuse (it was usually stated "aging and alcoholism" or "aging and drug or alcohol-related problems"), the confrontation was in phone calls suggesting that since I know something about alcohol, alcohol use, and alcohol abuse and about aging, I must know about the connection between the two. I would always respond, "Nobody knows so far as I know." That was a few years ago. Then the callers become more insistent. "There clearly is a problem, tell us about it." My response was, "I don't know what the problem is; why do you think there is one?"

My first reaction was to insist, "I have not seen any evidence of a problem but would myself be interested in such evidence if it exists." I occasionally became defensive, suggesting that if I wanted to be concerned about drug use and abuse among older people, my primary concern would be the use of prescribed drugs. Alcohol use in later life was not my primary concern.

The problem of aging and alcohol has refused to go away. I now see the problem differently, partly because of my exposure to the way in which ECA is approaching the issue. Alcohol abuse is a significant social problem and a minority--apparently a small minority--of older people are involved. A small percentage of the older population, however, can translate into a large number of individuals. Alcohol abuse not only complicates the lives of drinkers but also the lives of those who try to respond to their needs.

Robert Straus alluded to this point in his keynote address. If we concentrate only on the more flagrant outcomes of drinking, like alcoholism, we miss what, 25 years ago in research on drinking, we identified as a set of problems that is very troublesome to individuals and to society but that would not lead to a diagnosis of alcoholism. Consider, for example, accidents. Accidents have a very special meaning among older people. It is hard for me to believe that any older person who is drinking a substantial amount of alcohol, even at far below the level we would associate with alcohol abuse, is not increasing the risk of an accidental fall. We know that accidents are common in later life even in the absence of drinking. Drinking increases the risk of accidents.

Or consider alcohol and disease relationships. The idea that alcohol narcotizes not only the central nervous system but also other body systems needs emphasis. We do not know all the implications of sustained drinking for health in the later years. But we know enough to conclude that sustained heavy drinking increases both morbidity and mortality.

Jacob Brody asked us to consider who is complaining about drinking among older people. People who manage special housing facilities for older people are beginning to complain. One or two older residents with a drinking problem can be very disruptive in a relatively small, compact living community. Further, there is a kind of special visibility of an older person whose problem is complicated by drinking behavior. Disruptive behavior is bad enough. The disruptive behavior is superimposed frequently on other age-related problems that demand attention.

Alcohol abuse in later life is a problem. But we need to specify the nature of the problem. I continue to resist the notion, even now, that the problem is primarily alcoholism among older adults. Alcohol-related problems of a minority of older adults should be our primary concern.

I have been very favorably impressed by the ECA project as presented by Dr. Robins, Mr. Locke, and their colleagues. The objectives and procedures of the project have been presented with unusual clarity. Moreover, to an unusual degree, this project illustrates the meaning of science as a public enterprise. Science is a public enterprise in a double sense. It is a public enterprise in that peers have to be involved in evaluating findings. It is also a public enterprise in that society has to perceive that social interests are served in order to continue to commit public resources. I see in the ECA project an opportunity to make a useful and timely contribution to public discussions of an important national problem. The issue is not likely to go away soon.

I also stress another significant contribution of this project. It has brought together four major Federal agencies--NIMH, NIAAA, NIA, and the VA--to work cooperatively on a scientific and public issue. Such cooperation is not common and certainly is not common when substance as well as form are involved. I applaud the Federal leadership that made this workshop possible. I am pleased to have been a participant.

REACTION PAPERS

The papers and the related discussion in this workshop have repeatedly reminded me of a basic problem of scientific research. I call it the triangulation problem. The three interrelated parts of the problem are theory, available methodology and data analysis techniques, and the available data base. All scientific research is preoccupied with achieving some reasonable rapprochement among theoretically interesting hypotheses which can be tested with an appropriate data base with an appropriate technology for data analysis. In my experience, one or another base of the triangle is usually badly deficient. In recent years, certainly in the social sciences, analytic techniques have been much better than our theory or our data base. This may describe our situation in this workshop. How adequate is our theory of alcohol abuse in later life? How adequate is our data base for exploring the issue?

The ECA project may be important, not because it promises instant answers to complex questions, but because it attempts to deal in a balanced way with the triangulation problem by concentrating approximately equally on theory, data base, and research technology.

Part of the promise of the ECA project is that it may provide an appropriate--or at least a more adequate--data base. Moreover, its methodology appears to be basically sound. Finally, the theoretical formulation of the issues posed, while largely implicit at this point, can be made more explicit.

Personally, I attach considerable significance to the interdisciplinary composition of the workshop. I do not know whether the participants are representative of their disciplines. I am impressed with the rather high level of shared knowledge about theory, methodology, and data bases exhibited among the biomedical, behavioral, and social scientific participants.

The intellectual and affective climate of the workshop has impressed me. Rudolf Moos discusses organizational and contextual climates in his work. I am impressed both by the breadth and currency of knowledge about alcohol abuse and aging. I am also impressed by the good humor of the discussion. There is an awareness of sampling and the limits of generalizations. There is an awareness of multivariant analysis techniques and their limitations. There is awareness of cohort analysis and of a new Grade Of Membership (GOM) analytic technique. There is a sense of the state-of-the-art in research on alcohol abuse and aging. I am impressed with the competence illustrated here and a sense of humor about the limits of our competence.

Years ago, more years than I want to recall almost, I knew Morton Kramer, who has a current association with the ECA project at Hopkins. He had a passion for developing what he called model reporting sites. He believed that we lack critical kinds of information for planning and proposed model reporting sites as part of the answer. These proposed reporting sites would facilitate the development of professional and scientific networks. Further, because the reporting sites would be local, one would be able to get information simultaneously about individuals and the contexts in which they lived as well as the case system available to them. The ECA projects appear to have the characteristics of model reporting sites. If we believe that social context is important, then our research should reflect this fact. My only misgiving about the ECA project is that the study of the social context of behavior is not pursued more vigorously. Context remains relatively a black box.

What about the future? I think the ECA has been fundamentally well designed. The project will provide an important new data base and an opportunity to pursue a broad range of questions about aging and alcohol abuse. In the future, we must think about the outcomes of the use of alcohol in broad terms that go beyond our historic concern with its effects on the central nervous system. Alcohol abuse has social effects. Alcohol abuse increases the risk of morbidity and mortality. The biochemical effects of alcohol use are real enough, and we need to know more than we do about age-related changes in those effects. Alcohol abuse also has behavioral effects. The issue of accidents and falls, of particular importance to older people, and the issue of drug interactions in a society that has believed for so long in better living through chemistry warrant our attention urgently. The ECA project promises the opportunity to do this.

As quickly as possible, I hope that the ECA project data become public use data that will attract a growing number of scientific investigators.

Lee Robins

First, I would like to repeat that I think that a lot of what we are achieving and are thinking about has grown out of work that Matilda White Riley did many years ago, which sensitized us all to the importance of cohorts and the differences in their experiences over time. This is no longer a difficult concept. It has become a standard part of researchers' thinking. They think about it immediately when they start thinking about age. That was a long time coming. I am sure that the ease with which it is discussed here is partly a reaction of the group here. I don't fantasize that this change has affected the whole world, but at least there is a substantial group of people for whom this important concept is also now a comfortable concept.

We have criticism of the fact that we are treating age as a category rather than as a dimension, and that there are problems in that. I think that is a valid point. In earlier studies that looked at relationships between age and alcoholism in the general population, one finds a curious pattern: In almost every study, the oldest group, wherever the age cutoff is made, has the lowest rate of alcoholism. But, often the next younger group has the highest rate. That is, if the oldest group is defined as 65 or older, it may be the 55 to 65 year olds who have the highest rate of all. There are enough such studies to suggest that how you categorize the elderly is important because too early a cutting off point may combine the highest and lowest problem groups, hiding the differences. Analyzing the relation of age to drinking problems is a real problem, because relationships are not linear, but tend to be shaped like an inverted U, with the middle aged the most affected. We don't have good techniques for analyzing such distributions.

Another question raised was whether the DSM-III diagnostic criteria may not be more sensitive to alcoholism in the young than in the old; that could explain why we are getting the kinds of patterns that we are getting. There is probably something to that. Additionally, the diagnosis in DSM-III is focused on urban communities and industrialized communities. We are currently engaged in a very interesting project, trying to broaden the DIS for use on an international basis. To do that, we have added some questions that try to pick up kinds of alcohol-related behavior problems that would be typical in nonindustrialized societies. For instance, in addition to asking whether you have been fired from a job, we have asked whether drinking problems have interfered with completing chores, since people on farms, housewives, and children have chores, not jobs. The other addition, particularly relevant to drinking in the aging, is a question about accidents other than automobile accidents. In many parts of the world, few people drive cars and even in industrialized societies often the elderly have quit driving. The new questions ask whether the person has injured himself or anyone else as a result of drinking. This includes falls, which are now missing from DSM-III criteria, even though they are an extremely common complication of drinking.

The other issue that I would like to respond to is the opportunity the ECA sites have for capitalizing on knowing the local situation, with respect to local drinking patterns and treatment opportunities. I think some of the spinoffs from the ECA will emphasize the local environment even more than the ECA is conceptualized to do so far.

Despite all those upbeat remarks, I would like to emphasize that we still have some rather intractable methodological problems. One was not discussed in detail, but it is emphasized in Dr. Anthony's paper. When we find reports in interview 2 of symptoms of alcoholism not reported in interview 1, we don't know to what extent these symptoms are truly new or are only now being reported because memories have been jogged by the previous interview. Obviously, the absence of these problems in interview 1 is not lying in any simple sense, or they would not have been reported the second time. But respondents have had time to think the questions over since the first interview, and they may have been reminded of events they had forgotten. We have not yet found a way to separate new events from problems of stimulated recall. One of the exciting things about this project is discovering epidemiological issues that have hardly been touched in the literature. We feel this project is not simply contributing new information but contributing new methodology as well, which will result from our awareness of the gaps and the problems in standard techniques.

Another issue we have not yet resolved is whether it is possible to compare alcoholics with late and early onset. There is reason to believe that early onset alcoholism is different from late onset alcoholism, not only in the reasons for drinking and in associated psychiatric diagnoses but also in its prognosis. However, when you ask age of onset of people of different ages, obviously only the older group is at risk of late onset. I suspect studying the importance of age at onset is going to have to await a longitudinal study, because in a cross sectional survey the date of onset is so confounded with age at interview.

In short, I think we are very lucky to have an exciting data base, but we are also becoming increasingly aware of all the problems that remain and need solution. I don't think we are going to run out of things to think about or do for a long, long time. Thank you.

CLOSING REMARKS AND POSTSCRIPT

I would like to present a bit of history on how this workshop came about. I kept hearing that we do not know much about the nature and extent of alcohol-related problems among the elderly. This suggested that what was needed was a workshop devoted to papers that presented empirical evidence on this question. The key event that permitted the workshop to unfold was the realization that the Epidemiologic Catchment Area (ECA) Program of the National Institute of Mental Health had collected but not yet analyzed nor reported data on alcohol problems among the elderly. When I went to Mr. Ben Locke, who is responsible for the ECA program, he encouraged me to develop the workshop and I want to thank him for that encouragement.

In addition to papers from the three sites of the ECA Program (which served as the nucleus for the workshop), we were also fortunate in being able to draw upon data presented by Dr. George Warheit of the NIAAA-funded center at the University of Florida in Gainesville, Florida, which was activated in December 1982. We also drew upon data from the Veterans Administration-sponsored Normative Aging Study, with papers from Dr. Robert Glynn and from Dr. John Hermos. The paper from Dr. John Helzer provided additional longitudinal perspective on an elderly alcoholic population. Dr. Robert Straus's keynote address provided some especially insightful comments. I would like to thank all these individuals and the various discussants for their contributions to this meeting. On behalf of NIAAA, I would like to thank Dr. George Maddox and Dr. Lee Robins, both for their substantive contribution to this meeting and for their invaluable editorial efforts with respect to the proceedings. I would at this point also acknowledge our thanks to Dr. Robins and to Washington University for hosting the meeting. Technassociates, the NIAAA contractor for support services, was most helpful in the arrangements.

POSTSCRIPT

Subsequent to the workshop, having had the chance to study the papers, I note that there is not an overall percentage to describe the prevalence of alcoholism among elderly Americans. Although of uncertain accuracy, an overall percentage can be computed by combining data across the three ECA sites that oversampled the elderly. Since the estimates are based on household survey data, they do not include individuals whose residence is in a a nursing home, a hospital including those of the Veterans Administration, a single room occupancy dwelling, or a prison. If individuals from these missing facilities had been included, especially those from nursing homes and hospitals, the estimates of alcoholism obtained might have been higher than those observed in households.

There is a more serious limitation to using the ECA data in that we are extrapolating from only three sites to the entire United States, with the attendant risk that the prevalence of alcoholism may vary considerably in other locales. This is underscored by the fact that one of the sites (New Haven) differs considerably in the estimate of prevalence from the other two. Since we have no reason to consider data from one site more representative than from another, it seems that our best estimate is obtained by averaging estimates from the three sites.

The Holzer paper provides separate estimates for each of the three sites for the prevalence of alcoholism in the over 60 age group, separately for males and for females. Some might have preferred defining the elderly population as age 65 or older rather than 60 or older. Including persons aged 60 to 64 in the elderly group increases the prevalence estimate somewhat.

What should be clearly understood, however, is that the estimate is based on the Diagnostic Interview Schedule (DIS) definitions, and the estimates obtained here are really not comparable to estimates based on quantity-frequency alcohol intake data obtained in other household survey studies. The DIS criteria are defined exactly in the Lee Robins paper in this volume, and we should keep these definitions in mind as the prevalence estimates are presented. Since the DIS is designed to uncover clinically significant cases, estimates for prevalence based on it would be expected to be significantly lower than estimates based on heavy drinking, since heavy drinking is a necessary but not a sufficient condition for problem drinking.

There is one other matter that needs comment. The Holzer paper reports data based on the preceding 6 months' prevalence estimates. The rationale for this is that it should improve reliability of recall to limit the time frame to the last 6 months rather than to the last year. The 6-month estimate is necessarily lower than the 1-year estimate, since individuals who were problem drinkers more than 6 months ago but less than a year ago are not included.

By weighting the percentages in table 3 of the Holzer paper (this volume) by the number of interviewees, one obtains an estimate of 2.8 percent for the males and 0.3 percent for the females. (The male:female ratio may be on the high side in this age grouping in comparison with the under 60 population.) However, these estimates should be regarded as tentative, and as first approximations, for the reasons cited above. If we use 1980 census data, we can obtain a very rough overall percentage rate. We compute that 419,000 males over the age of 60 meet the DIS criteria, and 62,000 females do. The total of 481,000 represents 1.35 percent of the over 60 population in 1980.

How important a problem, then, is alcoholism for the over 60 population? For males, the absolute number would seem to be in the hundreds of thousands and would clearly merit attention by NIAAA. Brody (1981) has suggested in a paper for the White House Conference on Aging that preventive efforts for the 55 to 64 age group would be worthwhile. Preventive efforts involving increased case finding can be applied to both males and females, so that even for the relatively small number of females, alcohol-related problems can be addressed.

There are a variety of types of research that need to be undertaken for the elderly population. It should be clear that estimates of prevalence of alcoholism for this group need further elucidation. There is a need to confirm the reported finding that elderly alcoholics are responsive to treatment and that therapeutic methods that are of little use in earlier years are successful for both early onset and late onset alcoholics. It has also been suggested that premature aging takes place in an alcoholic population. This needs to be more reliably established than is currently the case, and the mechanism by which this occurs, if it does, needs to be elucidated. It is also true that memory deterioration is found in an alcoholic population, and some memory problems are common to both an alcoholic and elderly population. The mechanisms involved in memory abnormalities in both groups need to be better understood; some of the palliative measures may be the same, in any case.

The above are intended only as examples of research questions, and there are many others in the papers and discussion of this volume. This workshop is intended as a first step toward stimulating research in the alcohol-aging area. We look forward to the opportunity to support projects that will advance our currently limited understanding of alcohol-related problems among the elderly.

Nathan Rosenberg, Ph.D.
Health Scientist Administrator
Division of Extramural Research
National Institute on Alcohol Abuse
and Alcoholism

Springer publishing company

ANNUAL REVIEW OF GERONTOLOGY AND GERIATRICS
Carl Eisdorfer, Editor

Volume 1
432pp / 1980 **Contents (partial):** *G. Sacher,* Theory in Gerontology, Part 1 • *L. Hayflick,* Cell Aging • *D. Cohen/S. Wu,* Language and Cognition during Aging • *T. Hines/J. Fozard,* Memory and Aging • *R. Besdine,* Geriatric Medicine: An Overview • *E. Bierman,* Diseases of Carbohydrate and Lipid Metabolism

Volume 2
432pp / 1981 **Contents (partial):** *R. Walford et al.,* Immunopathology of Aging • *D. Gelfand,* Ethnicity and Aging • *L. Troll/E. Parron,* Age Changes in Sex Roles amid Changing Sex Roles: The Double Shift • *R. Riedel,* Behavior Therapies • *J. Yesavage/R. King,* Drug Treatment of Cognitive Impairment in the Elderly

Volume 3
448pp / 1982 *"These annual review series set a standard in their field and this volume is no exception."*—Clinical Gerontologist
Contents (partial): *G.W. Siskind/M.E. Weksler,* The Effect of Aging on the Immune Response • *L.A. Morgan,* Social Roles in Later Life: Some Recent Research Trends • *R. Kastenbaum,* Time Course and Time Perspective in Later Life • *U. Lehr,* Social-Psychological Correlates of Longevity

Volume 4
304pp / 1984 **Contents (partial):** *J. Crawford/H. Cohen,* Aging and Neoplasia • *S. Goldstein/R. Schmookler Reis,* Genomic Plasticity in Aging Human Cells • *S. Glatt/R. Katzman,* Multi-Infarct Dementia • *B. Baum,* Normal and Abnormal Oral Status in Aging • *H. Asuman Kiyak,* Management of Oral Problems in the Elderly

Volume 5
M. Powell Lawton and **George L. Maddox,** Guest Editors
352pp / 1985 **Contents (partial):** *B. Starr,* Sexuality and Aging • *M. Powell Lawton,* Activities and Leisure • *M. Smyer/M. Frysinger,* Mental Health Interventions in Institutional Settings • *B. Arnetz,* Physiological and Psychological Variables in Interventions: European Studies • *J. McArdle,* Aging and Intellectual Function: The Evidence for Longitudinal Studies in WAIS Performance

Order from your bookdealer or directly from publisher.
Springer Publishing Co. 536 Broadway, New York, NY 10012

Springer publishing company

Productive Aging
Enhancing Vitality in Later Life
Robert N. Butler and **Herbert P. Gleason,** Editors
This pioneering volume considers a largely undeveloped topic: productivity in old age. Contributors and their topics include: *Robert Butler,* Health, Productivity and Aging: An Overview; *Alvar Svanborg,* Biomedical and Environmental Influences on Aging; *James Birren,* Age, Competence, Creativity, and Wisdom; and *Betty Friedan,* The Mystique of Aging. 176pp / 1985

Aging and Public Health
Harry Phillips and **Susan Gaylord,** Editors. Reviews essential services in health, housing, and nutrition from a public health perspective. Also explores biological, environmental and psychological issues. 352pp / 1985

The Duke Longitudinal Studies of Normal Aging 1955-1980
An Overview of History, Design, and Findings
Ewald W. Busse and **George L. Maddox**
Over two decades of landmark research on the complex multivariate process of aging are chronicled in this work. It serves as an introduction to and overview of the studies, highlighting the findings on the biological, behavioral, and social aspects of normal aging. 192pp / 1985

Mental and Physical Health Practices of Older People
A Guide for Health Professionals
Elaine Brody
Examines the day-to-day mental and physical health practices of older people and describes for the first time the direct bearing of their behaviors on the provision of effective treatment. 288pp / 1984

Addictive Behavior and Its Treatment
Jesse B. Milby
An in-depth discussion of addiction, its foundations, factors leading to dependence, behavioral manifestations, epidemiology, and medical and psychosocial approaches to treatment. 288pp / 1981

Retirement
Causes and Consequences
Erdman B. Palmore, et al.
This book reports the results of the most comprehensive and definitive study of the causes and consequences of retirement ever undertaken, drawing on data from three national and four local longitudinal surveys. 208pp / 1985

Order from your bookdealer or directly from publisher.
Springer Publishing Co. 536 Broadway, New York, NY 10012

Springer publishing company

The Aging Network
Programs and Services, 2nd Ed.
Donald E. Gelfand
Revised and updated to reflect the changes most important for the 1980s, this essential text describes the key components in a multitude of programs serving the aged on federal, state and local levels. 320pp / 1983

The Elderly in Rural Society
Every Fourth Elder
Raymond Coward and **Gary Lee,** Editors
A complete overview of America's elderly population in rural areas. Included are studies of kinship structures, housing patterns, and health services, along with problems related to alcoholism, mobility, and income maintenance. 288pp, illus. / 1984

Managing Home Care for the Elderly
Lessons from Community-Based Agencies
Anabel O. Pelham and **William F. Clark,** Editors
These studies document important recent experiments in providing care at home for the elderly. Contributors describe alternatives to institutional care which are less expensive and more appropriate to the needs of the individuals involved. 208pp / 1985

Social Support Networks and the Care of the Elderly
Theory, Research, and Practice
William Sauer and **Raymond Coward,** Editors
Examines the role of family and community support networks in maintaining the social, psychological, and physical well being of the elderly. 288pp / 1985

The Older Person as a Mental Health Worker
Rosemary McCaslin, Editor
Describes and evaluates models and existing programs for the training and utilization of elderly people in the mental health system. "An excellent sourcebook for professionals seeking guidance in the area of programs development for the older client and worker . . . Well organized and easily understandable." —*Clinical Gerontologist.* 176pp / 1983

Order from your bookdealer or directly from publisher.
Springer Publishing Co. 536 Broadway, New York, NY 10012